MESSAGES FROM AN OWL

But ask the animals, and they will teach you, or the
birds of the air, and they will tell you; or speak to
the earth, and it will teach you, or let the fish of the
sea inform you. Which of all these does not know
that the hand of the LORD has done this?
In his hand is the life of every creature
and the breath of all mankind.

—Job 12: 7–10 NIV

MESSAGES FROM AN OWL

Max R. Terman

with photographs by the author

PRINCETON UNIVERSITY PRESS · PRINCETON, NEW JERSEY

Copyright © 1996 by Princeton University Press
Published by Princeton University Press, 41 William Street,
Princeton, New Jersey 08540
In the United Kingdom: Princeton University Press,
Chichester, West Sussex

Library of Congress Cataloging-in-Publication Data

Terman, Max R., 1945–
Messages from an owl / by Max R. Terman ; with photographs
by the author.
p.   cm.
Includes bibliographical references and index.
ISBN 0-691-01105-2
ISBN 0-691-04822-3 (pbk.)
1. Great horned owl—Biography. 2. Owls as pets. 3. Animal
radio tracking. I. Title.
QL696.S83T465   1996
598.9′7—dc20   95-31091

This book has been composed in Trump Mediæval

Princeton University Press books are
printed on acid-free paper and meet the guidelines
for permanence and durability of the Committee
on Production Guidelines for Book Longevity
of the Council on Library Resources

Second printing, and first paperback printing,
with a new epilogue, 1997

http://pup.princeton.edu

Printed in the United States of America

10 9 8 7 6 5 4 3

TO THE MEMORY OF MY PARENTS

BEN F. TERMAN

WHO LOVED BOOKS AND WOULD

HAVE LOVED TO READ THIS ONE

AND

VIOLA S. TERMAN

WHO LOVED ANIMALS AND

NURTURED THIS LOVE IN ME

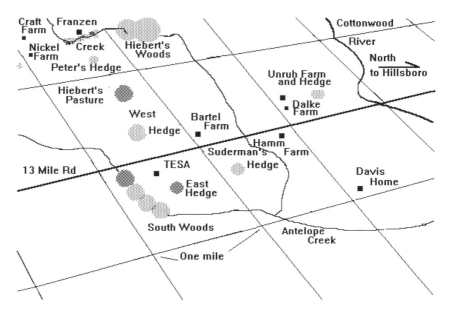

Map of area described in book.

◈ ◈ ◈ CONTENTS

FEW OWLS warrant an entire book. Most are hatched, fledged, live their shadowy hidden lives, and die with no note from the human world. Some, however, such as Bubo, an owl reared by biologist Bernd Heinrich (see his book *One Man's Owl*), touch people's heart and deserve to be immortalized in print. They are unique individuals that have interacted with humankind in a way that stirs the imagination and sets new perspectives.

As I worked with my special owl, Stripey, I began to recognize in its experiences some illustrative messages about the basic themes of life—experiencing youth, training for adulthood, leaving home, and securing a place in the world. The owl is an example of an organism finding its niche, a role in life that in microcosm reflects our own struggles. I decided to record the episodes of Stripey's behavioral development in captivity—and later in the wild—in a journal and on videotape. I wanted to capture the story of the owl's life by use of radiotelemetry, the use of radio tags. I hoped that the tapes and detailed field notes would add new information about the natural history of owls and the effects of human contact on their development.

This book relates my experiences training and tracking a captive-reared great horned owl. The long-term study of a hand-reared individual by telemetry is to my knowledge unique. Like Bubo and Bernd Heinrich, Stripey and I developed a special relationship. Wherever Stripey wandered, I could follow. I was able to "look over my owl's shoulder" as it flew from fence row to fence row, wood to wood, encounter to encounter. I was present when crows bantered and mobbed, when other owls launched fierce attacks, and when a prospective mate caught Stripey's eye. For nearly seven years, I was (and am still) an unlikely companion to this amazing creature.

Owl-watching may not rank highly as a means to contemplate the basic issues of life. But those who have been taught about the workings of the machinery of nature recognize a commonality in the struggles of all organisms. It is particularly enlightening to consider the world through the eyes of an owl equipped with a wild genetic program but reared by the hand of man. What is it like to be a wild owl living on the edge of survival, constantly driven to seek food and, in season, to reproduce? Genetic predisposition and species-typical training endow these individuals with the ability to secure food and a place to mate and breed, to secure a nest and pass genes on to the next generation. Scientists generally believe that an owl nurtured by humans is forever deprived of this wild heritage because it is forced to focus on the wrong entity as mother, mate, and social peer. Coldly termed an "imprint," the hand-reared owl becomes an ill-adapted creature woefully inadequate for meeting the challenges of life in the wild. Most imprints, if not "put out of their misery," are confined to a cage or aviary to live out their days as incorrigible "misfits," guided not by their will but by faulty wiring.

Even if one is legally sanctioned, one should think long and hard before adopting a wild creature. With Stripey, however, I had no choice. And besides, I had a mission: I wanted to explore this generalization—is an imprint really unable to survive in the wild?

As a scientist hoping to study great horned owls firsthand, I welcomed the opportunity presented by an abandoned owl chick. However, I was only a detached observer until I probed nature from an owl's back. As an animal behaviorist, I customarily approach the study of an animal with a question, a hypothesis, and a plan for testing the hypothesis—the technique of a working scientist—logical, manipulative, and powerfully revealing. Although a potent method for searching out truth, this view sometimes supplants what the naturalist learns by simply watching and listening. I believe in the experimental approach and I am not advocating its abandonment. My intent was to follow a different tack with this bird, however: data on its life should come freely, in an unrestrained environment rather than a laboratory arena. Indeed, this bird put flesh and bones on ideas and theories that I knew about but had never explored. When I began to survey life from the perspective of a wild creature, a new understanding emerged. Details of the private lives of wild creatures are secrets they keep well hidden. But now I had recruited a spy on the wild, an animal reared by the hand of man yet ruled internally by the commands of nature.

From the time it fledged, my owl roamed unrestrained—killing prey, competing for territorial space and for mates, all the while sending messages—messages telling of hunts and kills, fence-row romances, and intense battles over real estate and perching rights. Yet, with me it was tame, its aggression restrained—its natural wariness held in check. How did this owl transcend the gap between its world and mine? Was it just luck that it maintained its natural force, yet returned repeatedly to be with me? Perhaps I acquired Stripey at just the right time, at the end of the critical period when the species identity was set but not hardened. I suspect that by the smallest of odds, this was an owl with a crack open to humanity.

Many people were a part of this adventure. Tabor College is a small institution with a big heart, and I appreciate the time given me to research and write about my owl. My wife Jan and daughters Katy and Kerry deserve my unlimited praise for enduring all the indignities that naturally accompany a great horned owl. My students in animal behavior and ecology at Tabor College, especially Peter Johns and Carl Dick, helped immensely in rearing and radio-tracking activities. The late Virleen Bailey, naturalist, friend, and colleague who died in 1993, helped edit the manuscript and provided many words of encouragement to a sometimes discouraged owl-watcher. Viola Gossen, a true friend of our family and a long-time teacher, also read and critiqued the manuscript. Her straightforward demand for clarity no doubt made many paragraphs more readable. Craig Weatherby, fellow owl researcher at Adrian College in Michigan, helped immensely in providing advice and information basic to tagging and following Stripey. Richard Wall and Allen Hiebert, friends and colleagues at Tabor, provided much encouragement and more than once lent a helping hand in working with Stripey. Special thanks go to those friends in the scientific community who were excellent sounding boards for the veracity of some of my explanations for Stripey's behavior. I also appreciate the help of Jack Repcheck and Alice Calaprice of Princeton University Press, and the reviews of Bernd Heinrich of the University of Vermont and Peter Grant of Princeton University. Finally, I want to thank my neighbors whose hedgerows, pastures, and barns were so casually invaded by Stripey and me. I particularly appreciate the help and goodwill of Dan Dalke and John Unruh, on whose properties Stripey now resides.

TESA, Hillsboro, Kansas
May, 1995

MESSAGES FROM AN OWL

The most important requisite in describing an animal is to be sure and give its character and spirit, for in that you have, without error, the sum and effect of all its parts, known and unknown. You must tell what it is to man. Surely the most important part of an animal is its anima, its vital spirit, on which is based its character and all the peculiarities by which it most concerns us. Yet most scientific books which treat animals leave this out altogether, and what they describe are, as it were, phenomena of dead matter.

—Henry David Thoreau, *The Journal*

AUNCHING NEW LIFE

YOUNG HORNED OWLS THAT ARE RAISED IN CAPTIVITY AND
SUBSEQUENTLY RELEASED IN SUITABLE BACK-YARD SUR-
ROUNDINGS INVARIABLY REMAIN DEPENDENT ON THEIR
HUMAN FOSTER PARENTS UNTIL WELL INTO AUTUMN. MUCH
CAN BE LEARNED FROM WATCHING THESE CAPTIVE YOUNG-
STERS, WHOSE BEHAVIOR AND DEVELOPMENT PATTERNS
CLOSELY PARALLEL THOSE OF WILD HORNED OWLS. BY SUP-
PLEMENTING RANDOM FIELD OBSERVATIONS OF YOUNG
HORNED OWLS IN THE WILD WITH DETAILED OBSERVATIONS
OF CAPTIVE ONES, A MORE COMPLETE EXPLANATION OF THEIR
ACTIVITIES AFTER NEST DEPARTURE IS MADE POSSIBLE. THESE
STUDIES HELP TO AVOID MUCH SPECULATION ON NUMER-
OUS QUESTIONS THAT MIGHT NEVER BE SETTLED BY OBSERV-
ING WILD OWLS IN THE DARKNESS OF THEIR NATURAL
SURROUNDINGS.

—G. Ronald Austing and John B. Holt, wildlife ecologists

❖ ❖ ❖ Occasionally, but not often, the lives of
wild animals become entangled with our own. When a young great
horned owl in a park in a small Kansas town fell to the ground, there
began a story of teacher becoming student, of subject informing
scientist.

One sunny March day in 1988, a local minister became involved
not only in the affairs of his congregation but also in the seren-
dipitous aspects of nature. This is noteworthy because some men of
the cloth tend to be so driven by spiritual motives that they seldom
tune in on natural phenomena. Pastor Dennis Fast was not one of
these. When he discovered a fallen owlet, the instinct to "rescue the

perishing" prevailed. Immediately he called me to say that a young owl, nearly starving, was huddled at the base of a tree in the Hillsboro city park.

As a professor of biology at a small college in a country town, I often receive such calls, and over the years have cared for a plethora of snakes, raccoons, opossums, and other small denizens of the wilderness. Many of these animals became research subjects for my ecology and animal behavior students. None of the previous laboratory inhabitants, however, would enrich my life like this one owl.

I was reluctant to go out after an owl that probably was only waiting to be fed by its foraging parents. However, there was a chance that this animal had indeed been abandoned and I was the only person in the area with legal certification to collect wildlife specimens. On my way to the car, I met Richard Wall, a fellow biologist and my colleague in the department. Never too busy for the intriguing moments in life, Richard quickly jumped in my van and drove with me to the city park.

Near the park entrance, three young boys clustered around the base of a Siberian elm. All were pointing to a squawking ball of grimy cotton with a gaping black beak. It was thin and gaunt and had not been fed for some time. "That bird's in trouble." Richard's voice reflected his gentle, concise manner—a demeanor humble in appearance, that masks his considerable talents. Richard is a tall, robust man with a full reddish beard, one of my students from my early years of teaching. As frequently happens in towns like Hillsboro, he had come back from the big university to his roots, to continue growing where he sprouted.

After informing the boys of the little bird's species and its future disposition, we stooped to inspect the defiant black eyes and clacking bill that confronted us. I reached in front of Richard for the noisy little owlet. At once the beak clacked louder and the dagger-sharp talons raised skyward. This bird was already in full possession of its species' fierce disposition. Since I had handled owls previously, I knew how to grasp the young raptor safely by the legs above the talons. Such a move takes practice and cool nerves. Eventually, the little owl balanced itself on the surface of my hand, amazingly content and quiet for one being handled by an alien species.

Our subject was about four weeks old. I estimated its age by my knowledge of a series of photographs from a 1940s study done at the University of Kansas, "the prairie Harvard." In this study, a pair of

owls had reared their young near an upper-story window of the Natural History Museum, where two alert professors photographed
them as they developed. It was research of considerable worth performed on a very common but neglected species. Great horned owls
are noted for their ferocity and cryptic habits, making them unpopu-
lar candidates for Ph.D. theses and short-term grant proposals. This
ferocity is reflected in an account given to naturalist A. C. Bent (in
Life Histories of North American Birds of Prey) by a resident of the
state of Washington in the early 1900s:

> As a young man, in Tacoma, the writer once lived in a house which
> immediately adjoined a large wooden church. My chamber window
> looked upon a flat kitchen roof, through which projected a brick chim-
> ney some ten feet away. At three o'clock one morning a horrible night-
> mare gave way to a still more horrible waking. Murder most foul was
> being committed on the roof just outside the open window, and the
> shrieks of the victims (at least seven of them!) were drowned by the
> imprecations of the attacking party—fire-eating pirates to the number
> of a dozen. Pandemonium reigned and my bones were liquid with
> fright—when suddenly the tumult ceased; nor could I imagine through
> a whole sick day what had been the occasion of the terrifying visitation.
> But two weeks later the conflict was renewed—at a merciful distance
> this time. Peering out in to moonlight, I beheld one of these Owls
> perched upon the chimney of church hard by, gibbering and shrieking
> like one possessed. Cat-calls, groans, and demoniacal laughter were var-
> ied by wails and screeches, as of souls in torment—an occasion most
> memorable. The previous serenade had evidently been rendered from
> the kitchen chimney—and I pray never to hear its equal.

While they universally excite our nights with their multifarious
calls, they are themselves a consummate mystery. What if just one
of them could communicate with us? What messages about the
world of the night would it reveal? The idea of rearing my own emis-
sary to the wild began to take form in my consciousness.

I judged the bird to be a male because of its small size and comparatively subdued manner (females from the beginning tend to be
larger and noticeably more aggressive). The owlet was obviously in
food distress and appeared to be abandoned, but young birds on the
ground may be merely waiting for the parents to bring them food.
Apparently both parents feed the young, a noteworthy event in itself. Great horned owlets commonly leave the nest at about five to

six weeks of age to inhabit the nearby brush and rank grass, where they are later located and fed by the parents. Great horned owls are noted for being very protective of their young—even to the point of attacking and seriously injuring persons approaching nests or chicks on the ground.

A thorough search of the area where we found our owl showed no sign of the parents. Given its emaciated condition and the obvious absence of either parent, I decided that this baby owl had indeed been abandoned. At the same time, the realization began to take shape that this owlet provided an excellent opportunity for a behavioral study using radiotelemetry. Through my work in outdoor biology, I possessed the proper state and federal permits and had for some time been looking for an animal on which to do a long-term telemetry study. This would be an ideal project to base at my rural home on the prairie about five miles away from campus. But first, we would have to nurse him back to health in my lab at Tabor College.

My plot of prairie, which I call TESA (an acronym for Terman Environmental Study Area), is a beautiful fifteen-acre sliver of native grass salvaged from the plow and the cow. My house is a passive solar earth-covered structure (an underground house with one side exposed to the sun)—a mere smile in the side of a hill—blends perfectly with its surroundings of big and little bluestem and prairie wildflowers. Pheasants, quail, wild turkeys, and a host of other natural "tenants" regularly visit the front yard and the nearby pond, seemingly unaware of the low-profile human habitation. With its hedge-bordered expanse of grass and the nearby wooded creek, TESA would be a great place to release the owl. However, the area was inhabited by other great horned owls—a fact that was to have a major impact on the future of my owl.

Bernd Heinrich, a University of Vermont biology professor and author, had written a book about a similar adventure with a hand-reared owl. I studied the pages of his *One Man's Owl*, relishing the communality of experience. Heinrich, however, had not been able continually to follow his owl, Bubo. Armed with the technology of radiotelemetry, I would be able to climb on the back of my owl and through the magic of radio waves accompany it wherever it went, an idea I found exciting.

After loading the little owl into a cardboard box, Richard and I carried it back to the college. Tabor College is an institution much like its harboring town of Hillsboro—small, seldom noticed, but

Aerial photos of TESA and solar earth-sheltered house: (*top*) looking east; (*bottom*) looking north.

good at turning Midwestern sons and daughters into articulate servants of society. Such a student was Pete Johns, the tall, angular offspring of a USDA official from Colorado. As a student in my animal behavior class, Pete was given the young owl for his course project.

What about a name for this bird? This was no small matter. In the words of philosopher Francis Bacon: "Name, though it seem but a superficial and outward matter, yet it carrieth much impression and enchantment." As a scientist, I knew this business of giving names seemed anthropomorphic—forcing humanity's mode on those not human. However, everything has to have a name or we cannot refer to it in any specific way. Even the biblical Adam was directed to give names to creatures as one of his first tasks.

The new arrival was visited by many "Adams," each exercising a basic urge to bestow a name on the little orphan. Owls, by their very appearance, literally demand to be called "Henry" or "George" or some other name that would fit an old, rather wise and stodgy gentleman. Owls have always fascinated humans—their wide blinking eyes, ear tufts, powerful beaks, and mournful voices both endear and repulse. Because owls are often perceived as both beautiful and sinister, wise and evil, something like a love-fear relationship has arisen. No simple task, giving this owl an appropriate name!

Pete decided to call it—simply enough—Stripey. Not too imaginative, but possibly indicative of how owls recognize each other in a fence row. Subtle differences in spots or stripes or angles of the feathers may allow for individual recognition. This owl later proved that he could and did recognize individuals of his own and other species. For Stripey, the name was appropriate, for his stripes were strongly evident.

Stripey's progenitors were of the Midwestern race of the widespread great horned owl species. Each race, of which there are twelve in North America, is adapted to its local environment. Stripey's genes reflected the contributions of thousands of owl generations that may have survived and passed on their heritage simply because a stripe on the breast resembled, to prey or predator, a beam of sun across a shielding cedar tree. As a hatchling, Stripey had certainly been exposed to the behavioral heritage of his mother, a phantom winged tigress who inhabited the local golf course and city park. While golfing, I had often come across the scattered remains of her victims, a circular pile of feathers in the middle of the fairway—all that remained of a dove or quail that was not quick enough. Certainly this grand hunter could impart through her genes a disposition amenable to developing what it took to live with humans.

Would Stripey function like the owl he was, or would he be an "imprint"—a technical term describing an individual with a mistaken species self-image. Had I sentenced Stripey to this mental pur-gatory somewhere between identity and confusion? Raptor rehabil-itation centers go to great lengths to prevent human contact with the many young birds that are brought to them; we have all seen the mother puppets used in the California condor release program. The conventional theory is that imprints are unable to relate to others of their own species once they are imprinted and thus cannot be re-leased to the wild. In the few observational accounts available, im-printed owls are described as loners, always in the corner of the cage, never interacting normally. There are no accounts, however, of the fate of imprints released to the wild and followed for any length of time.

With Stripey perched contentedly in a large aquarium in the back of the laboratory, Pete and I sat in my office planning his future. The idea was to rear this owl with maximum human contact, then re-lease him and keep tabs on his activity through telemetry. I warned Pete: "You'll almost have to live with Stripey—feeding him, touch-ing him, and basically substituting yourself for his mother. We must be certain that he has adequate opportunity to identify with humans."

My now wide-eyed student intently considered the implications of what I had just said. Pete was a lover of nature and the chance to interact with an owl excited him far beyond the natural bounds of a course project. After briefing him on what to look for in Stripey's emerging behavioral repertoire, he left my office in joyous kinship to Jane Goodall, or at least to Grizzly Adams. Within the hour I saw Pete and his girlfriend in the back of the lab finger-pecking the bill of the young owl in a gesture of mutual "grooming."

Owls are funny about grooming. Even wild owls will caress the top of a human head presented to them. Owl rehabilitators will often coax a reluctant invalid owl to feed in this way. A fearful wild owl will, supposedly, be calmed and placated by this sign of friendship, bow to its caretaker, engage in grooming, and then eat. Although my hair was often groomed by Stripey, I would be reluctant to try it with a winged tiger whom I did not know.

Stripey was now squarely in the world of humans. He had been thrust into one of the most interactive of human institutions—a col-lege. At Tabor College, much important communication is accom-plished by people who never plan to bump into each other but conve-niently do—a characteristic of the milieu created by the small size and intimacy of the place. Important decisions are more often made in hallways than committee rooms, a situation that eventually culminated in the decision to let Pete and me keep Stripey.

Feeding the owlet was the first significant problem we faced. Within days, we realized that the appetite of the white fluffball with the gaping bill was well along to outstripping our ability to trap cotton rats, deer mice, prairie voles, and whatever other rodents resided on my bit of prairie. We were already spending most of our spare time trapping food for this insatiable bird. What more could we do? Pete and I did not want to completely sacrifice our home and social lives to ease the hunger pangs of one small owl.

The answer came to me after noticing a huge pile of raw meat scraps that remained after one of the college's special steak dinners. If we could occasionally give the owl a mouse to maintain his search image (which later proved to be very important), perhaps we could keep Stripey satisfied with leftovers from the cafeteria. It was worth a try.

Substituting meat for mice was no problem. The owl thrived—literally growing exponentially while filling the lab with long, attention-grabbing 'cheeeeps' or begging calls. In the wild, these cheeps are emitted by young owls who have left the nest; the cheeping stops as they mature. The parents, hearing these vocalizations, can then readily locate and feed their offspring. Stripey never ceased giving these calls, even as an adult. Somehow, the image of this large Lord of the Night, cheeping from the limb of a stately oak, seemed both ill-suited and altogether hilarious.

We soon appreciated the amazing amount of effort expended by parent owls to fledge just one of their offspring. This labor characterizes parenting in general, especially relative to the formidable costs involved. For wild animals, life strategies are set by the comparative costs (energy requirements) of reproduction. If food or other resources are in short supply, reproduction is halted and reserved for a better time. The fine-tuning of environment and physiology is set with no greater precision than in procreation. We humans, removed from the direct effects of natural selection and living in our own created world, often forget the tremendous implications entailed in deciding (or not deciding) to produce offspring.

In the weeks that followed, Pete and his girlfriend played endlessly with the growing owl. At least twice a day, Stripey was taken out on the lawn and his cage was opened. He strolled out like a chairman of the board. If this owl was innately afraid of humans, he covered his fear with the bravado of a novice bullfighter. This bird was a joy to be with, and his public appearance was often the premier event on campus.

With the eyes of an animal lover and naturalist, I found this playtime with Stripey delightfully gratifying. Here was the bird we had rescued now developing into a sturdy owl specimen. As a scientist, however, I wondered whether I was observing the development of an owl or the transformation of a wild animal into a human plaything.

$\mathscr{B}$ASIC NEEDS AND BASIC TRAINING

GIVE ME A DOZEN HEALTHY INFANTS, WELL-FORMED, AND
MY OWN SPECIFIED WORLD TO BRING THEM UP IN AND I'LL
GUARANTEE TO TAKE ANY ONE AT RANDOM AND TRAIN HIM
TO BECOME ANY TYPE OF SPECIALIST I MIGHT SELECT—DOC-
TOR, LAWYER, ARTIST, MERCHANT CHIEF AND, YES, EVEN
BEGGARMAN AND THIEF, REGARDLESS OF HIS TALENTS, PEN-
CHANTS, TENDENCIES, ABILITIES, VOCATIONS, AND RACE
OF HIS ANCESTORS.

—*John Broadus Watson, behaviorist*

◈ ◈ ◈ Winter's final grip had released the Kansas
countryside, and all sorts of wild things were busy filling the fields
and grasslands with offspring, following the driving motif of nature—reproduction. Yet only a small percentage of the young of any
animal ever mature to adulthood. Most die in the jaws of a predator
or from exposure to the elements. Even the owls, near the top the
food chain, lose many of their broods to accident, disease, or other
predators. Stripey, dumped prematurely from the nest by a March
windstorm, probably would have been numbered among the lost,
relegated to anonymity in nature's never-ending struggles. But with
the help of the college food service and the local rodent community,
Stripey grew quickly—trading white feathery down for the pin-
cushion appearance of a juvenile. He had provided much data for
Pete's project, and now Pete, like his subject, was leaving the (academic) nest for a summer job. The owl would pass solely into my
hands.

As I continued to observe our adolescent predator, I reflected on
how this owl, perched contentedly in his lab cage, existed only because I had prevented it from being another statistic in the mortality
tables of owls. Because this one owl lived when it should have died,
did the natural world go out of alignment? Did my action result in

any significant directional change? Are chance and circumstance the only factors determining whether any particular individual endures? I think not. Any creature's existence depends on the fine thread of probability weaving in and out of the fabric of generations. I believe the Weaver of this eternal cloth allowed this bird and me to meet. Many who ply my trade tend to be skeptics and depend solely on the human mind to construct answers to infinite questions. A proper respect for humility convinces me that much of reality might well transcend human thought.

Stripey as
juvenile.

One day after a particularly tough lecture before a largely somno-lescent classroom audience, I yielded to an intense need to escape the stuffy halls of academe. I decided to take Stripey out to TESA, my piece of the open prairie. After we arrived, I introduced him to a cage in my open-faced pole barn. The 4 × 6 foot wooden cage was constructed by a student years ago for a wild adult owl that had lost a wing to a shotgun blast. That owl survived four years before suc-cumbing to an unknown malady. Possibly those four years away from flight and freedom were all it could endure. Sadly, up to 90 percent of great horned owls may die at the hand of man. Too often, fear, superstition, and outright meanness overwhelm good sense. Now, the cage for one who should not have died so soon was to be the launching pad to freedom for one who should not have lived.

Stripey immediately took to his new home, apparently comfort-able in the wood-and-wire cage with a tree limb for a perch. In the manner of his kind, he sat stoically for hours, only occasionally moving to view his surroundings. But when mobilized by the pangs of hunger, he rocked back and forth like a feathered metronome. He literally demanded food and I responded by giving him meat scraps and mice. Small items were gulped down whole. Larger pieces he dismembered with talons and beak.

Rodents were foremost on his list of culinary delights. I served them up at every opportunity in order to develop his search image for proper owl prey. Captured field mice, killed by me first, were then handed to Stripey, who grabbed each one with his beak, instinctively broke its neck, and swallowed it whole. Later, I presented live mice in a large wooden box and allowed him to do the killing. In about a month, his accuracy improved to where he was able to pounce on a free-ranging mouse about 50 percent of the time. Older mice could usually avoid capture, but young ones were invariably snared (the old and sly survive while the young and careless perish—a graphic illustration of the character of natural selection). Both species morphology and behavior are shaped by the need to avoid detection and being eaten, a potent message that demonstrates the paramount importance of predators in the workings of the natural world.

Interestingly, Stripey drank water from a dish. I had assumed that most moisture would be derived from the prey. Later, I observed him visiting TESA's pond regularly and dipping his beak thirty to forty times in one drinking bout. He was amazingly easy to handle—open the cage door, present a forearm, and an owl immediately appears, anchoring himself in place with his formidable talons. With Stripey on my gloved wrist, I often threw a mouse out on the lawn and watched him dive after it. He soon learned to anticipate the diversionary tactics of mice, and his aim improved daily. Stripey grew to almost his full adult weight of 1350 grams (about 3 pounds) in the first two months of his stay at TESA (see the Appendix).

Since owls, like people, learn from observing the behavior of the parents, I wondered whether he could ever develop the considerable skills needed to locate and capture prey without exposure to an owl that was actually hunting. Successful hunting seems to be largely an inherited ability, reinforced by innumerable opportunities for practice. Eventually, practice pays off. Stripey later demonstrated that he could pounce on a deer mouse fifty feet away on a dim night. While much of Stripey's behavior was genetically determined, I later appreciated how learning fine-tuned his existence, especially in his selection of prey animals and his use of habitat. Although internally driven to hunt, he had to learn what perches he could effectively use and which prey could easily be dispatched without undue risk to himself.

Stripey was continually given to stretching his wings and going through the motions of flight. My twin daughters Katy and Kerry greatly delighted in helping with his trial flights. Gently, I tossed the young owl into the air. About twenty yards downwind, he'd crash, right himself, then calmly stroll up to the girls to groom their shoes with his beak. Being eight years old with a full measure of developing adult caution, the girls backed off, and ran away. Undeterred, Stripey gave chase but soon returned, cheeping, to sit on my foot and groom my pant legs.

This toss-and-glide training lasted until one day in early June when Stripey suddenly was no longer content to land on the ground, but instead flew into a tree forty yards away. His cheeps became longer and more highly pitched after this—perhaps reflecting his entrance into a new dimension.

$\mathscr{O}$F GENES AND ENVIRONMENT

❖ ❖ ❖ Considerable differences separate the traditional pet from the wild animal reared as a pet. A dog or cat is the
product of generations of domestication—compatibility with the
aims of man determining which individual will breed and which will
not. Stripey was born wild, his behavior throughout our association
only slightly removed from the unrelenting parameters set by the
process of natural selection. The avoidance of humans was wired
into Stripey's system, but the owl chick's chance exposure to humankind during a critical time of species identification resulted in a
short-circuit in the wiring. In other words, the distinct possibility
existed that he was imprinted on me.

This possibility raised a number of questions: Was he *really* imprinted on me? Would he develop as an owl or as a feathered human
mimic? Or would the genetic programming from ages past prevail?
This question essentially typifies the "nature-nurture" debate. Is it
genetics or environment which sets the course and fate of owls and
humans? Stripey, with a talon in both sides of the issue (so to speak),
could teach me much about this eternal argument.

He was thriving—and showing both human and animal characteristics. Owls, perhaps more than other birds, reflect our humanity
back to us. Even as a scientist, I felt a desire to keep him simply as a
pet. However, my intent from the beginning was to release him because he was a wild animal and therefore entitled to the freedom
decreed by his heritage. Stripey's ferocity when I fed him convinced
me that he could develop the necessary skills to survive, but his
friendliness at other times made me doubt his chances for making it
on his own. Regardless of his behavior, there was no alternative—in
time he had to be released.

The big question then—when should I let him go? By mid-June of that first year, the routine of feeding, playing, grooming, and returning him to his cage was quickly becoming tiresome. And Stripey, beginning to exhibit signs of a yen for freedom, had attained his full size—eighteen inches in length and about three pounds. The time seemed right. The first order of business, then, was to fit him with a small radio transmitter—a seemingly simple task that quickly became tangled in a web of complexities. Should I attach the transmitter to the leg, to the back with a wire passed around the chest, or clip it to one of his feathers? My first decision favored fastening the transmitter to his leg.

With the help of my wife Jan (who richly deserves a place in the annals of wives who went the extra mile for their husbands), the transmitter was secured. I held fast to the legs and talons while Jan adjusted the plastic loop around the squawking owl's leg. Others who have worked with owls have indicated their disbelief that Stripey could be so easily tagged. Actually, since leather gloves give scant protection against long talons, Stripey must have withheld his rage while we subjected him to this affront. However, he did use his beak to pinch and pull at my fingers—even though wild owls are not known to employ their beaks as weapons when handled.

Convinced that the leg band holding the five-gram transmitter was loose enough for comfort, I placed Stripey back in his cage to observe his reaction to his new anklet. After a few initial tugs, he decided to ignore it. This adaptability greatly magnified his value

Leg-mounted transmitter.

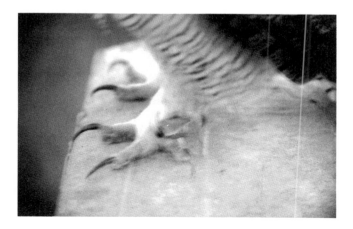

as a subject for telemetry. Other researchers have reported that some individuals simply will not adjust to a transmitter. Apparently unhampered, Stripey continued to catch and kill rodents with ease. But nobody's perfect: in a few weeks he removed this first transmitter—which I never found—and I opted for a more secure plastic band to hold the device, and this worked much better.

The June heat set in early. In Kansas, summer—regarded as the year's most uncomfortable season—means a burning sun in a cloudless sky, and man and beast alike are compelled to seek the nearest shade. The oppressive heat certainly might be a negative factor in Stripey's survival. Yet the cheeps of wild great horned juveniles emanating from the nearby woods were both encouraging and comforting sounds to me. Their parents had released them; perhaps I should release my charge too.

So I launched Stripey, now about three months old and wearing his transmitter, simply by opening his cage. The door was left ajar so that he could return at will for food and water, in the shade and security of the barn. After a quick check of the signal with the receiver, I concealed myself—watching like an anxious papa as his child first ventured forth into a cold cruel world. Stripey immediately hopped to the door frame, cheeped, then flew over to the nearest perch—the wheel of my old Ford 8N tractor, about five feet away. There he sat and looked for the mouse or meat scrap that heretofore had accompanied the opening of the cage door. No snack forthcoming, he ruffled his feathers in the total body shake uniquely characteristic of owls, and flew out to the hedgerow fifty yards to the east.

Scarcely into the trees, he was attacked—mobbed actually—by three bluejays and one absolutely mad mockingbird who relentlessly shrieked and dived at the bewildered owlet. Then I observed what must be an instinctive reaction, since this mobbing business was new to Stripey. Without hesitation he jumped to the center of the tree where the branches were thickest. Here his pursuers were at a disadvantage—no room to fly or dart about. One by one the raucous foursome departed. The mockingbird was the last to give up, intimating of more to come from his quarter.

Mobbing is one of the enigmas of nature. Why do so many small birds squander energy attacking those larger birds usually considered threatening to lesser species? Hawks, owls, and crows—even blue jays—are all frequent targets. Bernd Heinrich hypothesizes that

Mobbing mockingbird.

mobbing serves to chase off predators that could possibly kill the smaller birds and their young. Great horned owls certainly kill these birds by surprise attack at night, and the benefits of mobbing may outweigh the costs.

A. C. Bent, the great bird watcher and naturalist, describes the relationship between owls and their mobbers:

> Horned owls have plenty of enemies that cordially hate them, but none of them are dangerous, except man and occasionally one of their own species. Crows are their chief enemies, with blue jays a close second and all other small birds following. I have often been able to locate an owl by the clamor of a noisy and excited mob of crows. If an owl is discovered by a crow, the alarm is immediately given and all the crows within hearing respond to the call, gather about the owl, flying around or perching in the tree as near to the owl as they dare go, cawing loudly and making a great fuss. They seldom are bold enough to strike the owl, though I have seen them do so twice. The owl stands all this with dignified indifference, until his patience is exhausted, when he flies away with a string of crows trailing on behind; perhaps he has to move several times before he shakes off his tormentors or finds a secluded hiding place, where he can doze in peace. The owl seldom retaliates by striking one of the black

rascals; in fact, I doubt if he ever does. But he gets even with them when they are in their roosts at night; I have heard of several crow roosts that were broken up by a great horned owl living in the vicinity; and many an owl has eaten crow.

This being the case, the songbirds of TESA were gearing up for the new threat in their midst. Their concern proved to be premature. After an hour I located Stripey by the signal from his transmitter. Huddled against the base of the same sheltering tree, he was a sorry sight, and looking far from ready to go it on his own. Every vestige of self-confidence was dimmed in those yellow eyes. He literally came running to me and leaped onto my arm. Cuddling him, I returned him to the barn. As he snuggled against my chest, I could almost believe the experts. Was an owl that's imprinted on humans ruined for a natural existence in the wild? Surely the owlets in the nearby woods did not behave this way! I feared the instincts for survival were gone, replaced by some abnormal bond. With a decisive cut of the tin snips, I removed the transmitter from his leg and returned him to his cage in the barn—a place I now doubted that he would ever leave.

During the following two or three weeks Stripey would undergo a marvelous transformation. This was not so much a physical alteration (he already had attained the size of an adult male owl) but a psychological change. He appeared to blaze with new fire, as if his brief taste of freedom had ignited a spark of wildness, deep down, that had lain hidden and smoldering. Possibly his short exposure to the wild switched on some internal program. Animals loitering in his surroundings were no longer ignored but became objects of intense scrutiny. His yellow eyes gleamed with a depth of ferocity that I had noticed only in wild owls, and he no longer sat contented in his cage but rocked back and forth in agitation when I approached.

Stripey's unrest provided me with an obvious reply to an equally obvious question: Should I release him again? There was no longer any reason to hold back—he had become a bird of a different feather.

$\mathscr{P}$LAYING OUT THE INTERNAL PROGRAM

❖ ❖ ❖ Do we really have free will or are our actions ultimately determined by our genetic makeup? How many of our decisions are really unforced and unencumbered? When opportunities in life arise, are we totally at liberty to choose which road we will follow? I do not presume to know the answer for humans, but I suspect owls go on automatic pilot for much of the first months of their lives.

I refitted Stripey with a new leg-mounted transmitter and then carried him to a centrally located tree on TESA, a larger than average osage orange with widespread shade. With the sun in late June a major factor to be avoided, I did not want Stripey to begin his tenure dry and thirsty. Also, I wanted to give him every opportunity to discover the nearby pond. As I walked from the barn to the tree, Stripey remained on my arm although he could now fly well for long distances. Perhaps this propensity for staying near home and security would make the job of radio-tracking him more doable in the weeks to come.

When we arrived at the release site, Stripey—with some prompting—found a perch on the nearest branch. Mercifully, the mobbing crew was absent. He stayed there all day, one with the branch on which he sat, same position, not moving a feather. As evening closed in, I wondered whether he would be around in the morning. Before I went to bed, I took the radio receiver outside, where I set the correct frequency, pointed the antenna toward the tree two hundred yards away, and flicked the switch. The receiver beeped reassuringly—Stripey had not moved.

The next morning was Sunday, and while the family was getting ready for church I picked up the receiver and walked outside. No signal greeted me from the tree down by the pond. Frantically, I rotated the antenna until it fielded a faint beep coming from somewhere. A complete turn to the east brought it in stronger—apparently from the barn. Losing no time, I ran over there. There, sitting on the old home cage, was Stripey, his partly closed eyes suddenly alert at my approach.

Moving from side to side like a pendulum, he promptly began cheeping for food. I found my leather gloves on the tractor, pulled them on, and caught up a deer mouse from the cage where I had been keeping trapped rodents. A deer mouse is a mouthful for a young owl, but Stripey, after killing it by breaking its neck and crunching its skull, gulped it down with ease. This manner of killing, characteristic of wild owls, appeared full-blown in Stripey. He had inherited at least this share of his wilderness legacy.

After finishing five deer mice, Stripey was content to sit quietly on top of his cage. In his brain, this spot in my barn was where he was supposed to be—near the familial nest or rearing site. Owls feed their young for several months after they leave the nest. These "branchers," who hide among tree branches or in the grass, must stay near the nest if the foraging parents are to find them easily. Stripey's internal guidance system had not failed him, nor would it over the next few days. He was invariably around the barn, the garden, or house. Early in his life, food was available to him *ad libidum*. Now, when he was free-ranging, his hunger occasionally went ungratified for short periods, and like a spoiled child he began to cry incessantly until I fed him.

The piercing cheeps of a hungry young owl were designed by nature to bring immediate reward from already overworked parents. I found it impossible to ignore them, and after a couple of nights of these nerve-shredding squawks I established two feeding stations— one on a swing set in front of the house and another on the barn roof. The house feeding station was for table scraps and an occasional rodent. The barn-roof station was for larger food items such as rabbits and road kills. These I placed in a large raccoon live-trap with the door wired open. I hoped Stripey would routinely enter this trap, which would allow his recapture should I lose radio contact with him. He soon learned to visit these stations regularly, thus reducing his midnight cheeping orgies and restoring the family's regular sleep patterns.

I am convinced that the feeding stations (a "halfway house" where food was always available) were a prime factor in his eventual road to complete independence, allowing him to try out his hunting skills without the dire consequences suffered by many wild juvenile owls. He always had an ace in the hole—a place to refuel when prey and talon did not meet. Stripey gradually began widening his explorations of the area around TESA, and as his absences increased in number and length, his visits to the feeding stations became unpredictable. Occasionally, food would sit for two or three days and become rancid and riddled with maggots. I would clean this mess away only to have Stripey show up the next night, very indignant that his food insurance had been canceled.

(*Left*) Stripey's feeding station on top of the swing in front of the house. (*Right*) At night on top of the swing.

I knew the transmitter's battery would eventually expire and I would lose the signal and my link to Stripey. Would he continue to come back, and if he did, could I catch him to replace the transmitter? If it became necessary to trap him, I could activate the raccoon trap/feeding station on the barn roof.

Near the end of June the receiver no longer picked up the signal from Stripey's leg transmitter. A small unit, its range was limited to about half a mile. Evidently he had embarked on his first dispersal flight, leaving the safe confines of the barn, garden, and house for the beckoning adventures of the unknown.

I located him in a wooded stream just below TESA, in the South Woods (see map). Young owls, like the offspring of other animals, cannot remain in their parents' home range. With only so much food available, eventually the young will have to strike out on their own and find other hunting grounds.

Stripey in trap on barn feeding station.

Broad meadows, dotted here and there with osage orange and cedar trees, surrounded TESA. Why did Stripey ignore these trees and fly instead to the dense confines of the South Woods? Owls may have programmed in their brains a model of the right habitat in which they should live. Perhaps as he flew about, Stripey surveyed trees, fence rows, and pastures, comparing these images to an internal blueprint. The South Woods flipped all the right switches.

Great horned owls are habitat generalists, living in all sorts of places, so the limitations placed on Stripey by his neural circuitry were few compared to other birds such as the Kirtland's warbler in northern Michigan. Survival for this little bird is dependent on jack pines of just the right height in woodland glades of a specific size. The Kirtland's "pickiness" is leading it to extinction in a human-dominated landscape while the great horned owl's generalist habits have allowed it to prosper.

Responding to whisperings within, Stripey flew many times to the South Woods. I was excited when he did this because it indicated that his affair with humans had not violated this aspect of his wild heritage. He was doing the right thing about going to the right places.

In Kansas, woodlands are found mainly along streams; the prairies and wheat fields control the higher ground. However, these wooded

The South Woods next to TESA.

areas are prime owl habitat and usually are already filled with their quota of great horned owls. The South Woods was no exception—a pair of horned owls patrolled its borders, especially during the fall and winter. Now in late June, the hormone levels in these local residents had subsided and they were either gone or more tolerant. Stripey, for the time being, had visiting privileges.

Stripey reveled in the tall walnuts and oaks. For me, it was an uncommon joy to roam those woods and have one of the most secretive of all wild creatures fly down to greet me. Occasionally, the owl would even follow me out of the woods to TESA and roost on the barn roof.

Radiotelemetry gives the scientist an unusual advantage over his subject. Wherever the tagged animal goes it can be located, thus superseding most hiding strategies. Stripey must have been amazed at how easily I could find him. Variously, I located him under cedar trees and in ranks of tall grass, in hedgerows and along creek bottoms, and even tucked under concrete rubble. Hiding in such places allows young owls to avoid predation, and it must be that the printing presses of natural selection have indelibly inked these instructions inside the skull of every great horned owl. Throughout the remainder of his first summer, Stripey and I played hide and seek on the prairies and in the woods around TESA.

The owl had yet to show me any sign that he was hunting and killing his own food, and I found it necessary to keep food supplied at the feeding stations. Mother Nature had given him so many automatic mechanisms—I could not believe that she would leave this most important one to the uncertainties of the learning process. Would Stripey ever be able to support himself? Apparently, teaching Stripey to hunt was going to be up to me—but how?

$\mathcal{O}$N BECOMING INDEPENDENT

IT TAKES A LONG TIME TO BRING EXCELLENCE TO MATURITY.

—Publilius Syrus, philosopher

❖ ❖ ❖ Wild owls generally force their young to leave in late summer or early fall by refusing to feed them—supposedly the young by then have learned enough to fend for themselves by watching their parents hunt. However, most studies reveal that a majority of these young owls perish in the first year. Natural selection deals a rough hand. I wanted to give Stripey better odds. Because he was imprinted on humans and had only the briefest exposure to his mother, he had to learn to hunt from scratch, with a little natural help from his genetic endowment. The outlook for his survival seemed grim indeed. Every time I observed him, I looked for some sign that he was feeding himself.

The first clue came one night in late July as Katy, Kerry, and I were following him as he flitted from perch to perch. Stripey had called us out of the house with a loud cheep from his feeding station. The pantry was bare and he wanted us to know it. Shouldering the radio equipment and arming the girls with flashlights, I led the way. Off he flew to the garden, where he landed on a fence post and cheeped again. Following the signal of his transmitter, we approached him. Instead of waiting for me, he soared to the TV antenna on the roof of our earth-sheltered house. In the dim moonlight, he flew down and snatched a June beetle (*Phyllophaga portoricensis*) as it crawled across the ground, then carried it up to the roof over the entry where he crunched it down. I never suspected that owls ate insects but here was proof that at least one enjoyed an occasional arthropod. Later, my students and I were to find many insect remnants in the pellets of both hawks and owls—evidence that insects and other invertebrates are frequently eaten by birds of prey.

Later in the summer, I detected a distinct whiff of carrion on his breath. Was he finding and feeding on dead animals? Many predators, such as eagles, are not averse to eating carrion should live prey become scarce. Owls are not ordinarily given to eating carrion, preferring fresh kills. Maybe Stripey was killing and storing food and eating it later, thus acquiring the smell of rotting flesh. Was he actually storing food? I had to put him to the test.

I decided to give him all he could eat of his favorite delicacy, mice, at one feeding. The one hundred traps I set yielded twenty-two mice, a good catch indicating a high density of natural prey. These I fed to Stripey on his next visit to TESA. One after another, as soon as he could crush their skulls, he gulped down the mice. One, two, three, four—up to six mice in one feeding. When I offered him the seventh, the food-caching switch was thrown. Caching food is a complex behavior that requires assessing food type and condition, establishing a cache, and remembering the hiding place so that the food can be found again. Most scientists assume that this behavior depends on some teaching from the parents. By observing my hand-reared bird, who had no opportunity to learn from his parents, I was able to establish that caching behavior is genetically based. Stripey exhibited all the known characteristics of food-hoarding behavior. He decided when to cache, surveyed the surroundings, stored the items, and invariably retrieved them. His food-storing behavior appeared to be inherently programmed from start to finish.

Owls, like predators in general, will utilize a patch of prey until diminishing returns force them to move on. Animal ecologists are learning more about how animals make decisions on how to use their time and energy. This field of study is called "optimal foraging." Measurements are taken of pursuit time, search time, giving-up time, travel time, and handling time in an effort to predict how long an animal should stay in any one area (residence time). Perhaps my observations of him will add some more information into the growing volume of optimal foraging literature.

As time passed, I noticed that Stripey often hung around his caches of stored food. As far as I know, he was only caching the excess food that I gave him. Obviously, a substantial cache of surplus food would keep an owl in the vicinity since he would need to watch and defend it. Stripey's comings and goings grew more predictable as I became adept at monitoring the state of his food savings accounts.

He often dropped in for a visit on summer nights, and we eagerly looked forward to these friendly encounters. One night as Jan sat stargazing on the lawn, Stripey suddenly flew down, sidled over, and began nibbling her toes. His silent approach and unanticipated pedal grooming took her completely by surprise. She managed not to scream or jerk away. Jan's mild, controlled demeanor (fast-rooted in her own genetics) allowed the rest of the family to watch and marvel at the affable nature of this unique bird.

Stripey's curiosity and his rollicking manner lasted throughout much of the summer and into early fall. He regularly dive-bombed our cats, retracting his landing gear just prior to impact, sending them rolling. Since his sorties were flown at dusk or nightfall, the

Stripey
caching a
duck (*top*) on
the barn;
(*bottom*)
under a tree.

cats had no warning of impending attacks and became completely unnerved. Consequently, they began to scan the skies much more frequently than they had "before the owl."

Farmers often complain that owls attack and kill their cats—especially the light-colored ones. At this time, Stripey had no such designs on ours—he merely buzzed them (although at a later time he attacked a cat that wandered too close to his food cache). For now, he was in the practicing mode—attacks were launched against everything from hedge apples to corn shucks. While on the ground, he often stalked the cats and the dog, walking with his shoulders hunched, head forward, peering into every nook and crevice. When

Stripey on the barn, our cat on a stepladder.

Stripey interacting with author.

he located one of them, he would hiss and, with wings spread to make himself look large and fierce, he'd fly to the nearest perch. There he flexed his wings, shook and ruffled his feathers, and cheeped. No doubt Stripey very much appreciated the family pets— ready targets that they were.

Great horned owls can be dangerous, especially when defending nests. Contrary to occasional newspaper accounts about wild owls threatening joggers, Stripey neither dive-bombed nor "play attacked" me or other adults during all of our years together. By contrast, Bubo, Bernd Heinrich's hand-reared owl, occasionally attacked strangers visiting Heinrich's cabin in the woods. Why was Bubo aggressive and Stripey passive? Maybe it was due to individual differences. However, Stripey was not wild, at least not yet.

This young owl's relationship with me could be characterized as that of a pet. I could walk up to him and coax him to perch on my arm. He especially enjoyed having his beak and head scratched. Often, Stripey would fly down and land on my foot and groom my ankle with his beak. Such grooming never hurt. His touch was so gentle that I could even trust him to groom my hair and ears. It is said, however, that even an injured wild owl will groom the hair of a person brave enough to bend a head. Perhaps here was another switched-on behavior that awaited a specific stimulus.

Stripey's exuberant interaction with the pets might have been the natural unleashing of genetic directives designed to hone hunting skills. But why the unusual grooming of a human? A possible explanation is that his developing sexual urges were being misdirected and that he had viewed me as a potential mate. Basically, I feel this was true, but there seemed to be more happening here than out-of-context manifestations of behavior patterns not yet triggered by increasing hormone levels. Can behavior in any organism really be dissected and sorted into such simple, clearly defined components? I doubt it, but as a working explanation, this is the best theory that science has to offer at present.

ACHIEVING ADULTHOOD

To be adult is to be alone.

—*Jean Rostand, biologist, writer*

❖ ❖ ❖ Summer's monochrome passed into the multicolored days of autumn. Great horned owls mate in the dead of winter but begin carving out a territory and searching for a mate during the cool days of late fall. Stripey was hunting now and broadening his food choices to include reptiles (skinks). He was also responding to the calls of nearby wild owls who began showing themselves in prominent trees at the edge of TESA. He continued to stay near home base but the signs of fear were unmistakable—he was tense, jittery, nervous, with tufts erect and an ear tuned in to the challenging hoots from the South Woods.

My pet was changing. The strafings on the cats increased in violence and were punctuated with hisses and lunges. Nor was our dog Buffy excluded as a target. Yet tempering this aggression were interludes of amiable behavior. One night Richard Wall, who had helped me acquire Stripey back in March, stopped by, and Stripey accorded him all the friendliness that he usually reserved for me. Pete Johns, back in school for his senior year, was also welcomed by Stripey during an outdoor ecology lab session. The reunion went well although it was evident to Pete that his former pet had changed. The output of Stripey's hormone pump was definitely on the increase.

Meanwhile, his absences from TESA were increasing—undoubtedly influenced by the aggression of the resident owls. It was mid-November and the onset of the mating season for mature great horned owls. Around TESA, wild owl pairs were beginning to duet together—the male producing a rapid staccato hoot sequence and the female responding antiphonally with three soft and longer vocalizations. Great horneds are monogamous, though the meaning of this term in nature is probably different than it is with humans. Monogamy with owls is a practical affair dictated not from a human ethical system but by the raw reality that it takes two to rear the young. Owls that survive from year to year probably will continue to stay together, but should one die, the survivor finds another mate.

There seems to be a continual probing of habitat space by young dispersing owls trying to find a hole in the social fabric of established mated pairs. As Stripey matured—growing to be more like his kind—he became increasingly aware of the presence of the other owls around TESA.

With white-footed mouse in talons.

He would often stare at the nearby woods—especially when the woods-dwellers began hooting at dusk. Once he even appeared to be in a trance—I touched his beak with my hand, and he showed no indication of awareness. Soon after, he left for one of his longest absences. For more than ten days I could not pick up a signal from any of the usual places. Nothing from TESA or the South Woods—his most common perches remained unvisited. The usual owl-tracking lab projects for my biology classes had to be suspended because "there's no signal." Where had he gone?

Systematic searches by car—driving the back roads and stopping on hilltops to scan the area with the radio receiver antenna—yielded no signal. We even visited the city park in the improbable event that Stripey's genetic program might have led him back to his place of origin. No luck. Compounding our frenzy, Ron Hiebert, a neighboring farmer, informed us that he had spotted a dead owl in a nearby pasture.

Jan and the girls rode with me over to the pasture to inspect the owl's carcass. It *could* have been Stripey—down to the last barred and dotted feather! The beak, the feathers, the state of decay—this corpse in my hands wrote the end of the story. I was given one glimpse of hope that this might not be Stripey—the beak bore evidence of long use. Stripey was too young for a beak worn like that. Once home, we searched the videotapes we had made of Stripey to get a close-up view of his beak. We found a close-up of him eating cherries in the TESA orchard. Sure enough, below his facial disk, his beak was smooth and shiny. The dead owl could not be Stripey. But we were not totally relieved.

There was something weird about the spot where we found the dead owl. Alongside the bird lay the body of a rabbit. The owl's legs had been hacked off at the ankle above the talons. Although collecting the talons of any raptor is illegal, it still happens. This owl was probably lured to the rabbit bait and then shot for its talons. Sometimes, human behavior is hard to swallow. Such feelings confirm Aldo Leopold's words: "One of the disadvantages of an ecological education is that one lives alone in a world of wounds."

As luck would have it, the following week I received a call from a TV station in Wichita, asking if I would consent to do a news clip on my owl research. Here was fame in my grasp, but no owl! The dead owl wasn't Stripey. Stripey was out there somewhere, flying around his haunts—maybe he had even found a new haven. At any rate, almost certain that I could find him, I took a giant step of faith and, with nontypical bravado, told the reporter, "Sure, come on out. Will tomorrow be okay?" I would call him if the owl did not show.

That night I went to bed, alert to every sound. Sure enough, when the rest of the world had grown quiet, we heard the familiar cheeps out by the swing set. Stripey had returned, and now I couldn't let him get away. Grabbing a flashlight and a handful of franks from the refrigerator, I hurried outside. His transmitter was gone. Apparently he had again bitten it off. He was so hungry that he could hardly wait for me to hand him a hot dog. After feeding him four or five, I was

Stripey in his cage.

able to coax him on to my arm. With the TV crew coming the next day, I decided that the best place for my wandering owl would be the large walk-in cage by the barn.

Screeching, he flapped and fought as I held him against my chest and carried him to the cage. Getting the door open with my arms full of frantic owl was an adventure in itself. A quick push closed him inside where he flapped around the walls for a minute or two, then surprisingly he settled quietly on the perch.

In the morning, Stripey had another surprise for me. He had deposited a pellet in the cage. A pellet is the regurgitated remains—hair, bones, nails, and so forth—of whatever prey the bird had ingested. Since he had received only hot dogs from me, Stripey's pellet presented a record of what he had been eating during his ten-day absence. By teasing the pellet apart under a microscope, Pete Johns and I found that he had been eating shrews and birds. This was the first proof that he was hunting for himself, although somewhat inefficiently, since he was obviously in food distress.

When the TV crew arrived, the day was sunny and calm—perfect for photography. Pete had come out from the college and was also interviewed and filmed with Stripey. Stripey's behavior was exem-

Owl pellets, the regurgitated, undigested part of an owl's meal.

Television crew filming interview, with Pete Johns holding antenna and receiver.

plary. He handled so easily that his screen test was a rousing success. But we could not coax him to hoot. In fact, I had yet to hear him hoot, although he had occasionally emitted some rudimentary guttural sounds. An owl hoots to proclaim posession of a territory and to woo a mate, and perhaps for Stripey this would come later. As a smashing finale to the news clip, I released Stripey, who promptly lifted his wings and flew away into the sunset.

That evening, Stripey came back to the house and settled on a favorite perch—the shade cover above the glass patio door. Occasionally, he would drop to the ground and walk up to the door and look in before resuming his perch. We went to bed, content to know that this member of our family was home safe. But about 2:30 A.M. we were awakened by very loud hoots outside the window. They did not emanate from Stripey—he was gone! I could not raise a signal from his new leg transmitter. It had to be a resident owl, then, hooting from one of the trees close to the house, proclaiming victory over the intruder on his realm.

Stripey stayed away three days, and I could not locate him even with an extended antenna on the receiver. Where had he gone?

Researchers in South Dakota had lured great horned owls to an area by constructing platforms of twigs in trees. So, earlier in the summer I constructed an artificial nest in one of the trees near the barn in the hope that Stripey might feel attracted to it and maybe one day adopt it as a nest. Great horned owls do not construct nests of their own but commandeer those of hawks, squirrels, or other large nest builders.

When Stripey returned this time, this nest is where I found him. Tempting him down with a mouse, I decided to remove the leg transmitter since it had such a limited range and Stripey had already removed it twice. Transmitters are expensive and my research budget was tight at best. Of course this meant that I would be without a link to him until I could come up with a more satisfactory unit. Luckily, Stripey stayed around, showing up at the feeding stations so I could keep tabs on him. However, I had to find a better way of putting a transmitter on him.

As I searched for a more suitable transmitter and attachment device, I heard about an owl researcher, Craig Weatherby of Adrian College, near the home of Jan's parents in southeastern Michigan. Again, how fortunate could I be with this owl project of mine! I needed some help and perhaps the only one who could give it to me was located less than thirty miles from where we were going for Christmas vacation.

Could Stripey survive on his own for two weeks while we drove to Michigan to visit relatives and confer with Dr. Weatherby? We de-

Stripey on patio looking in.

cided to take the chance, and before we left, the feeding station on the barn was stocked with three pounds of meat, ten rodents, and a frozen duck to tide him over.

Craig Weatherby greeted me in the science building at Adrian on a cold December morning. Immediately, we felt the camaraderie that only arises when people are linked by an unusual interest or experience. Even though great horned owls are common, very few scientists work with them. Weatherby straightaway showed me the various forms of equipment used by him and his students to capture and radio-tag wild owls. We then traveled to a close-by marsh and located a wild owl he had been following for several months. As I trailed this owl of the North Woods, I thought of Stripey back on the Kansas prairie. The crisscrossed elastic harness with which Craig Weatherby had fitted his owl seemed appropriate for mine as well. I returned home to Kansas, hoping that Stripey would fly down to greet me when I arrived. Two weeks is a long time—would he still be around?

While he was not exactly "waiting at the gate," Stripey was indeed still around. A quick check of the feeding station revealed that all the food was gone except one mouse. Of course the larder could have been raided by a hawk or another owl, but because of the proximity of the stations to the house, I doubted it and refused to worry.

Elastic harness and transmitter.

Elastic harness on owl's back.

A few days later he showed up on the wire trash burner behind the barn. He immediately dive-bombed the cats, very much into perfecting his perch-and-pounce skill. After he alighted on the barn, I brought him to me with a mouse, then grabbed and held him against my chest. He neither struggled nor attempted to rake me with his talons—which was amazing since he had been on his own for so long. Consigning Stripey to the large cage, I tackled the problem of changing transmitter and harness. I wrote letters to every radiotelemetry company I could find and had the good fortune to be contacted by Dan Stoneburner of Advanced Telemetry and Consulting in Watkinsville, Georgia.

Large cage on TESA.

Dan is a rare individual in the world of science—he not only understands the need for competent science but appreciates the relationship that can build between scientist and subject. Over the next several months, he sent me not one but many transmitters, each time improving on the design to where both antenna and transmitter could withstand the ferocity of even a great horned owl. Richard Wall and I fitted the first transmitter on Stripey at the end of December. Since we did not have Dr. Weatherby's elastic, we used the wire harness that Dan had supplied with his first transmitter. But two hours after we released Stripey, he bit through the wires.

When I finally located him that night, the transmitter was dangling from his side. Luckily I was again able to catch him with a mouse (a powerful stimulus for an owl) and refitted him with a stronger wire. After shutting him in the garage for the night and acknowledging his disgust, I opted for Weatherby's elastic harness.

The next morning Jan donated some elastic bands from her sewing kit. Once again I was forced to call on her resourcefulness to help me fit this new "bra" on a less than eager owl. Deftly she threaded the

Stripey with
wire har-
ness—he's
unhappy.

Jan and Abby
tracking
Stripey on
TESA.

Hiebert's Pasture, Stripey's home area during the second half of his first year.

elastic bands around wing and feathers to tie them to the transmitter on Stripey's back. At the last instant, Stripey's frustration threshold spilled over and jerking from my grasp, he lunged out with a talon, piercing Jan's finger tip. I felt guilty because I had not suffered so much as a scratch in the countless times I had handled him. Still, Jan tied off the elastic and the transmitter was mounted. What a wife! Few women could live with an owl biologist, let alone help in the research! We then released Stripey in the garage to adjust his new harness while we treated Jan's painful wound with peroxide.

Elastic, once stretched, rebounds with surprising force, as Stripey learned quickly. After the initial fitting he pulled at the straps, got snapped as a result, and soon left the harness alone. From then on this was our harness of choice, with no apparent ill effects on the owl.

To hear a signal beeping so strongly from Stripey after so many weeks was singularly comforting. With the new stronger transmitter, I discovered that he was flying about a mile and a half to the west of TESA (see map) to an overgrown pasture belonging to the science division head, Allen Hiebert. Stripey could not have chosen a better habitat—it was rich in prey and bristled with perch sites. Ideal for an

Peter's Hedge, an area west of Hiebert's Pasture.

owl! I followed him often around his new home, relishing the ability to track his movements. But now, for the first time he became unapproachable.

Stripey expanded his wanderings to include a hedgerow bordering a wheat field another half mile to the west of the Hieberts, an area called Peter's Hedge. This area was close to an extensively wooded creek, and I eventually tracked him to these woods as well. It is here that he bit off the wire antenna of the first Stoneburner transmitter. The signal greatly weakened, I worried again about losing him. For whatever reason, he was acting very unsociably, and there was no guarantee that I could ever coax him within reach so I could replace that damaged transmitter.

$\mathcal{S}$TRETCHING THE BOUNDARIES

TO THE FARTHEST LIMIT HE SEARCHES OUT . . .

—*Job 28: 3*

❖ ❖ ❖ If a species is to be studied in depth, an investigator must devise a method of capturing one or more specimens. There are several interesting ways to catch owls. Some researchers use traps—either spring-loaded nets or pole-mounted springs—that draw nooses up around the legs. Another technique is to place a live prey animal in a weighted wire cage coated with entangling nooses of fishing line. When the owl tries to grab the prey, it becomes ensnared in the line. Alternatively, the owl is lured with a live prey item, usually a pigeon, and then is caught in a large net placed in the exit path. "Owl fishing" is a unique technique that involves tying a dead mouse to the end of a fishing line, casting the furry bait out in front of a probable owl perch, and reeling it in. When the owl snatches the mouse, the "fisherman" grabs the owl with a net.

In early January, Stripey's signal registered with sharp clarity on a house-mounted antenna and receiver-automatic recorder unit that I had set up for the purpose of acquiring a continuous record of his movements. He was back on TESA! Since the malfunctioning transmitter had only a limited range, I knew Stripey must be very near.

Automatic
recording
apparatus.

I decided to employ "owl fishing" in an attempt to catch him. And catch him I did, but not in the manner anticipated.

The transmitter continued to emit sharp, staccato clicks as I left the house with my gloves and mouse-baited fishing pole. Stripey was sitting in an osage orange tree near the utility pole which supplies the house with electricity. He looked hungry, as he often did after a prolonged absence. I lifted the fishing pole, and the dead mouse swayed back and forth in full view in front of him. Stripey saw it, cheeping and bobbing his head with intense interest. Casting the mouse out on the lawn, I slowly began to reel it in, whereupon he promptly leaped out of the tree and snared the mouse. Cautiously, I walked up to him. With the end of my fishing line firmly gripped in his talons, he hissed and clacked his bill, then emitted a loud chattering to warn me off. I tried to coax him onto my gloved hand so that I could grab him. But he wanted nothing of this and, dropping the mouse, flew up to the transformer on the utility pole.

On the prairie, perches are in short supply and are highly valued. Telephone and utility poles are especially prized by hawks and owls. Ecologist Richard Brewer added perches to a grassland and found that birds actively competed for access to them. Stripey's desire to use this one was understandable, but this stubborn behavior almost brought my owl project to an abrupt end. For as Stripey spread his wings to land on the transformer, his feathers touched both of its electrical contacts. Sparks the size of meteors flared and crackled. Stripey plummeted to the ground. Breath and heart deserted me as I bent to pick up the limp body, sickeningly aware that many birds of prey meet death by electrocution on power lines and transformers. But not this tough bird! Utterly amazed, I saw his large eyes blink and heard his beak begin its customary clacking. The burned ends of wing feathers revealed the contact points of owl and transformer. He had probably been spared by the weak connection of his dry feathers with the transformer's poles. Had he landed more firmly, he would have been fried for sure. As it was, he was temporarily stunned, giving me the opportunity take him to the garage and re-place the transmitter.

Stripey was groggy, cowering on the garage workbench. I called Jan to help me remove the damaged transmitter. Cutting the elastic bands around his breast, she quickly lifted the antennaless transmitter off the owl's back while I held him. I replaced this transmitter with a smaller unit which used replaceable hearing-aid batteries—a definite advantage but good for only one to three months. It would have to do until I could get another transmitter from Dan Stoneburner.

In a couple of hours Stripey began to eat and showed some of his old spunk. Since he seemed to have fully recovered from his brush with electrocution, I decided to release him. He flew to the hedge-row east of the barn, ruffled his feathers indignantly, gave his new harness a snap, fluffed his feathers again, and settled in for a nap. Never again did I see Stripey use that utility pole for a perch.

Utility pole
on TESA,
where Stripey
was almost
electrocuted.

Later that night he flew west to Hiebert's Pasture, no doubt spurred along by the hot-blooded resident owls who were in the midst of mating and therefore intolerant of inconsiderate interlopers.

The following day I called Dan Stoneburner in Georgia. He suggested that I return the old transmitter and he would replace the antenna that Stripey had bitten off with a stronger, owl-proof model. Although the smaller transmitter worked well, the signal was weaker. Meanwhile, Stripey homed in on the lush confines of Hiebert's Pasture, only occasionally returning to TESA. He seemed to be hunting for himself now, but still visited the feeding stations once in a while. Since he had to brave the attacks of the wild owls to return "home," I wondered how good a hunter he really was.

To test his hunting prowess (and to provide him with practice) I live-trapped and presented mice to Stripey whenever he showed up on TESA. He would attack the animals as they ventured from the traps and had a successful capture rate of about 85 percent. Only the old and very experienced prey were able to zig and zag their way to safety and avoid his talons.

Once, I released an old cotton rat who bolted from a leaf pile to a log with the owl only inches behind. No doubt thinking it was safe, the rat met death when Stripey suddenly reached under the log with his talons and snared it. A fraction of an inch could mean the difference between survival and death for a rat and a meal for the owl. Stripey would go through all the motions of stalking these animals— flying down, stopping, listening, and then lunging. Squeaks from the mouse indicated a successful hit.

The offer of food, I thought, should make him more friendly. However, the owl was becoming more difficult to approach, especially when he was not on TESA. Once when I was following him in Hiebert's Pasture, he flew from a large elm, across a hedgerow, and out into a field of cut sorghum stalks. I trailed his signal and got close enough to see him crouch behind the stalks. There he hunched down and crawled on the ground in an attempt to avoid me. This was hard to take—like an old friend suddenly and obviously avoiding me. But owls, after all, are loners, and to them feelings of friendship must be entirely foreign. Paradoxically, he could become chummy and approachable at times and on his own terms, especially when he was back on TESA after a long absence.

January ended with a period of frigid but sunny weather. Bundling up in layers of winter gear, I followed Stripey's signal out past Hiebert's Pasture to Peter's Hedge. When I approached, an owl flew to the north but the signal was still beeping from the hedgerow. It seems that another owl had been sitting there with Stripey. Did he have a mate so soon? If so, the significance of an imprinted owl mating in the wild would shake the foundations of the imprint hypothesis. I had to be very careful in drawing any conclusions.

As matters stood at this point, most of the ornithologists with whom I had communicated could not believe that Stripey was hunting for himself. The acquisition of a mate by an imprinted owl they would hold to be even less likely. And reproduction? Fat chance! At any rate, Stripey was at last acting like a true owl. And so I wondered if he would stay away permanently now that he had been attracted to one of his own kind. But I need not have worried—he continued to hit TESA regularly for hand-outs.

One frosty February 1989 night I followed a strong signal to the barn. There, perched on the cage where he was reared, was my owl, fluffed out and unabashedly neighborly. Even though he had a new companion over at Peter's Hedge, the warmth of his old nursery barn must have beckoned. I had long since discovered that creature comforts were a prime attraction for Stripey. In summer, he favored

Stripey in
the barn.

shady creek bottoms, while winter frequently found him huddled in deserted buildings or out of the wind in secluded woodlots.

When Dan Stoneburner's new transmitter arrived, Stripey was sitting on the trash burner near the barn. He usually flew down to these low perches when he wanted my company or—more likely—food. I extended my gloved hand, whereupon he settled his powerful feet gently on my fingers. When Stripey was younger, I handled him without fear. But now, full grown and more than half wild, he commanded from me a healthy respect and I found myself more hesitant. Still, with my heavy winter coat for protection, I scooped him up and, overriding his objections, hauled him to the garage. There

Jan and I removed the old transmitter and replaced it with the new one. I was grateful for his ability to quickly recover from these wrestling bouts—with no remembered malice. An owl's life is marked by episodes of sudden violence, so perhaps a tolerant nature is advantageous.

Fitted with the new transmitter, Stripey was again released to the elements. In what was now a familiar maneuver, he adjusted the straps with a powerful tug, experienced the snap-back, shook himself, and flew off, emitting signals with gratifying clarity.

BOTH TAME AND WILD

OF ALL WILD BEASTS PRESERVE ME FROM A TYRANT; AND OF
ALL TAME, A FLATTERER.

—*Ben Jonson, writer*

❖ ❖ ❖ For the remainder of the winter, Stripey divided his time between TESA and his nearby haunts. Much of this hide-and-seek existence was forced on him by TESA's resident owls. Late March 1989 found him checking out new, more distant areas—Franzen Creek and the associated farmstead and hedgerows. Great horned owls generally do not mate until the age of two so I did not expect Stripey to secure a mate or territory yet. TESA continued as home base, but as he extended the scope of his explorations, the home ties gradually grew weaker. Stripey was at once both wild and tame, his odd ambivalence variously contingent on his location relative to TESA and the state of his hunger. Drawn toward the wild, he was still dependent on the advantages of his relationship with me.

About this time our daughter Katy, who has epilepsy, was referred by her physician to a medical group in St. Paul, Minnesota. Since a nationally known Raptor Rehabilitation Center affiliated with the University of Minnesota was near St. Paul, I decided to take the opportunity to make a side trip to visit the facility and its director, Pat Redig, to find out more about reestablishing imprinted great horned owls. Redig is widely recognized for his work on reintroducing birds of prey into their natural environment. After stocking Stripey's two feeding stations with a supply of meat, I left for Minnesota to meet Jan, who had already taken Katy up two weeks earlier to begin her tests.

The tests were being done to determine if Katy was a candidate for possible brain surgery to cure her seizures. To our disappointment, the CAT scans, EEGs, and MRIs proved to be inconclusive—the doctors could not pinpoint the locus of Katy's seizures. On the positive side, Katy did respond to some new medications that reduced the frequency of her convulsions. A father's anxiety and a scientist's curiosity produced a strange mix of emotions within me as I journeyed between hospital and raptor center.

The Raptor Rehabilitation Center, located at the edge of the university campus, is a modern building with wide halls, many windows, and well-kept caging and veterinary areas. Pat Redig informed me that while many people have been involved in rearing great horned owl chicks, none that he knew had followed the released adult owls for any length of time. The postrelease imprints that had been observed (usually a year or less) were so abnormal in their behavior (trying to mate with the hands, feet, heads of their human caretakers) that most scientists assumed they would never make it in the wild. Imprinted great horned owls kept in an aviary with wild owls in the rehabilitation facility never associated with the wild owls, huddling off in an area by themselves. While he obviously doubted whether Stripey would ever achieve independence, Redig nevertheless encouraged me to keep track of him, since very little is known of extended postrelease behavior.

He also recommended that I read the reports of Katherine McKeever of Vineland, Ontario, who founded the Owl Rehabilitation Research Foundation. Perhaps the best-known authority on hand-reared owls, McKeever has written extensively from vast experience. She has cared for hundreds of great horned owls as well as many injured owls of other species. In her book, *Care and Rehabilitation of Injured Owls* (4th edition), she writes: "The whole process of imprinting takes place during a relatively short time—from the second or third week of life to about the sixth—yet the social identification acquired during this brief period is a permanent orientation, lasting the owl's lifetime. One can see how vulnerable this phenomenon is to disorder; the wrong model, during those brief weeks, dooms the raptor to perpetual antipathy towards his own species." She later writes: "Any juvenile raptor deprived of the sight, sound or touch of an animate being during this critical period is best euthanized at the time of admission. Such unfortunate birds are totally disordered, unable to relate to any other creature and antagonistic towards all life forms."

Needless to say, I returned to Kansas and to Stripey, apprehensive about both his and Katy's future. Our hopes for a cure for Katy's epilepsy had taken a blow, but her good response to the new medications encouraged us. Likewise with Stripey. His prognosis was grim but there was still hope. The uncertainty in this imprint business bolstered my resolve: I had to keep working with him—I felt that he was at a crucial point, a transitional stage. To stop now would forever consign him to the artificial niche of unique pet. And since so little is known about postrelease imprinted owls, my research could add needed information about an apparently common but little-studied rehabilitation disorder.

It was good to be home, and I set out at once to look for Stripey, hoping that his behavior would somehow ease my anxiety. I found him in the barn, where he hailed me with a strange mixture of clucks and drawn-out cheeps. He flew from his perch on the cage to an open box, crawled inside and, hunching in a corner, displayed a choking behavior much like that of a nesting gull. The cat, coming up to investigate the ruckus, startled him, and he left the barn on a whisper of wind from his soft-feathered wings. To me this seemed to be abnormal behavior. Was it a symptom of the social disorder of imprinting, or was it a normal sexual urge? Possibly he was only conducting himself in the normal manner of a developing great horned owl. No one has observed great horned owls narrowly enough to know.

Later that week Stripey's exploratory sorties took me two miles west to Franzen Creek, a densely wooded area on the far edge of his range. For whatever reason, he was now behaving like an owl that's totally wild. As soon as he spotted me, he zoomed off, rapidly flying away as if desperately trying to escape a predator. Watching him adroitly dart and weave among the tree branches, my spirit surged. Now—was this owl normal or what?

Throughout the spring and summer of 1989, Stripey see-sawed schizophrenically, running tame on TESA and wild over the other parts of his range. When we returned from our vacation in June (an eighteen-day absence), he was still operating in the same pattern—elusive off TESA but quite docile when he flew in for food. Although on his own and apparently functioning as an adult owl, he occasionally enjoyed being handled and nuzzled. I did notice that his friendliness was directly proportional to the depth of his hunger and the amount of the food I provided. When large road kills such as rabbits were available, Stripey stayed around longer than when mice were the only fare. Even though it was solicited, I still relished his presence.

Stripey was now over a year old and exhibiting some sexual behavior, frequently grooming my hands and feet, and sitting on an artificial nest I had constructed for him. He even deposited pellets there. Attraction to a nest would be normal for an owl his age because next year's mating would center around a nest. Was he now playing out his adolescent mating urges, like any wild owl? I wondered about the business of mate selection—could he even recognize another owl, let alone a female? But then, I had already seen him with one. In late August I was granted an opportunity to observe Stripey owl-to-owl for myself.

On the road bordering TESA on the west, I found two great horned owls that had been hit by traffic—one severely injured and barely alive and the other, dead. I first presented the injured owl, which died the next day from loss of blood, to Stripey. Right away he recognized it as an owl—he nervously bobbed his head, clacked his bill, defecated, and then flew off. In a couple of hours, upon his return, I propped the dead owl on a pole near where Stripey was perched. This time he did not fly off and merely ignored it after some cursory surveillance. Possibly, there are certain stimuli—sounds, head and eye movements, for example—that are necessary for owls to recognize and respond to one another. Stripey's behavior intrigued me, and later I would further pursue his reactions to stuffed owls and owl carcasses.

THE WAY TO THE WILD

❖ ❖ ❖ Although this owl project was rapidly becoming more fascinating, the research continued to raise more questions than it answered. The process of behavioral development in great horned owls was more involved than I had ever imagined. A complex interplay exists between brain and environment. Wired-in behavior patterns, stimuli, innate reflexes, learning, and changing environmental situations all mix with individual differences to provide a panoply of results. None of these can be predicted for an individual bird with any degree of certainty. Stripey was a great horned owl, but he was also a unique individual. He possessed all the evolutionary programming of the collective brain of his species, yet exhibited many traits not apparent in other individuals of his kind.

In classic scientific terms, Stripey was imprinted. An imprinted animal has formed a behavioral identification to only one type of animal or object (e.g., Stripey to me). Imprinting occurs during a specific and somewhat narrow time frame. The animal develops an attachment to the other animal or object during the sensitive period. A certain segment of this sensitive period, when the attachment response and reinforcement are strongest, is called the *critical period*. An early study of mallard ducklings by Gottlieb indicated a sensitive period of five to twenty-four hours after hatching, with the critical time slot defined as thirteen to sixteen hours after hatching. Stripey was approximately three to four weeks old when I collected him so he may have already identified with his parents.

Several kinds of imprinting have been noted. *Filial imprinting* is the term for the development of a social attachment for a particular object—usually a parent. If the actual parent is not present, then the youngster may imprint on any animate object, including humans. Two aspects of filial imprinting—visual and auditory—are crucial to recognition of the animal's own species, a necessary social association important for survival. In nature, young birds seldom have contact with any but their own species (their parents) for some time after hatching, insuring that they will imprint only on their own kind.

Sexual imprinting involves a longer period of exposure to the stimulus object than does filial imprinting. Stripey's sexual development was most certainly influenced by human contact. With clucks and twitters, he often made advances toward my shoes and arms that resembled courtship behavior. Other types of imprinting that have been identified include the selection of specific habitats and types of food. Therefore I was careful to present natural prey items to Stripey whenever possible.

There is a scientific axiom that advises us to seek simplicity but to distrust it. A clear accounting of Stripey's actions would evoke many of the aspects of classical imprinting theory. However, this is too simplistic an explanation for the wide variety of behaviors that this owl exhibited. Many of his behaviors were inherited, but others were learned and uniquely individual. This is the dilemma presented to those of us who engage in the nature-nurture debate. How much of an animal's behavior (or a human's, for that matter) is genetically determined and inflexible? How much is pliable and under the control of the will, determined only by the unshared initiatives of the individual? At the very least, we can say that behaviors unfold in a manner consistent with helping their owner find a niche or role in the ecological community. And since niches are both common yet different, so are individuals.

Stripey also seemed to be able to differentiate between me and other humans. How? Again, the answer was somewhat clouded. Time after time he flew from strangers who came too near, but not from me. He also fled from some of my students but tolerated others. By way of speculation, I wonder if there are key features among humans to which owls respond.

Humans find it almost impossible to distinguish one great horned owl from another. What are the features that an owl might use to identify one of us? Is it height, breadth, eyes, or even clothing? Stripey seemed to recognize me no matter what I wore. When my colleague Allen Hiebert, who somewhat resembles me, approached him with food—as well as the antenna with its beeping receiver—Stripey did not shy away either, but pounced on the mouse Allen tossed on the ground. I believe that a critical element is the way humans move and carry themselves. Body size is probably important, but the behavior must be the key factor.

When Dave Mahan, of AuSable Institute of Environmental Studies in Mancelona, Michigan, visited me in Kansas late that summer, he naturally asked to see Stripey. Dave exhibits all the attributes of one familiar with wild creatures—slow and cautious in his movements, carefully avoiding eye contact, alert to surreptitious rustlings in the brush. As we looked for Stripey, his transmitter signaled to us from Peter's Hedge. When we approached the area, he came toward us (which was unusual), then veered off into a plowed field next to the hedgerow. Just then we saw another owl leave the same tree and watched it fly about three hundred yards to the northwest to a second hedge, where it emitted the soft "hoo, hoo, hoo" typical of the female owl. Dave hid in the hedgerow while I walked over to Stripey. After repeated attempts, I coaxed my owl to hop onto my arm. When I started back toward Dave, Stripey, noticing the presence of another human, flew to the ground. On my command, Dave hooted, and Stripey, like a frightened child, hastily retreated to my shoulder! This he had never done before. Evidently, he associated me with security. Yet the times when he was attacked by the TESA owls, he did not fly to me for help. Why here? Why now, when he should be independent?

Totally unnerved, Stripey huddled close to my head as he scanned the hedge where Dave was hiding. When Dave suddenly stepped into view, Stripey flew about fifty yards to the plowed ground and squawked. He acted as if he were starving, which probably accounted for his chumminess with me. We made a quick trip back to TESA for some cotton rats, and surprisingly, he was still around when we got back. Dispatching two cotton rats with his talons and beak, he gulped them down, then flew again toward the near hedge.

As Stripey's powerful wings carried him aloft, his signal noticeably weakened. "Time to change transmitters again," I told Dave. But since he had been so approachable, I was hopeful that he would return to TESA so that I could refit him with another of the Stoneburner transmitters.

Because so much of Stripey's behavior paralleled that of Bernd Heinrich's owl Bubo, I wanted very much to compare notes firsthand. The next day it rained, and with the mud of the back roads precluding any interaction with Stripey, I decided to call Heinrich at his home in Vermont. My first question was whether he knew the fate of his owl. He believed there was a good chance that Bubo had still been in the area many months after being released to the wilderness near his cabin in Maine. Although he could not be certain that it was his owl, Heinrich said that a "tame" owl had often been seen in a nearby town. As we talked, it became evident to me that a great horned owl had better chances for survival in Kansas than in Maine. According to Heinrich, barred owls are much more abundant in the forests of that state, where a great horned owl is seldom encountered in an entire night of searching. In Kansas, every mile of hedgerow harbors a pair of great horneds. Stripey, it seems, had better odds than Bubo for finding a niche. Several factors supported this assumption—the common occurrence of field and hedge habitat, the rodent-promoting aspects of grain farms, and the openness of the landscape which facilitated flight for large birds. Unlike Bubo, Stripey could let me know through radiotelemetry what was happening to him.

About this time the batteries expired, and the only link I had with Stripey was my knowledge of his previous movements. The major drawback of radiotelemetry is that batteries are too short-lived for long-term studies, but a hand-reared animal offers a measure of compensation: if one is lucky, the animal can be recaptured from time to time and the batteries replaced, and I hoped my owl would cooperate.

Since a transmitter costs about two hundred dollars, I anxiously waited for Stripey to return, frequently walking the trails, listening for his calls. Before this, whenever he came home, he would usually make known his location by cheeping. One morning I heard the familiar notes coming from the osage orange tree in front of the barn. The signal from his transmitter scarcely registered on the receiver's sound meter, indicating that the batteries were alive—but barely. The thin tie of our unusual relationship had reunited us once again.

But when I offered him a dead cotton rat, Stripey would not fly down to accept it. He remained in the osage orange, interested but not yet committed. It was not until evening that I was able to coax him onto my arm and carry him to the garage, where Jan was waiting to help me refit him with a new transmitter. When we released him, we could hear the hoots of the resident owls in the South Woods, and I thought to myself that Stripey's stay on TESA would probably be short.

With September came the opening of school, but as the college had granted me a sabbatical leave for research, I could ignore the call of the classroom. Instead, I eagerly welcomed the opportunity to spend all possible time with my growing owl. Field research was a welcome change of pace from the necessary but sometimes mundane paper pushing and class preparation that dominate my time in the office. I looked forward to getting into my field clothes, loading the antenna and receiver in my van, and driving out to rendezvous with Stripey.

On a cool, still day, Stripey's signal again sounded from Peter's Hedge, which had recently become a focal point for his activities. Migrating monarch butterflies by the hundreds clustered in the trees as I rambled through the clear autumn morning along the hedgerow for a close-up view of Stripey.

Until now, I had been regularly live-trapping rodents and releasing them so that Stripey could sharpen his hunting skills. In an amazingly short time, he had become perfunctorily efficient at catching them as they bolted out of the traps into the nearest vegetation. Now, as he caught the animals, he exhibited a pronounced aggressive wingspread display over his prey, similar to the territorial claiming action of an eagle. He was becoming more assertive in his attacks on and defense of his prey. Hisses and beak clapping replaced the amicable twitterings which he had previously directed at me after being fed. This owl was becoming more wild, and before much longer he would surely be supporting himself, hunting on his own.

Stripey's behavior was also displaying more adultlike sexual characteristics. His clucking around the artificial nest at TESA increased (when the ties with home prevailed over the warning taunts of the local owls), and his first prolonged hooting occurred one night while he was perched on the nest. Almost from the first I had assumed he was a male, and his hoots now seemed to confirm this, since they were short and staccato rather than long and soft like those of a female. (Later, Craig Weatherby and I would further examine his maleness with a sonogram of his hoots.) Occasionally, Stripey also flew to my shoes and climbed on my head in apparent courtship behavior. He was rapidly developing into an adult. My chief concern: would he be a *normal* adult?

Stripey's absences from TESA become more prolonged. Most of this time he was headquartered in Peter's Hedge. Cotton rat populations were high and I caught many of them. So, apparently, did Stripey, as he visited the feeding stations less and less. As the fall progressed, he became unapproachable off TESA, and his behavior at home was noticeably more aggressive. On those occasions when I did handle him, his beak bit harder on my gloved fingers and his tolerance for me was short. His hormones were obviously running at high levels.

Adult great horned owls are renowned for their fierce attacks on humans in a variety of situations. Many researchers report violent attacks by parent owls when they try to mark or tag the young in the nest. Some confrontations are seemingly unprovoked. For example, joggers and skiers wearing fur hats have been suddenly pounced upon by great horneds who were either defending territories or on the alert for prey. An Anchorage, Alaska, newspaper article recounts the story of a skier wearing a gray pile hat who was repeatedly and persistently attacked by a great horned owl. The skier believed that the hat was mistaken for a rabbit by the owl. Moreover, the owl attacked again and again, holding on tightly to the hat and, variously, to his gloves, sweater, coat, and even his ski poles. Amazingly, the owl did not release its grasp until the skier removed the items of clothing and left them behind. One rarely hears of such a persistent assault. Generally, great horned owls are known to be less hostile toward human intruders. James Grier, in his popular text on animal behavior, tells about a hand-reared owl that, released in a cemetery, disrupted a subsequent funeral. Happily, Stripey had yet to reach this level of involvement with the rest of the human community.

In mid-October I left a dead opossum at Stripey's feeding station on the barn, and Jan and I left for Williamsburg, Virginia, to visit my cousin Dick, an animal behaviorist at the College of William and Mary. During my visit I presented a seminar on my work with Stripey. Major questions raised by students and faculty attending the seminar included: Does this owl show species-typical behavior? Does it present any abnormal behaviors? Is its range comparable to that of a wild owl? Has it really imprinted on you or did it already imprint on its mother before you collected it? I replied that Stripey indeed exhibits behaviors characteristic of his species—he has species-typical preferences for prey items (small mammals), exhibits juvenile begging and hiding behaviors, caches his food, hoots, and shows dispersal movements. I acknowledged that Stripey continued his begging calls much longer than I expected. Major behavioral deficits were also apparent in the slow development of his hunting skills (wild owls abandon their young in August of the first year) and in his sexual orientation (since his courtship behavior was directed toward humans). Wild owls have a home range of about two miles in radius around a nest site, and I pointed out that Stripey's range was a close match.

I had to admit that Stripey was certainly bonded to a human, although this was intentional. Whether he was imprinted in the strictest sense was debatable. We agreed that the term "imprinting" is rather loosely used when referring to hand-reared great horned owls, since most owlets that are collected have been exposed to their parents for three to four weeks. A more accurate interpretation might consider the effect of human socialization on the development of juvenile owls. Nevertheless, most hand-reared owls do experience real behavioral difficulties, which Stripey seemed to be overcoming so far. I concluded with the statement that, to date, hand-rearing has not appeared to hamper his development.

When we returned from Williamsburg, Stripey was again in residence in Peter's Hedge. At my first approach he was stand-offish but eventually he flew down to my feet to eat the mice that I had brought along. He was evidently feeding himself but he was not yet too proud to come to my table!

In mid-October, Stripey was still teetering between tame and wild, but the balance was shifting toward the wild. In spite of the influence of human interaction, Stripey's development, I believe, was normalized by the presentation of proper stimuli (i. e., prey items) at critical times, and by gradual exposure to the natural environment surrounding TESA supported by supplemental food at feeding stations.

In mid-November I once again followed Stripey's signal to Peter's Hedge, where he was now spending nearly all of his time. Approaching, I could hear soft hooting, and as I got closer, an owl—not Stripey—flew out and away from the ragged row of trees. Then Stripey emerged, trailing the first owl. To my amazement, in mid-flight Stripey cheeped, suddenly veered, and in a complete reversal came wheeling back, to land on a nearby branch and look at me.

He still recognized me! Immediately he was mobbed by four crows. Stripey hooted at his tormentors—one of the rare hoots that I had heard him articulate in the wild. As I advanced, the crows flew off and Stripey came down to take a mouse from my hand. Within this one owl, both tame and wild natures struggled for the upper hand, with no sure evidence of which was winning. He was able to relate to a female and fend off crows while still recognizing some remnant of our relationship that allowed him to accept food from my hand.

For the remainder of the morning, I watched my owl, and we enjoyed the time together. There was no sign of the other owl. But as I left, gratified that Stripey had chosen my company over one of his own kind, I worried whether he possessed the drive to secure a mate and reproduce. After all, reproduction is the measure of success in the world of nature. Only if Stripey mated and reproduced would I be able to say that he had really made it out there. Courtship and mate attraction are complex affairs, and I was not at all sure if my owl was developing these skills. In other words, had his sexual imprinting been thrown out of kilter by his interactions with me?

Warmed by the morning's activities, I decided to go back that evening to observe Stripey some more. My effort was richly rewarded. This time Stripey showed me where he had selected a nest. Walking along the hedge row, I noticed that he was sitting in the same tree where I had left him earlier in the day. Evidently he saw me coming and came flying toward me, then abruptly veered to land in a tree whose forked branches supported an old squirrel nest. Stripey climbed into the nest, hunkered down, and began clucking—similar to his behavior on the artificial nest at TESA. Was he doing this because of an attraction to me, or to the other owl? Was this normal for great horned owls, or atypical? Did he and the other owl have plans? My hunch was that this was a symptom of abnormal sexual imprinting and that my presence had triggered Stripey's response.

Stripey was not the only owl responding to burgeoning amorous hormones. Now, with the passing of November, the TESA owls were again reconfirming their bonds with nightly duets. Although great horned owls are monogamous, the male and female pair up only for mating and care of the young. Courtship involves a complex exchange of hoots and pair bonding behaviors such as food offerings by the male to the female. Mating occurs in January and young are raised through late summer into fall. Little is known of the details of parental interaction while caring for the young. Presumably, both the male and female share in feeding and protecting the young but otherwise interact little with each other. After the young leave in late summer or fall, the couple split up to live solitary lives, presumably on the same general area until they again repair in the late fall or early winter.

As the crescendo of the songs heightened, so did the TESA owls' aggressiveness. The patrolling male of the local pair was frequently seen as he flew from outpost to outpost looking for signs of interlopers on his territory. Any intruder was forced into rapid flight. For young owls probing the TESA area, the quest for an open niche became a desperate game of hide and seek. This was the state of affairs for Stripey. As the home owl's patrol increased in intensity, Stripey became much like a thief in the night trying to avoid detection as he attempted to effect liaisons with me and the feeding stations.

The natural food supply seemed to be plentiful, judging from the number of cotton rats, deer mice, and voles I was trapping at TESA and in Hiebert's Pasture. Therefore, I reasoned that if Stripey were hunting for himself, he should be having little trouble in capturing prey. I suspected, however, that his efforts were not as effective as they might have been since he continued to brave the attacks of the TESA owls for a handout.

One evening, when Stripey came to check out the supplemental food supply, his state of hunger enabled me to lure him to my arm with a mouse. He was content to sit there as I walked along the north hedge trail. Suddenly, TESA's resident male owl shot out of the hedge with an odd, pulsing hoot that sounded like intermittent blowing across the opening of a coke bottle. Stripey launched from my arm and flew westward with the wild owl in hot pursuit. Knowing that owls may kill each other, I raced after them, yelling at high volume. The attacking owl quit the premises, and Stripey dived down into some thick buckbrush, then scuttled back toward me on the ground. I picked him up and smoothed his feathers. He was noticeably shaken—the gular patch on his neck fluttered like a flag in the wind. I was amazed at the intensity of his reaction! Evidently for an owl an attack of this nature is a major ordeal—unsettling its composure and its whole sense of place. From this time on, Stripey was an exile, unwelcome in his place of rearing and forced to seek a new home.

Locating a great horned owl is difficult because of the bird's cryptic coloration and considerable ability to hide. Stripey had always been adept at blending into his surroundings—ducking into brush,

Two views of Stripey in trees, showing how he hides.

crawling along grassy pathways, working into rocky outcrops, hugging tree trunks. With heavy lids he hooded the yellow of his eyes and positioned his horns to mimic the pattern of the tree branches. One hypothesis about the function of the feathery horns is that they aid in concealment by mimicking the branching outlines of trees;

Up a tree.

another suggests that the horns aid in species recognition and communication. One day in late October I found him tucked among the shaggy limbs of a cedar in Hiebert's Pasture. So undetectable was his form among the needles, I probably would have passed by without the aid of radiotelemetry. Rarely did Stripey fly from a secluded perch unless he was sure that I had already located him. Usually he would fly about a hundred yards in two or three short spurts, then recognize me and look for food. If he was hungry, I would be able to visit with him; if he was not, he'd fly away and employ one of his clever hiding techniques to avoid me.

His inclination to flee may have been influenced by the color of my headgear. One day when I wore a white baseball cap, I had difficulty getting near him until I removed it. White, in nature, is a color associated with communication between individuals of various species such as skunks, cottontails, and white-tailed deer. Great horned owls have a distinctive white bib below their beaks that may have great importance in their relationships with other owls. When an owl hoots, the bib becomes especially prominent and is flashed like a semaphore. Perhaps my white hat scared him off. This effect of color on behavior again illustrates the complexity of the relationships among wild owls. Sounds, signals, and morphology—all have special meaning in defining dominance and thus access to prey, space, and mates.

Ours seemed to be a simple one-way relationship: I sought his companionship while he sought solitude—unless he was hungry. But then, much of an owl's life is lived alone.

$\mathscr{T}$HE TESTING OF A NEW OWL

❖ ❖ ❖ Although great horned owls are common over an exceedingly broad range of habitat and a lot of work has been done relative to great horned owl ecology, it is surprising how little science knows of the details of the owls' day-to-day existence. The truly exciting aspect of radio-tagging my owl was the privilege to learn some of these details firsthand. If Stripey's behavior proved to be at all normal, he could add significantly to our knowledge of the fabric of a great horned owl's life. Courtship and mating, for instance, have rarely been witnessed, and if Stripey could attract a mate and rear young, this project could be full of rewards.

What do we know of great horned owl ecology? Great horned owls as a species are exceedingly adaptable to an unusually broad spectrum of habitats, ranging from central Alaska to the tip of South America. Depending on localized habitat configuration, they are fairly evenly distributed throughout their range. Twelve subspecies of great horned owls have been identified, varying mainly in size and coloration. Generally speaking, in the United States, large, dark owls are found in the north, and smaller, paler owls in the south. There are two subspecies in Kansas with a large area of genetic intergrading occurring in the central third of the state.

Characterizing typical great horned owl habitat is difficult since owls live in so many different types of climates. At the very least, they require nesting and roosting sites, and an area in which prey is available. Roosting sites are usually in conifers, or in other trees offering good concealment. Nesting sites include hollow trees, snags, and forks of branches previously used by squirrels or hawks. The average size of a nesting territory for a mated pair consists of about one hundred and fifty acres of mixed woodland and open field. Home range (the area over which an individual owl may roam—different from a defended territory) covers about eight hundred to nine hundred acres.

Winter may see some northern owls migrating hundreds of miles while their southern counterparts tend to stay in one area year-round. Prey availability seems to be the critical factor: territory and home range size vary with the amount of accessible prey, contracting when food is abundant and expanding when it is scarce.

Usually, great horned owls attract a mate and become reproductive during the second to third year of life. This intent is announced to the world by the frequent night-time hooting of paired owls, especially from December through March. With calls that carry effectively over half a mile, males try to secure both space and mates. The male's vocalizations are more prolonged and elaborate than those of the female. Late in the fall, a pair of owls engages in "dueting," a prelude to mating that probably serves to strengthen the pair bond. The female begins the duet, calling to the male, who then joins in with appropriate enthusiasm. Each duet lasts about three seconds and occurs at gradually increasing intervals, up to every thirty to fifty seconds.

An adult owl is solitary from July to about December, when pairs begin to form and to roost together. Courtship begins in January. While courtship in this species has rarely been viewed by humans, ornithologists know that the female and male sing their duet, fluff up their feathers, and perform a courtship flight in which the male pursues the female a considerable distance. Prior to copulation, the birds may rub beaks and emit whistling chirps along with some beak snapping. Actual copulation, evidently very brief, probably resembles that observed in European eagle owls. The female assumes a flat posture with the fluffed-up male treading on her back. Sometime during the month following mating, the female will choose a nest site, and she will noticeably restrict her activity to the immediate vicinity during the two weeks that precede egg laying.

Typically, in Kansas a young owl's life begins in late February to mid-March, when its mother lays a clutch of two to three eggs. The young remain in the nest until about late spring and are dependent on the parents for food until late summer—each chick eats almost a pound per day. When food is scarce, only one owlet may survive, with siblings occasionally killing each other in the battle for food—an often observed phenomenon in raptors and other large birds. Surviving young leave the nest after they have nearly achieved the adult weight of about three and a half pounds. Flying skills are well devel-

oped by the beginning of summer. Still, the young birds remain fully
dependent on the parents for food, hiding in the brush and grass and
emitting their incessant begging calls so the parents can find them.
In late summer, the young birds learn to hunt while still sharing
their parents' territory. Vulnerability to predators is particularly
high at this time, and the unlucky will perish. If a juvenile does survive, it must disperse from its parents' territory in search of its own
space. During late fall and early winter, therefore, there is substantial movement of first-year birds and the risk of death is high. Paul
Johnsgaard, in *North American Owls*, cites the grim statistics that
about 60 to 80 percent (even 90 percent in one study) fail to make it
through this dispersal period. Death is caused primarily by accidents
and by shooting or trapping. If an owl survives past its second year,
the annual mortality rate is still about 30 percent.

Stripey was about four weeks old when I collected him. From the
first he readily ate mice and meat scraps, rapidly achieving his adult
weight and developing along the lines dictated by the natural history
of his species. After I released him in June, he instinctively sought
out secluded areas in hedgerows and tall grass, and his begging calls
filled the air whenever I came near.

By summer's end he was making brief dispersal jaunts to the
nearby woods and along the hedges. His hunting skills were honed
through a great deal of play behavior and by mock attacks on corn
cobs, hedge apples, and annoyed dogs and cats. October found him
ranging widely, as much as a mile and a half away. The South Woods,
the West Hedge, Hiebert's Pasture, Peter's Hedge, Franzen Creek,
Hiebert's Woods, and the nearby farmsteads were on his list of stopping places. All fit the descriptions of typical great horned owl habitat—wooded sites adjacent to open fields, and sheltered areas out
of the wind. Stripey was living out a legacy not of his human foster parent but one imposed on him by his genes. On at least two
occasions during his first two years with me, he even struck up an
association with another owl. And he exercised an option normally
unavailable to young wild owls: he returned to the home feeding
stations when necessary.

Although Stripey was rapidly learning the ways of the wild, he
continued to let me handle him past the first year and a half, and
often he would show up to spend the night on the shutter covers
above our windows. This friendly behavior was transitory, however,

and would disappear amid excited hissing and bill clapping when I presented him with a road-killed rabbit or squirrel.

One chilly December night during his second year, I found him beneath a cedar sitting on a frozen squirrel carcass—possibly trying to thaw out the animal so that he could tear it apart. When I reached down to give him our characteristic greeting of a finger-beak peck, he hissed, fluffed up his feathers to look twice his size, and, still clutching the squirrel, flew off like a heavily loaded cargo plane to cache his prize somewhere else. About this time he was noticeably more aware of the presence of hawks and other raptors, glaring at them with all the contempt he could muster. He especially hated the native TESA owls, and they readily returned his sentiments. Stripey rarely ventured deeper into TESA than the pond bank on the western edge and the few times he did try to come to the house, a fight or chase usually took place.

On another bitterly cold night that December, I was surprised to find him in the South Woods, deep within the resident owls' territory, probably having returned to feed on a cached animal too heavy to carry off to Hiebert's Pasture. Immediately, the resident TESA owls gave chase, forcing him to cover in a cedar in my neighbor's front yard, across the south fence from TESA, a place he had never visited before. The next day he was again in the South Woods, and again he was routed by the irate territory holder. The angry TESA owl spotted me, veered off from his attack on Stripey, and returned to the woods. Stripey did not yield his claim to TESA easily, however. All through the month of December, he tried repeatedly to maintain a presence on TESA and in the South Woods. Apparently a battle of nerves was going on, with Stripey challenging the resolve of the resident owls.

The wintry nights of this second year were filled with the duets of the resident owls, now in the midst of the mating season. The love-struck male, amid the passion of his courtship ritual, was often forced to leave his lady to chase Stripey off the place. (The culmination of the resident male's wooing occurred about January 7, if the long squawks of a female splitting the cold night air were a reliable sign.)

During this time, Stripey roamed mostly around Peter's Hedge. He, too, may have been trying to attract a mate. I based this assumption on the female hoots I heard one night when I tried to locate him.

Since he was only twenty-one months old, I doubted whether he could actually lure and hold a mate. With owls, mating is a complex business learned incrementally through experience and may take two or more years. For example, prudent females apparently judge male owls by their hunting ability and the amount of prey they can present to the courting female.

Any sojourn of Stripey's on TESA was confined to the western boundary, away from the now constantly patrolling home owls. His visits were nocturnal; he'd drop in for a short time, then leave abruptly. If I were to see him, I had to go west of TESA to the West Hedge. This commute eventually led to the death of our dog, Buffy, my constant companion on my sorties to observe Stripey. She was hit and killed by a truck as she trotted onto the road to follow me.

Almost from the first, Buffy and Stripey had maintained a wary but otherwise harmonious relationship. The owl dive bombed her repeatedly in his training flights, but Buffy faithfully held to her pacifist posture as I recorded the progress of the owl's hunting ability. Often, after one of Stripey's attacks, she would quietly shift off to the side and lie down under a tree until Stripey turned his attention elsewhere. A better dog for a field biologist would be hard to find, and I have missed her. I buried her near the north border of TESA, beneath one of Stripey's favorite perches.

Christmas came in the midst of a record cold wave and I worried whether Stripey would be able to survive on his own while Jan, the girls, and I again spent two weeks in Michigan visiting relatives. I also intended to visit Adrian College once more to discuss my videotapes of Stripey's development with Craig Weatherby. Craig was especially interested in analyzing the content of Stripey's vocalizations on his new sonograph equipment.

The day before we left, Stripey was in a tree near the pond. I offered him a hot dog but he was not interested. Evidently the decline in winter prey had not yet affected him. I set out one pheasant, seven sparrows, and various amounts of meat scraps on the barn feeding station and, with some misgiving, we departed for the East.

When I walked through the door of the Adrian College science building, I found Craig with the controls of his new equipment. With it he intended to analyze the vocalizations of birds of prey for differences and similarities. Since from the beginning, I had recorded Stripey's calls on videotape, Craig and I agreed that he was a prime subject for study on the new sonograph. We talked all afternoon about the possibilities of a cooperative study, and about the intricacies of behavioral development in great horned owls—especially so-called imprints. His comments regarding my work were encouraging. Considerably more confident of the significance of a long-term study, I was ready to return to Kansas and Stripey.

IN SEARCH OF A NICHE

WHERE DOES THE JUVENILE [OWL] GO, AFTER IT TAKES UP A
WHOLLY INDEPENDENT EXISTENCE?

—Paul L. Errington, wildlife ecologist

❖ ❖ ❖ Driving over the Kansas prairie after having experienced the lakes, streams, and forests of Michigan, I was reminded of the daunting challenge faced by great horned owls who must adapt to the many variations in habitat throughout their range. For example, great horned owls in Michigan face severely cold winters while those in Kansas must endure extreme summer temperatures. How can one species adapt to such variations?

Loosely stated, individual owls adapt through a combination of instinct and experience. Either of these components operating alone is seldom enough to enable the animal to survive. Natural selection working on local populations has endowed individuals with the genetic ability to cope with climatic and physiological tolerances. However, each owl must learn to find food, select a home, avoid predation, and a myriad of other demands vital to existence. Stripey's career teetered for the moment on this central point: he had to learn to cope. He had to adapt.

When we arrived home, Stripey was again on TESA and I wondered how he had managed to avoid the TESA owls. Perhaps they were so wrapped up in the amorous adventures of courtship that they ignored him. Stripey had obviously been spending a lot of time here. All of the food that I had set out for him on the barn feeding station was gone, and, judging from the tell-tale droppings and pellets on the sidewalk, he had evidently spent many nights in front of the house. When I located him with the radio receiver in the hedge near the barn, he did not appear overly hungry and was actually easy to approach. Thriving in the midst of the camp of the enemy—why was he being tolerated? My only speculation is the "too busy loving" hypothesis. If this was the case, the string had to run out soon.

For the next couple of days, Stripey wandered in and out of the South Woods. As I trailed him through the trees along the creek bottom, I kept looking for an attack from the resident male owl. This happened inevitably when the patrolling male, circling close, spied Stripey, and hooting belligerently, sent him packing—his adult size and general appearance flicked like a red shirt at the tolerance of the TESA owl. With the increasing territorial pressure, Stripey was forced to head west to Hiebert's Pasture. He did not come back to TESA for a long time. Things had changed—the territorial imperative reigned and unauthorized owls were now being evicted.

From the time he began his outland explorations, Stripey returned every week or so to refuel at the feeding stations. But now the absences became more prolonged. Stripey may even have felt some growing urge to strike out in search of his own niche. Now, at the end of his second year, it was time.

Since Stripey was clearly shunning TESA, it fell to me to visit him wherever he was putting up. I followed him a little over a mile west to the area encompassing Peter's Hedge, which was rapidly becoming his home away from home. His signal seemed to be weakening, however, making it harder to locate him. When I closed in on him, I usually announced my presence with a long "cheep" to help him identify me, hoping he would not dart away. Whether he would be approachable and come down to eat the frozen mice I carried in my pocket or fly off like a wildling was anybody's guess. I missed the times when he would just sit and wait for me and I could merely walk up and observe him. He was the boss now, and my schedule would have to adjust to his vacillating mood.

Stripey now began to seek new horizons, first to the south of Peter's Hedge then farther west to a nearby farm. These new bases all possessed well-grown native grass cover and woody edges for perching. Stripey's habitat selection preferences seemed to be consistent. Invariably, during the day, he concealed himself among the hedge trees or in isolated cedars, and at night he roamed the open fields. But he always returned to Peter's Hedge.

Pheasant hunting in Kansas extends through January, and in the midst of the season, I discovered Stripey hunkering against a trunky old osage orange in Peter's Hedge. Amazingly, he refused to move, and did not even blink. Since he had lately adopted the habit of flying away from me, I had stopped carrying the usual frozen mice in my my pocket with which to coax him down. This time, then, to draw his attention I threw my key case on the ground. Catapulting from the branch, he grabbed the key case and flew off to the north. Car keys, house keys, keys to a dozen doors at the college—all my keys soaring away clutched in the claws of a hungry owl!

I ran after him with great speed, yelling at him frantically. About one hundred yards down a waterway, he dropped his plunder into the grass. I found the keys, then walked to where he had come down in a nearby tree. About this time, I noticed two hunters walking toward us from the north. Stripey also saw them and immediately took wing, traveling in a rare sustained flight (owls are mainly perch-and-pounce short flyers) for over half a mile to the west—safely beyond any threat from the newcomers, perceived or real.

Stripey's reaction was extremely gratifying as it confirmed my suspicion that he could recognize potential danger. Humans are by far the leading danger source to owls, and any owl who gives a human a wide berth will no doubt live longer. This made his relationship with me the more mysterious.

A few days later, I found him again in Peter's Hedge and came up with a new wrinkle—midair feeding. After the key case episode, Stripey no longer would fly down for food. But I believed that feeding him was imperative to maintaining our relationship, so I tossed a piece of meat into the air in front of him. To my astonishment, he launched from his perch and caught it in midair with his talons. I never realized that his foot-eye coordination was so advanced. Possibly, owls are not so clumsy as we think. Could they employ this means to hunt flying birds at dusk? This is a hunting skill not observed in owls until now. Nonetheless, Stripey and I now had a new way of relating to one another—but at a distance, as it were.

An example of his ability to adapt—was the way he utilized higher perch sites to give him more air space in which to catch my throws. I videotaped many of these aerial catches in the next few weeks and analyzed the tapes with my zoology students. We were amazed at the precise movements revealed by the slow-motion playbacks. But while Stripey showed the coordination needed to fend for himself, did he have the savvy or "street smarts" to live in the wild? Did he have the awareness of where prey animals were to be found and what their escape maneuvers were like? This kind of knowledge separates the starving from the well fed during the lean times.

Stripey's preferred hunting sites seemed to be pastures or grain fields bordered by hedges. So rarely did I find him elsewhere that I was surprised one afternoon to locate him on the edge of the Franzen Creek gallery woods, in a tall Siberian elm. As I stood along the road-side observing him, a car stopped and the driver and his passenger asked what I was doing. Fieldwork, especially with owls, frequently requires an explanation by the researcher for what seems to be his or her strange behavior. The owl biologist is forced to walk through plowed fields with a TV antenna at all hours, occasionally pausing under trees for what must appear to be inordinate periods of time. While I was proving my sanity to the car's occupants, Stripey flew across the road in front of us north toward Hiebert's Woods. They were impressed by his four-foot wingspread and the fact that I could find him whenever I wanted.

But as luck would have it, I could not find him the next day. Stripey's transmitter battery had expired again. Was he still in the area where the hunters and I had last seen him? Great horned owls are thought to prefer deep woods for nesting and rearing their young, and Hiebert's Woods, a tract of tall cottonwoods, harbored many po-tential owl nests. During this time, my students and I drove around the area with the antenna of the receiver outside the window of the van, stopping on hilltops, trying without success to raise even the faintest signal. We did observe two owls flying from Hiebert's Woods

Video
sequence of
midair catch.

Right:
The toss.

Below:
The grab.

to Peter's Hedge but could not tell whether one had a transmitter on its back. Inspecting the area on foot, we flushed an owl from a large cedar with two huge nests but again could not determine if it was Stripey.

For about two weeks I had absolutely no idea what had become of him. Was he gone for good? Would he be able to make it on his own? Now, especially since he was beginning to reveal some important aspects of owl behavior, I was decidedly frustrated at the loss of contact.

Then, and without fanfare, Stripey showed up on March 16, 1990, in the tree near the barn, cheeping and utterly famished. Running to the house for a frozen mouse, I hurried back to the barn to lure him down. Instantly, he saw the mouse, bobbing his head to bring it into focus. Satisfied that it was the real thing, he glided to the ground in front of me to snatch the mouse from my gloved hand. I quickly placed my arm beneath him as he strode forward single-mindedly, one foot in front of the other, to claim his prize. Once he was on my arm, I grabbed him, and carried him squawking into the garage, where I released him. Stripey flapped across to the workbench and sat on a hammer, clucking like a hen on a nest—a new vocalization for him.

What on earth were these clucks for and what significance was I supposed to attach to them? Possibly, a programmed behavior pattern had been released by the stress of his capture. He was acting as if one of his computer programs had been called up by accident. Again, this made me think that much of his behavior was hard-wired and subject to triggering by any number of stressful stimuli. After he calmed down and ceased his weird clucking, Jan and I repeated our customary routine for refitting him with a new Stoneburner transmitter. I, happily again, had the means for tracking my owl for at least another 6 to 8 months (Stoneburner transmitters lasted six to eight months and replaceable battery types lasted about 3 months).

Animal behaviorists Lee Drickamer (with whom I went to grad school at Michigan State) and Stephen Vessey, in their book *Animal Behavior: Mechanisms, Ecology, and Evolution*, write that an "ecological niche of an organism is its location and functional role in the ecological system: Niche refers to traits like nest sites, food habits, and seasonal and daily activity rhythms." "Niche" is a broad term that encompasses all the animal's habits and what may be referred to as its occupation in the wild. To illustrate this, ecologist Richard

Brewer (in his text *The Science of Ecology*) has compiled a list of bird niches found in a typical Michigan woodland. Black-capped chickadees are generalized foragers on shrub and low-tree insects and other invertebrates. Wood thrushes are forest-floor feeders, scarlet tanagers glean the forest canopy, while great crested flycatchers seize flying insects from lofty perches. Blue jays are large omnivores feeding opportunistically on anything they can find. Cardinals forage in openings in the forest. Great horned owls are large predators that select drier forests in Michigan. How this discriminatory behavior for different habitats develops is unknown.

Stripey was now a young adult owl and showed all the signs of an individual in search of a niche. Obviously, he was trying to claim TESA, but due to prior ownership by the resident owls, he was the odd owl out. He clearly had to seek other places in which to carve out a corner of his own. I suspected, however, that his hunting skills were still so undeveloped that he kept sneaking back to TESA for the handouts upon which he had become dependent.

The more wildlife ecologists learn about behavioral development in an individual, the more we realize that releasing naive, captive-reared animals to the wild is not the way to repopulate an area. If there is a surplus of such essentials as good nesting and escape cover, food, and water, natural populations will expand on their own. It is only as a last resort (no natural populations) that planted animals from captive breeding should be used. Planted animals simply compete with other animals already there. Ignorant of how to behave in the wild, set loose in a strange place, they rapidly die of starvation or fall prey to local predators. According to ecologist Richard Brewer, "stocking birds is like trying to carry 2 gallons of water in a gallon bucket. If you start with a hundred birds, add a hundred game-farm birds, and recensus a couple of months later, you still have a hundred birds. Most of the losses are found to be the stocked birds, many of which disappear too fast even to find out what happened to them." If I learned anything from Stripey, it was that if animals are to be released, they must first be trained to live in the wild—they cannot survive automatically.

Throughout the winter and spring, the excluding pressure from the resident TESA owls was especially severe, and Stripey was relegated to TESA's fringes—primarily to the West Hedge just across the road. The road was a main traffic artery between Hillsboro and Wichita, and I was concerned that Stripey might be hit by a car or truck on one of his midnight visits—the fate of many great horned owls. He evidently had learned to recognize and avoid motor vehicles as a juvenile on TESA. He especially loathed the noisy motorcycle that I used when checking trap lines. All I had to do was walk over to it and Stripey would go berserk beating against the cage walls. The noise of the engine may have been pitched at a particularly painful frequency for owls. As a result, Stripey was wary of any motor vehicle, and this probably saved his life many times.

Stripey's adventures proved to be handy learning experiences for my students in the ecology and animal behavior classes. Often it is difficult to explain such concepts as niche, competition, and habitat selection, but a free-ranging owl wearing a radio transmitter makes learning both easier and exciting. Several students followed Stripey on their own as independent study projects, and he never failed to provide memorable encounters. For example, one team of two students reported that Stripey led them on a game of hide and seek, diving into hedge rows, then flying to the middle of fields, and creeping along creek bottoms. The besieged owl no doubt was perplexed that so many people were able to follow his every movement. Owls, after all, are masterfully cryptical and accustomed to total anonymity most of the time.

One of the puzzling things about Stripey's behavior was his tameness on TESA and skittishness elsewhere. For this reason, I believe that a lot of his behavior was context-specific. Familiar people in familiar places are accepted, but familiar people in unfamiliar places are not. Again, wariness is a way of surviving, and fear and flight responses are probably instinctive. Whenever I interacted with Stripey, I had to keep in mind that a great deal of his behavior was beyond his control—he simply reacted to his internal state and external environment.

So much of his behavior seemed erratic on the surface, but in reality it was very predictable when I took the time to ask some very simple questions. Was he hungry? At a familiar place? Experiencing reproductive urges? Avoiding competitors? In a period of inactivity? The inclination to anthropomorphize animals is overwhelming and frequently leads to unrealistic expectations on the part of humans. If pet owners and others would try to understand and accept behavior in the context of an animal's survival value rather than in human social terms, they would be much more satisfied with their pets.

Such a misunderstanding occurred one Saturday morning when a neighbor called and asked to go with me to get a look at Stripey. The owl seldom allowed anyone else to walk up to him even when I was along, and I doubted if we would see him this time either. Nevertheless, the neighbor arrived and we walked to the West Hedge where Stripey was hiding. As soon as we came into view, he flew like the wind to a distant hedge, and we barely got a glimpse as he disappeared. Not understanding Stripey's need to flee and disappointed, my friend expressed sympathy that I had now lost my owl. I reassured him that the loss was only temporary and that things would be different another day and in another situation. Stripey blew both cold and warm, and his moods shifted dramatically from day to day.

In mid-April two years after I found him, Stripey, for whatever reason, left TESA for a month-long absence—spending most of his time around Hiebert's Pasture and the adjacent hedge rows. Apparently the TESA owls were being especially vigilant. Possibly young owlets were in the nest and consequently the demand on the TESA rodent population was extraordinarily high. Every mouse and rabbit in a reproducing owl's territory is precious, and there is absolutely no sharing. If the TESA owls had young, Stripey would most certainly be kept at bay.

About this time, I located a nest of great horned owls about five miles west of TESA near a farm pond. The nest was approximately twenty feet up, and two white fluffy owlets sat there rock still, their black eyes (which would later become yellow) perfectly motionless. Seeing these chicks brought back memories of finding Stripey. The contrast was evident: Stripey was starving—probably abandoned— while these owls seemed to be thriving. The ground under their nest was literally covered with pellets and the remains of rabbit and pheasant bones. Evidently they were blessed with parents who had claim to productive territory. Before long, these young owls would be out of the nest and the parents will have to work even more feverishly to feed them, launching two more owls into the eternal struggle for limited niche space.

As summer neared, the TESA owls slackened the intensity of their patrols and Stripey was able to come home more often. It was like old times—when he was hungry, I was able to walk over with either meat scraps or mice and even coax him to perch on my arm. Since he was now a full-grown owl with wilderness experience, our closeness became even more special to me. Anyone who has worked

Wild owl nest.

with great horneds would be incredulous to see one so humbly deny-
ing the solitary aggressiveness of its own nature. With each episode,
I wondered if his hormones would suddenly switch on, if he would
recognize his odd behavior and fly off for good. Bernd Heinrich's owl,
Bubo, left him in the third summer of their relationship, and I found
myself wondering if Stripey would do the same in this, his third
summer.

STRANGE BEHAVIOR

I ONCE HAD THE GOOD FORTUNE TO STEAL UNNOTICED UPON
A PAIR OF THESE BIRDS IN THEIR LOVE MAKING. THE CERE-
MONY HAD EVIDENTLY BEEN IN PROGRESS SOME TIME. WHEN
DISCOVERED, THE MALE WAS CAREFULLY APPROACHING THE
FEMALE, WHICH STOOD ON A BRANCH, AND SHE HALF TURNED
AWAY LIKE A TIMID GIRL. HE THEN FONDLY STROKED HIS
MATE WITH HIS BILL, BOWED SOLEMNLY, TOUCHED OR
RUBBED HER BILL WITH HIS, BOWED AGAIN, SIDLED INTO A
NEW POSITION FROM TIME TO TIME, AND CONTINUED HIS CA-
RESSES. ALL THESE ATTENTIONS WERE APPARENTLY BASH-
FULLY RECEIVED BY THE FEMALE. SOON THEREAFTER THE PAIR
FLEW SLOWLY AWAY SIDE BY SIDE.

—Lynds Jones, *naturalist*

❖ ❖ ❖ The end of May found Stripey back on
TESA in a considerably milder mood than he had manifested for a
long time. Once more I was able to feed him with midair tosses,
and he seemed to be as accessible as he had ever been. He appeared
to be centering his activities on the east edge of TESA and in the
South Woods. The resident owls were nowhere to be seen—perhaps
they had moved to a remote part of their territory, their reproductive
fires seemingly banked. Stripey's fires, however, apparently still
smoldered.

One afternoon as I was observing him in the South Woods, he flew
from a broken limb down to my foot, chirped amorously, and began
climbing my leg. When his talons penetrated my jeans, I yelped and
brushed him off. It was well past the mating season and if this was
displaced sexual behavior, it was totally unexpected.

He flew back to the old snag where he had been sitting and ruffled
his feathers in the way only owls do—a total shake from the tip of

the horns to the points of the talons. Like a spurned suitor, he tried to change the subject and sheepishly began to cheep for food. I tossed him a good-sized chunk of meat, which he caught in the air and then cached in the fork of a tree. Food storing in great horned owls is a topic worthy of much more study as it appears to be a common practice which if my speculations with Stripey are correct, has a genetic basis.

Later that same day I decided to try some behavioral research with what proved to be my surprisingly affable subject. I brought out a stuffed owl to where Stripey was perched, hiding it behind my back. Ever since my initial experiments, I've wondered how he would respond to another owl, so I decided to examine this question systematically.

Stripey was perched in an osage orange tree in the middle of the pasture that bordered the eastern edge of TESA. Placing the stuffed model about twenty yards in front of him, I stepped back with video camera to see what would happen. As the camera rolled, he promptly started to bob his head and surveyed every inch of the model's torso. I expected him to fly away as he did nine months earlier when I presented the injured owl to him. But Stripey was older now and he reacted differently—he stood his ground and glared at the model for an awfully long time.

Growing impatient, I hooted to see if sound would heat up the action. Without hesitation, Stripey hooted at the model twice and then attacked, driving his talons deep into the chest and back of the inanimate intruder. Getting no reaction, he released his grasp and moved a short distance away and hooted again. Frustrated by an owl that would neither fight nor flee, he flew up to a tree branch, ruffled his feathers, and patently ignored the trespasser.

The next day I found Stripey deep within the resident owls' territory in the South Woods. Should they return, they might attack him, so I grew anxious for his safety as I went out to look for him again the next day. Following a good strong signal, I tracked him to a pile of concrete rubble dumped in an eroded gorge. What on earth was he doing here? Great horned owls are not prone to rock climbing, but there he was, cheeping and bowing his head up and down as he sat on a huge triangular piece of concrete, looking for a handout.

I gave him a piece of meat, which he promptly gulped down. This made him very approachable, and I took the opportunity to scratch his head and poke his beak with my finger. These sporadic and unan-

Author radio-tracking Stripey.

ticipated times of amicability were a treat for me, especially now that he was getting wilder every day.

About a week later, I located Stripey in the barn. He had flown in from the woods to the southeast, as he often did after sunset. At seeing me he hopped to an empty pan on a nearby shelf and began doing a sort of courtship dance—he bowed his head, cheeped loudly, emitted a kind of clucking, and then stood up straight and looked at me. Was this a courtship pattern? Strange behavior!

I walked up to him and was able to handle him easily. After climbing on my gloved hand, he sat still while I talked to him and examined the contours of his head and even looked in his huge ear canals. No further displays. After ten minutes, he flew from my hand and made a beeline for the feeding station by the house. Grabbing a hot dog in his talons, he flew with it to the artificial nest I had made for him in the tree near the barn. Amazed and puzzled, I was pleased that he found this construction of wire and sticks to his liking. When I left, this owl, reared by a man, was sitting on the edge of a man-made nest. It seemed strangely appropriate.

The next afternoon I found Stripey on the ground near the edge of the South Woods. He was, as usual, hungry. I gave him a dead mouse, which he promptly grabbed, examined, and devoured in a smooth but somewhat energetic swallow. Katy, spying her dad "playing with the owl again" came running from the house. When she came within fifty yards, Stripey abruptly flew off and went deeper into the woods. Owls are loners, and any kind of company is not welcome.

Perhaps it was other owls that forced Stripey to leave the next week for Hiebert's Pasture, from where I picked up a moderately strong signal over the next few days. I wanted to observe him, but now other responsibilities were at the head of my list. Summer had arrived, and I had agreed to go up to AuSable Institute in northern Michigan to teach a course in animal ecology. This meant postponing further study of Stripey. What would happen in my absence? Would he leave the area? What if the transmitter died—could I ever find him again? I asked Jan to keep an eye out for him and packed my radiotelemetry gear and headed to the north woods. Stripey was now more on his own than he had been in a long time.

Artificial nest on TESA, near back of earth-sheltered house.

Teaching an animal ecology course at a field station such as AuSable Institute was a privilege. Nestled in the tree-covered hills and clear lakes of northern Michigan, AuSable is an oasis in a desert of man-induced destruction. Logging had long since devastated the tall white pine forests of the region, but some awesome tall giants still graced the grounds of the Institute. Eighteen prospective young ecologists were in my class. As we studied the principles of ecology, I often used my experiences with Stripey to show how animal behavior can be studied in the field. The use of free-roaming, hand-reared animals such as Stripey can do much to further our understanding of animal behavior under natural conditions, since a semiwild owl is much easier to observe than a wild one as it goes about its business.

Earth-
sheltered
science hall
at AuSable
Institute in
Michigan.

After my six-week stint at AuSable, I decided to take my video-tapes of Stripey to Craig Weatherby's lab at Adrian College. I wanted to use his sonograph to analyze Stripey's vocalizations. I was not really positive that Stripey really was a male (even though his court-ship antics were fairly suggestive of this). The sequence of notes in a sonogram might make it possible to determine the sex of a great horned owl. After viewing the hoots he made in response to the stuffed owl model on the sonograph, I became more convinced that Stripey indeed was a male, as they revealed the complex, shorter note intervals of a male owl. If Stripey had turned out to be a female, it's likely that my responses to "her" would have been different, and so might some of the interpretations I had made of observed behavior. I now felt more reassured but still felt some confusion about Stripey's gender.

As I left Craig's office, I contemplated the potential of sound recording and sonographic analysis for doing animal behavior studies. Craig and I had talked of doing comparative hoot analyses on owls from Kansas and Michigan. Because of the very different environments, owls from the two states should be doing different kinds of things—including hooting. Dialects in song birds are well known, and the time seemed right to study them in one of America's most widespread and well-known birds too. After my long absence from Stripey, more owl study was just what I intended to do.

KANSAS OWL

THE PRAIRIE OFFERS A MINIMUM VIEW OF THE EARTH AND A
MAXIMUM VIEW OF THE SKY. THE PRAIRIE VIEW IS, IN THIS
PARTICULAR, PRECISELY SIMILAR TO A VIEW IN MID-OCEAN.
—*Wallace Craig, North Dakota ecologist*

◈ ◈ ◈ On a hot wind-swept July afternoon, I arrived home in Kansas, land of incessant wind and wide-open vistas framed by clear blue skies. It is quite different from Michigan. William Least Heat-Moon, in his book, *PrairyErth*, which is about nearby Chase County, Kansas, describes the Jayhawker wind as coming "out of the lungs of the universe." Indeed it does, for when the universe exhales, it is as if Kansas and the central plains receive the entire brunt of the expiration—sometimes all at once.

About the only thing that hampers the winds on the Kansas plains is the hedgerows—winding, undulating lines of scraggy trees that, like a huge checkerboard, circumscribe what used to be unlimited, unobstructed prairie. Introduced around the end of the Civil War, osage orange (scientific name *Maclura pomifera*, named by botanist Thomas Nuttall after a wealthy friend, William Maclure) has become without doubt the most copious tree in a state known for grass. Originally intended to be a living fence, as envisioned by Thomas Jefferson, hedgerows helped organize and grid the wilderness. Barbed wire has since replaced the yellow-wooded tree as a protector of man's boundaries, but the squared-off landscape that is so striking from the window of a passenger jet is still here, its presence due to the unparalleled tenacity of this tough and wiry plant. Of considerable importance to Stripey, TESA's hedge trees formed ideal habitat for great horned owls. The thorny, thick branches are ideal roosting sites and many an owl has sat-and-waited on prey that habitually use the hedgerows as covered corridors of movement .

I had been gone for nearly two months, and foremost in my mind now with regard to the owl was to try and locate him. I immediately unpacked my radiotelemetry equipment and hooked up the antenna. After quickly resetting the frequency on the receiver to match his transmitter, I nervously set out to see if he was anywhere around TESA. Beep! Beep! He was still around and his transmitter was still working—hallelujah! I headed for the east edge of TESA, feeling like an old comrade come back from the war. I had thought that I might never see this owl again, and there he was—real as life, bobbing his head up and down looking for food.

Even though Jan and some friends had occasionally fed him, he looked thin and somewhat lighter than usual. Later in the evening, he flew to a favorite perch near the garden. As I approached him, he looked just a little more wild than normal—something in his demeanor indicated his graduation from tame owl to one that was on the edge of becoming independent.

As I held out a cotton rat to him, he quickly grabbed it, flew to the wire rim of our trash burner, and greedily consumed it, viciously tearing it apart in a way that I had not seen before. Thinking he needed more food, I threw a dead mouse on the barn roof. Our Siamese cat saw this and scampered up on the roof. Stripey immediately left his perch and attacked the cat, knocking it off the barn. The cat, visibly shaken, marveled at the "I mean business" demeanor of this new owl. When Stripey was younger, our cats had grown accustomed to his bluff attacks and soon learned to ignore them as a minor irritation. Fear in the eyes of the cat and the focused dead-still stare of Stripey marked a new understanding in their relationship.

Stripey strode around on the roof like a sentry, all the while keeping his eye on the cat, who was now carefully slinking away to the safety of the house. When the cat disappeared from view, Stripey flew to the TV antenna on the house for a better view to make sure the cat no longer threatened his feeding station or food. This was the first time that I had witnessed Stripey execute and complete a full-blown attack. Given this quantum leap in the owl's behavioral development, I decided to catch all the live prey animals that I could and test his hunting skills. First up was a live Sonoran skink, a type of lizard known for its ability to disconnect its tail when attacked—a predator defense strategy known as autonomy. Stripey was sitting on the barn in the evening about dusk—the usual time he'd fly in from the shady confines of a nearby tree-lined creek in the South Woods. Temperature regulation in the hot Kansas summer is a prime mover behind perch selection for great horned owls. One can almost guess where to find these big birds by using a thermometer and looking for shade at this time of the year. In winter, it's just the opposite. Look for a sunny perch out of the wind, and more often than not you will find a hoot owl.

Stripey in open raccoon trap on barn.

On the wing wall of our house.

Aldo Leopold, in his essay "65290" in *Sand County Almanac*, describes this phenomenon for chickadees: "In winter [the chickadee] ventures away from woods only on calm days, the distance varies inversely as the breeze. I know several wind-swept woodlots that are chickless all winter but are freely used at all other seasons. To the chickadee, winter wind is the boundary of the habitable world."

Hidden in a shady tree.

With Stripey following my every move, I released the skink from the metal live trap into which it had wandered during the night. Immediately Stripey launched from his perch, silent as light, and plunged down upon the scurrying reptile.

There are many ways to hunt. Some birds of prey such as northern harriers (commonly called marsh hawks) circle continually over an area, searching for prey. Others, particulary the large owls, sit and wait on the prey to walk beneath them. A sudden, silent plunge onto the unsuspecting prey follows. This perch-and-pounce type of hunting strategy is so well known that this kind of owl is called *shalak*— "plunger"— in Leviticus and Deuteronomy in the Bible.

SHA-LAK, the sound of this strongly syllabic word, stirs up the appropriate imagery—silent, sudden, violent death. Talon through the heart, air pressed out of the lungs, organs bulging— death. In this instance, however, shalak came up only with a writhing fragment of tail as the skink had employed it prime defensive move. The rest of the skink was fast moving away. In his younger days, Stripey would have continued to watch the moving tail, but not now. He dropped the wiggling tail, quickly looked around, and noticed the tailless gray body moving away from him. In one well-timed leap he grasped the real prize, pierced its skull with his beak, and swallowed it whole, the skink still writhing. This was strong evidence for substantial learning. During the summer, Stripey had been to the "school of hungry nights and long days" and its curriculum had taught him well.

I began to catch many rodents—cotton rats, deer mice, white-footed mice, and voles in the trap lines set on TESA. My doctoral program at Michigan State University had dealt with competition in rodents and I had acquired hundreds of traps in my research over the years—I was well set up to offer an owl its prime delicacy. I maintained the captured rodents in a wire cage near the barn. Stripey soon learned that this was a source of his favorite food and I often found him there in the early evening watching the mice and rats.

Upon my arrival he would act almost like a child at Christmastime anticipating a present. He was also fond of birds, so I also captured house sparrows for him to eat. These had to be handed to him during the day but I suspect he learned to pick them off their perches at night. On examining his pellets of regurgitated food remains, I found many feathers. Stripey also ate fish (a catfish) and a frog. The best way to describe the diet of an owl is probably a theme menu of rodents with variations of whatever else is available.

On occasion, I presented Stripey so many prey items that he became satiated (quite a feat as he was able to down up to ten mice at one sitting). When he was full, he would grab a mouse, hold it in his talons, and begin looking around—his swivel head closely surveying all landmarks for ten to twenty seconds. Selecting a hiding place such as a bush or tuft of grass, he then flew there and carefully deposited the excess prey with his beak, carefully covering it with vegetation. He had always cached items, even as a young owl, but his technique now was vastly improved. Here seems to be a common theme in behavioral development—the basic behavior has a strong innate genetic foundation that then becomes perfected through learning. Those owls who have the genetic template and learning abilities survive, while those who do not will die. The demands of nature on animals are severe and the line between survival and death is thin indeed——perhaps as thin as the difference between a well-hidden or poorly hidden item.

I must admit that, even as a biologist, I am occasionally put off by acts of predation. Why, for instance, are mice and house sparrows considered insignificant—even by me, now—when compared to the needs of an owl? A tough question. My best answer is that there seems to be a "food chain morality" in nature that imparts value and worth to all creatures based on its own balance and functional integrity. In nature's ethics, animals act out of need and not greed nor creed. Why we humans operate somewhat differently is an engaging mystery that occupies our finest philosphical and scientific minds, though certainly we have chosen our own prey animals too.

I was indeed gratified to see that Stripey had progressed so well in his hunting skills. What about his reactions to other owls? He had contended with the attacks of the TESA owls, and his attack on the stuffed model owl in the spring indicated that he was learning in this area as well. Stripey was always vigilant for signs of the resident owls, especially in the late fall, and it would be interesting to see how he fared with them come October and November. How would he respond to the model and playback of owl hoots now?

Evidently his sophistication had grown considerably over the summer of 1990, as Stripey did not respond when I presented him with the stuffed owl model on a warm Sunday evening in late July.

He observed it for only a few seconds, then ignored it completely. His response to owl vocalizations was more interesting, however. When I played a recording of owl vocalizations recorded in Canada, he listened but did not respond. However, upon hearing a recording of the hoots of the TESA owls, he immediately took off after being noticeably disturbed. Evidently, there is more in the hoot of an owl than merely a proclamation of its species—perhaps there is an individual identifier that says not only that "I am an owl," but "I am this particular owl." And Stripey knew these particular owls!

It was important to me to realize that Stripey was developing socially, since any owl that was to survive had to be able to avoid needless confrontations with well-established territory holders. With owls in the wild, the real estate market is first come, first owned, and other owls searching for a home respect these rights of priority—you simply move on until you find a place that is empty. The dispersing young owls in an area are like so many pegs trying to find an empty hole in nature's pegboard. Stripey's turn to play this game was approaching.

BEATING THE ODDS

❖ ❖ ❖ Stripey obviously liked it on TESA. The grasslands teemed with mice, rabbits, and other prey. He had access to many favorite perches in a variety of habitats. The tall trees and creek were cool in the summer and provided protection from the cold winter winds. He also had a human who fed him and offered a diversion from what must be a rather hum-drum existence. Do animals strive for adventure and different experiences like we do? I don't know the answer to this question, but Stripey faithfully flew into the barn each evening and I like to assume it was for more than just eating. It was nice for him and it was nice for me. We enjoyed each other, or at least I enjoyed him and he tolerated me. One hardly knows what another person really feels let alone another species, but between him and me the gap was narrower than for most.

In early August I began to hear the gentle low hoots of the TESA owls, and I knew that it would not be long before Stripey would have to deal with them. He seemed to be much more wary lately—often staring for long periods in a dazelike state at the South Woods where the resident owls lived. Would he have to leave TESA? Could he successfully dodge in and out and avoid the attacks of the TESA owls? At two and a half years, Stripey was a full-grown owl now, and it seemed doubtful that he could live this idyllic existence with me much longer. One August night as I watched him plunge after a white-footed mouse (which deftly froze its position and escaped— must have been an old pro), I wondered if this might be the last night that I would see him on TESA. The hoots were getting closer, Stripey's gazes more intense, and I even caught a glimpse of a shadowy figure setting on a tall tree in the middle of the South Woods.

Bartel farmstead north of TESA.

The next day Stripey flew to Hiebert's Pasture, where he remained for the next week. His next location was a new one—to the north, near the Bartel farmstead in a nearby pasture. Was he moving out, searching for his hole in the pegboard? This would be interesting, and I was thankful that the battery in his transmitter was doing yeoman work and still transmitting.

In mid-August I lost Stripey's signal. I could not locate it anywhere and I assumed that the battery had finally given out. I then began visiting Stripey's old perches in hopes of scaring him up. Owls pick out certain places to sit and use them over and over and again.

I decided to try looking for him at the new location near the Bartel farm. To my surprise I picked up a surprisingly strong signal. Stripey was sitting in a hedgerow about two hundred yards away. I rejoiced, but my happiness was short-lived. Three days later I could not find him again—not a sign of Stripey at the Bartel's. The next week I sighted an owl near the road west of the farmstead. It landed in the field and began cheeping—it was Stripey! The moment was bittersweet since I now could confirm that his transmitter was finally dead—no signal at all, and he was only one hundred yards away. I tried to approach him and he flew off to a distant clump of trees. I lost him. For the next week I could find no sign of him and, once more, feared that my adventure with this owl was over.

In desperation I placed some dead mice and sparrows on Stripey's feeding station back at TESA. Perhaps he would try to come back to TESA, and if he took the food, I would know he was around. The food remained on the feeding station and soon began to decompose. No Stripey.

School was back in session and my classes had begun at Tabor. I was now driving back and forth by the Bartel Farm every day, and I looked carefully for any sign of Stripey. One day on my return trip, my heart leaped into my mouth. There beside the road was a dead owl. Was it Stripey? I stopped the car and hurried up to the dead bird. It was a great horned owl about Stripey's size that recently struck a car or truck. Its eyelids were open and the eyes were still intact with a woeful stare—almost like Stripey's. I fingered through the feathers looking for the transmitter and harness. No transmitter—maybe this was not my owl. I then noticed that the feet and talons of the owl had been cut off. Someone had gotten to this owl before I had and had claimed his talons as a trophy. My thoughts went back to the dead owl I found in the first year that had the same fate. If this person had taken the talons, he may have taken the transmitter too. I wrapped the owl in plastic and took it back to my lab at the college and put it in the freezer.

My doubts tormented me for the next few days. How could I determine if this was Stripey or not? I searched for his signal again and walked every square mile of his past wanderings without a sign of him. I called my neighbor Paul Suderman, a long-time friend whose wife was a social worker who had helped us adopt our twin daughters. Paul recalled that he saw a brown car stop and a man step out and pick something off the road. He was busy getting to a field to plow so he did not look very long. He added that an owl was hooting loudly in the creek bottom near his house the night before. Had the fate that claims most dispersing young owls finally claimed Stripey too?

I carefully examined the dead owl's anatomy, noting every mark that might help me identify this bird as Stripey. I got out my photos and videotapes of Stripey, trying to match any distinguishing marks. There was a dark spot on his left chest and the dead owl had one too. Was *this* the end to the story?

As a last hope to find more information, I wrote a letter to the Hillsboro *Star Journal* asking if anyone had seen an unusually friendly owl in their backyards. I received several phone calls of people saying they had seen an owl fly across the road near TESA, but there was nothing definitive. At the end of September 1990, about two and a half years after finding Stripey in the park, I wrote what I believed to be the last entry in my field journal:

> *Sunday, 30 September.* After search of West Hedge and Hiebert's Pasture I conclude that Stripey is either dead or has left the area. I pray that it is the latter.

EUNITED

EVERY PARTING GIVES A FORETASTE OF DEATH, EVERY RE-
UNION A HINT OF THE RESURRECTION.

—*Arthur Schopenhauer, German philosopher*

❖ ❖ ❖ The next week was a sad one around our house as my family could tell that I was visibly shaken by the loss of Stripey. A scientist is not supposed to feel that way about the subjects of his study. Animals to an animal behaviorist are just that—animals. Animals are not friends but are subjects tested in unbiased fashion to get data to rule out null hypotheses and to answer questions. Well, that's the way I started this study, and I still believe that is the way to do science. Emotions and feelings can cloud one's judgment and can cause you to give anthropomorphic interpretations to behaviors that are merely being carried out so individual animals can increase their reproductive output. Organisms are, after all, packages of genes shaped by the successes of ancestors over millions of years. While this may or may not be correct, I cannot deny my attachment to this great horned owl of mine. He filled my days with anticipation and I itched to learn all I could from him. My main disappointment was that I feared that he would now never own a territory, attract a mate, or propagate his own genes into the great web of life.

But then, on Monday, October 8, 1990, at 6:30 P.M., something happened. I was working around the barn when I heard a familiar sound that, even though I was not listening, fired off some neurons in my brain that brought to my consciousness an immediate recognition. First a faint "cheep"—then a more pronounced "CHHEEEP." It was Stripey! He was sitting in the hedge row on the east edge of TESA near the barn. He looked very hungry. I knew that this was not only a reunion for us, but probably my best chance to capture him and refit him with another transmitter. I quickly ran to the house to get a hot dog, and Stripey followed me as before, landing on the swing set out in front of the house. Jan was inside and I could see the surprise on her face as she recognized that the dead had come back. Katy and Kerry were ecstatic, jumping up and down as they pressed their faces against the window to get a better look.

Katy and Kerry, our identical twins, with Stripey in a tree.

I quickly grabbed my leather gloves and two hot dogs and ran outside to where Stripey was sitting on the swing. Spying the hot dogs in my hand, he began swaying back and forth, moving his head in circles while trying to focus in on the meat that he so desperately wanted. I pulled the hot dog across the ground hoping that he would come after it as he used to when I was able to handle him. In those days, I used a mouse in one hand to lure him onto my gloved hand of the other arm. I hoped it would work now. If I could get him to sit on my hand I could grab him with my other hand around the legs above the talons and take him into the garage, where Jan and I could fit him with another transmitter.

Stripey flew to the ground and began to follow after the hot dog, clacking his beak, trying to snatch the tasty morsel. He did not, however, climb on my other arm. He backed off and just sat about a foot away from me. I decided to try a swipe at his legs—dangerous as that is because an owl can put a talon through your wrist in a split second. As I grabbed, he jumped and flew to a nearby cedar tree. I had missed—perhaps ruining my chance to refit him with a new transmitter. Still carrying the hot dogs, I followed him to the tree where he sat, still intensely interested in what I had in my hands.

I decided to try another method. I tempted him to the ground with small bits of meat. He flew down immediately and gulped down the scraps quickly. As he reached for another morsel, I made a quick grab for his legs. This time I got his legs securely above the thrashing talons. His huge four-foot wingspan flapped as he tried to loosen my grip. The lift generated by his wings was amazing but I held on tenaciously. Realizing that his efforts were futile, he settled down and meekly cheeped as I cradled his body to my chest. I walked toward the garage, where I released him inside. He flew to the front table of the garage and surveyed what must have been familiar surroundings. I had refitted him many times, but this time was certainly the most traumatic. I prepared the elastic band harness that Craig Weatherby and I had devised. The next task was to catch him again in the garage.

When he had been tamer this was a relatively easy task—gently approach him, slowly extend a gloved hand to his feet, and on he would jump. Now things had changed. He had felt the sting of nature's reality and he could no longer afford the gentleness he had once possessed. Stripey was now a fully equipped owl with a temper to match. The Bible refers to the owl as *tinshemeth*, astonishing hisser. I was now facing tinshemeth in my garage. Round and round he flew, from the table to the shelves to the car roof (scratching it with his talons). I had not planned on this part of the project being so complicated. At last he landed on the table, and I was able to get him to bite into the empty finger of my glove. While he was doing this I grabbed his legs with my other hand. Screeching and hissing, he calmed down as I put a cloth over his head. Jan had come in and put the new transmitter on while I manipulated and turned his body to accommodate the fitting of the harness. I checked to see that the harness was not too tight and I released him, again in the garage. I wanted to observe him just to make sure that he and his new harness were compatible. He seemed to be quite comfortable and I was glad that my owl sported a new transmitter, frequency 151.242.

Stripey had adapted quite well to having a harness. When it was first placed on him, he tugged and struggled with the straps for quite a while, but after the third or fourth refitting, the transmitter just became part of his anatomy and he stopped struggling with it. This is an advantage of hand-reared animals over wild ones. Wild owls spend an inordinate amount of energy trying to rid themselves of a harness, and some never accept it, which in turn decreases the value of any observations.

When I finally let Stripey go, he flew north to an open field and then to the pond. Later he went to the north part of TESA where he spent the rest of the night. I set up a second receiver in the house which attached to an outside antenna. It was a sweet sound to hear those beeping signals once again.

The next day found Stripey perching in the East Hedge near the barn. I put the large trap on the barn in the hope that he would again enter it to get food. I placed a dead mouse in it. That evening Stripey entered the trap (which I wired to stay open) and then flew over to the artificial nest I had made for him. It was good to have him back doing all the things he had done before.

I was, however, presumptuous in my hopes for a long stay at TESA. During the next few weeks Stripey stayed on TESA but confined his movements to the northern fringe farthest from the South Woods, where the resident owls were increasing their hooting. This was a new behavior and I was sure he was doing it to avoid the TESA owls but still derive the advantages of the feeding station.

One evening I located Stripey in the waterway in the wheat field north of TESA sitting on a hay bale. I gave him some rodents that we had caught in my ecology lab that afternoon. After eating his fill, he gently sat on my arm and I was again able to stroke and groom him like old times. I felt like a spurned but happy suitor who was allowed to come back after a long absence. I was on my best behavior that night, and knowing that I had an independent and fierce animal on my arm made the pleasure of our reunion all the more meaningful.

Then the next day, Stripey was all of a sudden gone, and I could not locate him at any of the usual places for over a week. It was as if the resident owls had been watching us the night before and decided to chase off this strange member of their species that cavorted with humans. Sometime later I drove north about a mile and stopped on a hill and searched for a signal. A beep came in from a row of trees to the north owned by Paul Suderman. Suderman's Hedge was a new location for Stripey. I walked up to the hedge and Stripey cheeped at me. I was surprised that he was approachable.

The next locations for Stripey were farther and farther to the north. I next found him another mile north of Suderman's hedge near the Davis home and then to the west near the Hamm farm. What was he doing in this area—just hiding, or was he trying to establish a territory? I assigned one of my students, Carl Dick, to spend an all-nighter checking his whereabouts every hour. Carl determined that he was flying in a triangular pattern from the Davis farm to the Suderman hedge to the Hamm farm. It appeared that he was trying to carve out a home range. Meanwhile, that same night I observed one of the TESA owls fly away from the barn—undoubtedly checking to see if Stripey was gone. How tenacious one can be when it comes to one's territory!

The next morning Carl and I found Stripey sitting in a hedge tree near the Hamm farm. As we approached, he exploded off his perch and flew to a distant tree, completely rejecting us. Perhaps it was Carl's presence that spooked him. Or perhaps he was cutting the strings that had united us. As we viewed his distant silhouette in a small tree across a wheat field, I wondered once again if he would ever come back to TESA.

No sooner had I thought that Stripey had a new home than he showed up again at TESA sitting on a brush pile near a wire cage where I was rearing three wild turkeys hatched from eggs that I had uncovered while bailing hay in July. What those eggs were doing there in July is hard to figure out—perhaps it was a second brood laid by an especially productive hen. The hen, I am sorry to say, had to pay the ultimate price for her commitment to reproduction—she went through the bailer and was instantly killed. Feeling that her effort should not go in vain, I collected the ten eggs and took them to a friend who had an incubator and had raised turkeys from eggs. I placed the hen's body on Stripey's feeding station.

After the turkeys had hatched and grown to about half size, I took two of my turkeys and one of my friend's and raised them in the large cage on TESA. I hoped to raise them and follow them by telemetry as well, to see if they would stay on the place of their birth. No doubt they had their own ideas about that, seeing a great horned owl sitting beside their cage.

Early November is a time when great horned owls are rather feisty since the mating game is just around the corner. The TESA owls were warming up for this, and Stripey knew that his stay was bound to be of short duration. He nervously surveyed the South Woods area after he flew to the barn. I gave him a hot dog by the usual midair toss method, and he missed it because of a hooting barrage from the South Woods. I knew in the morning that he would be gone, and he was.

A quick swing of the antenna from the roof of my earth-sheltered house revealed that Stripey was near the Bartel farm about a half-mile to the north. In the evening I found him, surprisingly, again on our barn eating some meat scraps that I had left out for him the night before. He had that trancelike appearance that he has shown before when the TESA owls were on his mind. This territory protection in owls must be a serious business. Stripey continuously scanned the South Woods when he was on TESA, ever vigilant.

The next day Stripey was down by the pond, which was an unusual place for him to be. The feeding stations near the barn and house were the customary focal points for his activities. It appeared that he was trying to stay on the fringes of the TESA owls' territory but not too far away from the feeding stations. He appeared to get chased off but, like a pesky salesman, kept returning, hoping to make a sale.

A wild owl, being close to its third birthday, would probably be miles away from the site of its rearing, setting up its own territory. Stripey, however, was not your typical wild owl. He had learned that the TESA feeding stations meant survival, and in the battle between hunger and destiny, a wrenching stomach no doubt kept him around TESA, in spite of its ferocious tenants.

Two red-tailed hawks flew around TESA in the next day—right over Stripey, who amazingly was still there, hiding in a thickly branched red cedar tree on TESA's northern boundary. As I watched the hawks fly with each other, I wondered if Stripey would ever be able to attract a mate and eventually reproduce. All the conventional wisdom about imprinting would give him little chance of pulling this off, since his human rearing theoretically distorted his

Stripey on shutter cover outside window.

sexual search image. This, after all, is likely to be the outcome of my experiences with my owl imprint. Or could he be an exception?

I had my doubts as I watched Stripey settle in on the shutter cover over our window the next night. He had been unusually sociable toward us—almost like during the first year. Perhaps I was going to have an imprinted owl who would always be around, and we could happily grow old together on TESA. That would be a bitter-sweet ending to this story. Still, as I went to bed that night, I relished the thought that an owl sat just outside my window .

I was not able to sleep well and I decided to get up in the middle of the night to see if Stripey was still around. At 2 A.M. he was still on the shutter cover and had dropped a pellet on the sidewalk. At 6 A.M. he was still on TESA but had gone from the house. An hour later I could not pick up a signal—even with the sensitivity on maximum. He was not only gone, he had flown far away.

At dusk I found Stripey in a wooded area about half a mile north of the Bartel farm—a new location. Evidently the resident owls of TESA chased him a long way and he flew beyond his usual boundaries. It is said that in late fall or early winter all young owls are chased off by their parents, so perhaps this was not so unusual. I couldn't help but think that Stripey's extrication was more severe, however.

The courtship of the TESA owls must have reached a feverish pitch, as I heard a long, loud squawk or yank call coming from the South Woods. Although great horned owls are common and much is known about their general natural history, the details of their love life are largely a mystery. My best guess is that this call is part of a continuing ritual to cement the pair bond between two owls, eventually leading to mating in January. Great horned owls are the first bird in North America to nest, and to do this in the midst of winter must require good evidence of a commitment. This loud "I do" only gave further indication that Stripey's exclusion from TESA would be permanent.

During the next week Stripey was located around the Dalke and Hamm farms. On the last day of November, he tried to sneak back on TESA in the evening but immediately flew away again. He eventually perched in the west hedge across the highway. I walked up to him and he was very hungry. I gave him a dead cotton rat that he downed in one gulp—something highly unusual given the size of the rodent. This was an indication of his hunger. All wild owls face times of severe food stress. Because of his imprinting, however, I doubt if Stripey would have survived if it were not for the feedings I gave him in times of dire need.

One of my students had put a radio transmitter on a young opossum that Richard Wall and his family had lovingly reared. It was becoming too big for them to keep, and Richard suggested that it would be interesting to see if it would survive on TESA, especially given the presence of Stripey and the other owls. On a Saturday night, my student Arlen Penner located both possum and Stripey in the north TESA hedge. Stripey paid no attention to the beeping marsupial even though he must have been hungry. Much is made of the ferocity of great horned owls—the consummate predator, as one wildlife biologist put it—but I believe that this ferocity comes only with experience. Young owls, like raw recruits in the army, must *learn* to be mean and aggressive.

I put plenty of food out on the feeding stations because it was wintertime and given Stripey's hide-and-seek situation with the TESA owls. He stayed unusually close to the house during his clandestine forays on forbidden ground. I gave him rodents and sparrows, and eventually began to exhaust the stores of my food supply for him. The only thing I had in the back of the freezer was the carcass of the great horned owl I had thought was Stripey. The thought of feeding him a member of his own species was repulsive, but the question lingered: Would he eat it or would the carcass repulse him also? There was only one way to find out.

I took the owl carcass out to the barn feeding station on a cold winter evening in mid-December. Stripey was down near the pond, and one of the TESA owls was flying to the south and eventually disappeared in the South Woods. I placed the carcass in the wired-open trap on the barn roof and went back into the house, thinking I had done something against nature—actually promoting cannibalism. Maybe this was just a human repulsion and wild animals have no such aversions. Later that evening I went out to the barn and found the owl carcass on the ground below the feeding station. Had he tried to carry it off or just thrown it on the ground—perhaps in a mock fight? I replaced the carcass in the trap and went back to the house. Stripey was sitting on the clothesline pole in front of the house. I approached and easily handled him. He had eaten all the meat on the feeding station except the owl carcass, and he seemed fat and satisfied.

My next location for Stripey was in the West Hedge across the highway. While walking toward him I spotted two other owls—one on the east edge of TESA and the other on a telephone pole near where Stripey perched. Upon my approach both flew off. Did I come in the nick of time to save Stripey from yet another expulsion from TESA?

The owl carcass was gone from the barn roof the next day. Stripey's signal came from the pond area. As I approached him I noticed the grisly sight of Stripey eating the remains of one of his own kind. How could he do this? As a human being, this was hard for me to understand, but as a scientist it made perfect sense. It was winter and food was scarce. An owl carcass is meat and a live owl can digest any kind of meat—why shouldn't he eat it? Should we expect nature to develop laws of behavior similar to those of our culture? Such thoughts are perhaps the height of anthropomorphic bias. The world does not revolve around us, and sometimes it takes something shocking to remind us of this very simple but humbling fact. When I drew closer to Stripey, he flew off but returned after I offered him a cotton rat.

Stripey stayed near TESA for the rest of December. I fed him some road kills (rabbits and opossums), which he removed from the feeding station and cached under cedar trees on TESA. It seemed that the TESA owls had relaxed their patrols—perhaps they were busy with other things since it was in the midst of the breeding season. For the first time in a while, I saw Stripey fly into the South Woods of the two owls! What was he doing? This was the last day that I saw Stripey on TESA.

HOME SWEET HOME

❖ ❖ ❖ Christmastime for us means traveling to Ohio and Michigan, where Jan and I have family. When you do not have relatives within a thousand miles of you, holidays take on a special significance, and the long and sometimes hazardous trip to America's upper Midwest seems less daunting. It would be nice to see my brothers, both of whom are teachers in the sciences. The sharing of my owl stories was a good icebreaker to overcome the long time that we had not seen each other. I often took time when in Michigan with Jan's family to visit fellow animal behaviorists at Hillsdale, Adrian, and Spring Arbor Colleges. Stripey was a subject of many conversations, and it was nice to share his adventures both verbally and on videotape.

Don Heckenlively of Hillsdale College is an animal behaviorist who trained under one of the leaders in the growing but controversial field of sociobiology, Richard Alexander of the University of Michigan. The theoretical questions surrounding the role of genetics in determining behavior and the functional aspects of imprinting laced our many conversations. We also explored the many implications of sociobiology for understanding human behavior, particularly its interplay with the religious aspects of understanding who we are as a species. Fascinating stuff, and my observations on Stripey were like a window into the world of animals through which I could contrast and compare aspects of my own behavior.

We were away from Kansas for twelve days and upon my return I was anxious as usual to see what had happened to Stripey. The last time I saw him he was flying into the teeth of the storm in the South Woods—I had felt like a parent seeing his daughter drive off to a heavy-metal rock concert; the possibilities for trouble seemed endless and my imagination just magnified the potential for bad news by a factor of ten. A quick check of the transmitter frequency for Stripey revealed a weak signal coming from the north. He was at the Hamm farm and obviously had had to leave TESA, as I saw the resident owls flying near the barn and hedge areas.

One of the benefits of being a college professor and ecologist is the opportunity to take students on field trips to distant places to study different habitats. This January was my turn to take a group of seven students to the southwestern deserts of Arizona and New Mexico, with excursions into old Mexico. While I was looking forward to this, I hated to leave Stripey during his time of greatest trial, the winter. He was, however, a fully grown owl now and it was time to be on his own. Still, I asked Jan to occasionally put some meat out on the feeding stations in front of the house, in case he was able to penetrate the defenses of the TESA owls, who surely were in the thick of mating activities by this time.

The deserts of the American Southwest have a ghostlike quality about them. They are apparitions of habitats that lived in former times. Most deserts are very much alive—I don't mean that they were dead—but they have the remnants of animals and plants that existed in other conditions millions of years earlier. The adaptations are starkly evident. Plants with spines, waxy coats, small leaves, and green stems, and roots to extract every precious drop of water from the stingy, sandy, rocky soils. Animals live in burrows and come out only at night or don't even bother to come out at all, such as the rattlesnakes in winter. Even here, though, you find the great horned owl.

Natural selection has taken the Duke (as Jonathan Maslow so aptly calls great horned males in his book *The Owl Papers*) and changed his coloration and size to suit the desert condition. Desert great horned owls are lighter in color and reduced in size. Supposedly they blend into the background better and are more able to live on the limited resources and with the climatic extremes. It is these extreme desert conditions that make them such a good laboratory of evolution. When I returned to Kansas and the beauty of the rolling, grass-carpeted expanses of the Flint Hills three weeks later, I again grew anxious about the fate of my owl. Shaped by millions of years of evolution and by a few years of my teaching and care, had he been able to survive the extremes of the windswept Kansas winter?

The last week of January 1991 found Stripey in what was to be his final home and territory. After much searching, I was pleased to find the frequency 151.242 beaming strong and loud from John Unruh's farm about two miles due north of TESA. Stripey had found an empty hole in the pegboard of owl territories that knitted together the fabric of owl society south of Hillsboro, Kansas.

It is appropriate that when I found Stripey, Levi Suderman, long-time resident and farmer, was with me. He had spotted me along the road with my attenna and receiver and stopped his pickup to inquire about what I had found. Together we drove onto John Unruh's farm, which was really only a pasture with an old barn—the house had been torn down long ago. Sure enough, Stripey was there and he flew off as Levi and I approached.

Levi then told me how he had grown up near this place and had driven a team of horses to plow the surrounding fields. As he looked across the fields of wheat and at the hedgerow and lowland swamp to which Stripey had flown, he waxed eloquently about the character of this land, the breadbasket of the world. This prairie had given so much to his family, and he said it seemed only right that an owl, studied by me, was using it as a home. I was moved that Levi knew of those things that motivated people like me to spend time chasing down an owl. I could be doing a thousand other productive money-making things. The land, the creation, and the Creator—these are the things that count with me, and it was gratifying to find this old Kansas farmer in tune with this. As the two of us stood on this patch of prairie with the large orb of the sun dropping off a horizon of orange-glowing curtains we looked at a distant hedgerow and a large bird of prey nestled in its branches. Man, nature, and nature's God together closed one more day in the age-old story of life and living.

Blending into the background seems to be a high priority for owls. Stripey, equipped to do so both behaviorally and morphologically, was adept at carrying off this amazing disappearing act. Not only did he blend in with the coloration of his feathers, but he arranged his profile to fit the background. If he was in a cedar tree, he moved his "horns" to fit the angles of the twigs, and he would scoot close to the middle of the tree. If he sat on a branch of a large cottonwood tree, he scrunched his body into a short, thick knob to mimic the branches. He not only did this, but he also covered over his yellow eyes with his eyelids to reduce any contrast. Camouflage is a thing achieved at any cost, and no doubt this is a prime factor in the selective forces that have designed the horned owl.

Stripey in a cottonwood, with eyes covered.

Without telemetry I could not hope to observe Stripey as I did. With its aid, I was able to ferret him out among the many hiding spots he used on the Unruh farm. His favorite perches seemed to be in a thick, bristly hedge tree near a dry, dug-out pond, in a hedgerow near an old squirrel or hawk nest, in a lowland area on an old cottonwood snag, near the old barn, and on an old silo whose roof was missing. He flew to many other places, but more often than not, I could find him perching in the daytime on one of these roosts.

Why did Stripey choose the Unruh farm when there must have been many other areas big enough to support his food demands? Certainly the fact that it was unoccupied by another great horned was of prime importance. If it were not for the resident owls, he would still be on TESA. The presence of an open pasture and grassed waterways certainly were important for the prey species (mice, rats, squirrels, birds such as quail, rabbits, and other small animals) they housed. The presence of many perches and hiding places also must have attracted him. The many potential nest sites—old squirrel and hawk nests—certainly appealed to the model of an appropriate habitation that was located in his brain. Finally, I think the presence of farm buildings similar to those on TESA must have played a role.

Here we see what is the most logical answer to the nature-nurture controversy. An observed behavior, in this case the occupation of a

Haying and silo at Unruh farm.

habitat, is a product of both genes and environment. Stripey no doubt has natural innate tendencies that allow for many potential sites, but he might have chosen this site on the basis of what he had learned in the past. The barn on TESA provided many rewards in terms of free meals and shelter. Should he not look for a barn in his new home? The pond provided water and the hedgerows furnished perches and protection. The grassy fields offered prey. All of these stimuli entered his data processing equipment and perhaps the logical choice was made—if this place is unoccupied, I will settle here.

Why did this rather nice area not already have an owl that defended its borders against young owls like Stripey who were searching for a home? Probably the previous resident had died at just the time Stripey came on the scene. Indeed, it may have been the dead owl I found on the road (the one Stripey had eaten). If so, this owl not only gave its body to Stripey, but also its home. What more poignant coincidences could this tale possess? The cannibalized harbinger of Stripey's death now heralds his success? The death of one, the salvation of the other—almost theological in tone.

Another possibility is that this area was used as a skeet-shooting range, and a wild owl may not have been able to live with the commotion and human presence. Stripey was accustomed to both, and perhaps this tolerance of humans enabled him to select and stay on this piece of real estate. Other young owls, hearing the shooting, would pass it by for a quieter spot.

Ecologists know that for all the owls that venture out from their parents' territory, only a small percentage will find a home and survive. This, of course, is one of the principle tenets of the theory of natural selection that drives the processes of evolutionary change. Charles Darwin's simple but elegant rendition of this in 1859, in his book *On the Origin of Species*, is the foundation of biology and of modern approaches to ecology. Organisms produce more offspring than can be supported by their environment; a struggle for these resources (such as owl territories) ensues, and individuals such as Stripey who are fortunate enough to meet opportunity with ability will survive while others perish. If Stripey reproduces, and if his survival instincts and learning ability are heritable, he will pass these traits on to his offspring, who may in turn be able to meet opportunity with ability better than other owls.

This view of nature is a human convention. Like other aspects of our society, it is built on how humans think things work, based on what they see. It is possible that mechanisms that we have not thought of are at work in making animals like Stripey look and act the way they do. As an aside, I never observed what could be called hatred or animosity that led to sustained combat in Stripey's relationships with the TESA owls. He tried to stay on TESA; but they were there first, he failed in his attempts to stay, and so he searched for some other place until he was fortunate enough to find one. I wonder what the results would be if human relationships were so easily resolved?

It was now February, and Stripey was continually at the Unruh farm, near the old nest in the hedge row. In ecological terms, this is called site fidelity. In the past, in other areas, he lasted about a week before he moved on. Here, he stayed put for what was now going on three weeks. It really appeared that he was home.

HOOTING

THE LANGUAGE OF BIRDS IS VERY ANCIENT, AND, LIKE OTHER
ANCIENT MODES OF SPEECH, VERY ELLIPTICAL: LITTLE IS
SAID, BUT MUCH IS MEANT AND UNDERSTOOD.

—*Gilbert White, British naturalist*

❖ ❖ ❖ During the nights that followed, much hooting occurred on the Unruh farm. When I stopped by on my way home from Tabor, I heard distinctive male owl calls near the barn and hedgerow areas. Was Stripey doing this? The only time he hooted in the past was near the artificial nest and when he attacked the stuffed model on TESA. These could hardly be compared to the almost ceaseless hooting that was emanating from the dark recesses of Unruh's farm now. It almost had to be Stripey, but I could never observe him vocalizing even though I tried many times in the evening. When I found him, he was silent or flew off.

Following an owl at night is an adventure. Even with telemetry, it is almost impossible to observe an actively moving owl for any length of time. On some occasions I had the eerie feeling of sitting down in a hedgerow on a cold dark winter night, hearing a faint radio signal, and having it increase in intensity and loudness as Stripey flew toward me. I knew it was him and that I was in no danger, but something in my genetic or experiential makeup caused fears automatically to rise within me as that beeping became louder and louder. Movie makers, I believe, have taken real advantage of this fear in making soundtracks for horror movies. I endured this type of thing, however, because catching him in the act of hooting would be a noteworthy event since this almost certainly indicates the ownership of a territory.

For the most part, Stripey was unapproachable and difficult to observe in his new home. Usually when I would come upon him, he would sit until my eye caught his eye, then he would fly away, usually circling around about a thirty to fifty acre area bounded by hedgerows and pockets of trees. This happened unless he was hungry. In mid-February 1991 I carried a piece of meat to him and he flew down to the ground near the barn and took it from my hand. When I tried to pick him up, however, he flew away and did not come back. So much for the old conventions. Things were different here than back on TESA. After this I fed Stripey by the midair catch method described earlier. It's amazing how such a big bird is able to do this with such grace. This technique of hunting on the wing must be an important aspect of his hunting strategy, and I wished I could observe it happening naturally in the wild—an improbable occurrence even with our unique relationship.

I wasn't the only one with whom Stripey was building a relationship with at the Unruh farm. There were signs that he was in a reproductive mode. On February 9 I watched him take a mouse I had given him to an old, empty squirrel nest in the fork of an elm tree by the barn, and he put it down. What was he doing—caching? I didn't think so, because he performed an odd head-bobbing movement while emitting some guttural sounds as he pranced around the nest. This was some sort of feeding or courtship behavior played out in my presence, but without the aid of a female owl (or maybe I was the intended mate). Again, was this observational evidence for some sort of behavior pattern or engram being released by the season (February) and the presence of a nest? Was this abnormal, or did all young owls practice like this? I could find no mention of this kind of behavior in the scientific literature.

The next evening Stripey's signal came from a hedge tree near the dry pond. As I walked up to him, I was surprised by another owl flying up from the grass and heading north across the field! Was this Stripey's mate? Stripey, however, did not follow his companion but flew to the barn area and began begging some food from me with his usual cheeping. Since I had none with me, I decided to go home and get some, hoping he would still be there when I got back.

Upon my return, Stripey was in a tree near the barn and immediately began cheeping as I approached him with some frozen chicken scraps. Then the second most amazing thing in the course of my observations of Stripey happened—he flew to the hay loft of the barn and began to walk around in a circle, performing choking motions much like gulls do when threatening each other on a beach. I was able to observe this by climbing up an old bale-loading conveyor belt that led to the barn loft. When I put another piece of chicken on the floor, he immediately came up to me, grabbed it and flew out of the barn through another side door and across the pasture to the north.

Again, what was going on here? My best guess is that hormonally Stripey was in the courtship mode. Any number of stimuli could summon his hard-wired habits. He was in the presence of another owl (probably a female—she looked larger than Stripey), and maybe he was performing the choking behavior before I came. Why she was on the ground and he in the tree, I don't know. When I came, he was in the primed mode—perhaps the active mode of male owl courtship behavior. He then transferred his affections to me when I gave him some food. The presentation of food, especially by the male to the female, is probably a major part of owl courtship. Being young and hand-reared, Stripey was probably not very good at this. Again, maybe he showed perfectly normal behavior, and my presence was the only odd part. I have a hunch that the truth is somewhere in this explanation, but more observations on great horned owls are needed to ferret it out for sure.

The most memorable event in Stripey's life with me until then happened the next week. He was sitting in the usual spot by the dry pond, and I got out of my Aerostar van and walked toward him as I usually do. He flew a little way ahead of me—sort of leap-frogging from tree to tree as I followed him, leading me to the wooded creek bottom that led off to the northeast, a place where I had never found him. He flew into a clump of large cottonwoods and I lost sight of him. While I stood looking at my receiver controls trying to get a fix on his position, I heard some loud hooting coming from the same trees into which Stripey had flown. Had he moved too far and roused another neighboring owl?

Quickly I ran up to where I had heard the hooting—about seventy-five yards away. Stripey was sitting high in a tree watching me approach. Obviously he had not been chased away. Then suddenly another owl flew from a nearby stump—a huge one that looked like a female. It flew to the east and settled into a tree about one hundred yards away. Then it happened. Stripey hooted! I mean he really hooted! I had never seen a great horned owl really hoot before, and it is quite a performance. One of the most vivid descriptions of great horneds hooting is given by Jonathan Maslow of his owls Duke and Duchess dueting at Pelham Bay on a winter night in New Jersey:

> It grew marginally lighter. The owl flitted from tree to tree, describing an arc around the hemlocks, aligning itself each time to face the direction of the other owl's call. When he made his call, this Great Horned bowed as deeply as any Japanese ambassador and raised his

white rump till the tail feathers stuck straight up in the air. As the bird craned forward and hooted, he seemed to shake every last ounce of hoot from his puffed body. Then he waited for the return call with a concentration bordering on anxiety. The hoots coming back out of the forest from the female owl excited the male into partially lifting his wings, which I could now see were shivering. Then he repeated the entire performance.

As I watched Stripey through my binoculars, I could not believe my eyes. This imprinted owl reared by humans was loudly proclaiming his place among the wild owls of central Kansas. But this chain of extraordinary events was not over yet. Stripey flew closer to his mate, and in full view of my field glasses began a hooting duet with her. The love song lasted for only a few seconds, but was additional evidence of a sexual relationship. I was overcome with excitement.

Next, Stripey flew to a tree on the edge of his territorial claim. It was on an opening in the creek bank gallery forest next to an open wheat field. Across the field lay the Thirteen Mile Road that went into Hillsboro. We were about a quarter mile away from the barn on Unruh's farm. As I watched from about twenty feet away, Stripey hooted for about ten minutes. It was as if he was showing me that he had arrived—"See, I am a full-fledged owl now, and this is my land and she is my mate."

Anthropomorphic? Yes, and I freely admit to reading too much into this event. However, allow me to go on doing so a bit more. It began to grow dark and I was quite a distance from my van and did not want to go stumbling in the dark through thorny hedge trees and over barbed wire fences. I began to make haste following the creek bed to where I thought it led back to Unruh's farm. I did not recognize that the creek forked and a branch led away to the Cottonwood River on the north. I mistakenly took this branch and found myself in unfamiliar territory. I was unable to see over the darkened tree tops to get my bearings. Which way was it back to the van? It was then that I saw Stripey hooting on a tree to my left, about seventy-five feet back at the fork of the creek. It was as if he were calling to me as he looked straight at me. I went toward him and followed him as he flew south to a hedge bordering the creek bank that went to the Unruh farm. Was he leading me back?

After I found my way to the pasture and dry pond of Unruh's farm, I turned around to see that Stripey had followed me. He was sitting in a tall elm hooting once about every thirty seconds, directing the hoots right at me. What an incredible experience—rescued by an owl!

I was never again the beneficiary of this kind of treatment. The rest of February found me locating, sometimes feeding, but never getting friendly with Stripey. Each time I threw a piece of meat to him he flew off, and I would not see him anymore that evening. Was there a nest somewhere, or young? This search became my next quest.

$\mathcal{F}$ITNESS, THE FINAL MEASURE OF SUCCESS

GOD BLESSED THEM AND SAID, BE FRUITFUL AND INCREASE
IN NUMBER AND FILL THE WATER IN THE SEAS, AND LET THE
BIRDS INCREASE ON THE EARTH.

—*Genesis 1:22*

❖ ❖ ❖ Had Stripey really become a wild owl? Could he make it on his own now that he was nearly three years old? Could Stripey hunt, secure and hold a territory, attract a mate, and reproduce? These are the final measures of his success.

The first three requirements were met. Stripey's hunting territory at the Unruh farm was well established. He had stayed there a long time now, and I had mapped his movements to within a well-defined area of approximately eighty acres. I had direct observational evidence that he was hunting (pellets around his roosts) and that he was hooting at the borders of his home range. He was seen often with another owl and observed in hooting duets. Only the presence of his chicks in a nest was necessary to secure the final measure of his return to wildness.

It was in the midst of winter in the third year of Stripey's life that I began to look for a large nest. As I walked along the hedge row and scanned the trees along the creek and lowlands of the Unruh farm, I found many potential owl homes. Owls generally look for a nest away from human disturbance although some nest in barns in remote rafters and beams. Great horneds, unlike many other birds of prey, seem to be able to tolerate humans by remaining secretive during the day and skulking around their buildings and barns by night. Besides the many tree nests, there was the possibility of a nest in the Unruh buildings, or in those of the nearby Dalke farm. Indeed, it was near the old Unruh barn that I had first noticed Stripey and his potential mate.

On my way to the college, I drove the short quarter-mile jog off the main road to Unruh's farm. Entering on a short driveway, I approached the barn. Two owls flew out of the elm where Stripey had

Unruh farm and old barn.

deposited the mouse I had given him. As they left, they looked like huge brown apparitions, at first flapping their big wings rapidly, then gliding like bombers low to the ground, pulling up at the last instant to zip into a tree in the hedge area. One of the owls was indeed Stripey—his signal came through clearly on my receiver. Before leaving to meet my first class, I watched them for about ten minutes as they sat in the distant tree.

Were they going to nest in the elm or in the barn? Surely not, because there was a significant amount of human activity around those buildings when John Unruh operated his farm machinery. John was not there often, but when he was, the noise and commotion were considerable. Also, this area was near the road, and many a young couple pulled into this drive to watch the lights of Hillsboro and go through courtship rituals of their own. If that was not enough, there were the occasional skeet shooters and hunters honing their shooting skills. Though at times it was quiet and serene, it was unexpectedly harried and pressured at others, so the Unruh farm building area seemed an unlikely site for the romantic adventures of owls.

When near the barn, Stripey and his mate were probably like two lovers who, thinking they have found a secluded spot, discover that intruders destroy their privacy at unexpected times. Owls, like many birds of prey, have to go through elaborate courtship rituals in order to prepare themselves for mating. I suspect that the many disturbances (including me) that occurred around the barn would pretty much rule that spot out as a nesting site.

Also, Stripey's abilities to carry out a full and successful courtship display may have been severely compromised by his long association with me and lack of interaction with other owls. Still, if these critical amorous steps to his reproductive programs were hard-wired into his brain, then why should it make any difference if he was reared by another species? His opportunities to *observe* the proper ways to court were probably limited to brief glimpses at the TESA owls, but I doubt he learned much since they always chased him off during the time they were mating.

Perhaps young owls under natural conditions get a chance to observe the courtship of their parents or other owls, and these observations help mold the innate sexual drives that lie within them. Great horneds, on the average, do not successfully mate until the second or third year of life and maybe it takes that long to get the courtship rituals properly practiced. Throughout this last year, Stripey was surely showing me what appeared to be rudiments of courtship that were out of context—the mounting of my foot, the clucking in the barn. I hoped he would get it right, for the future of my study (and his reproductive fitness) depended on it.

The term "reproductive fitness" is of prime importance in understanding animal behavior and ecology. Fitness in this case does not refer to any particular aspect of bodily health as in being "physically fit." Rather, it is a term that speaks of numbers of offspring, of successful reproduction. In this sense, fit individuals are those who have reproduced and their offspring have survived to pass on the genes of one generation to another. Animal ecologists reason that almost all of behavior is driven by the need to reproduce. An owl is aggressive and hoots because it is securing a territory. Why? So it can attract a mate and reproduce. This modus operandi rules because those that survive and reproduce pass on these abilities to their offspring. Those that do not reproduce, for whatever reasons, do not. This, of course, is but an extension of evolutionary theory, and these speculations need confirming evidence through observation and experimentation. If commonly found to be true, the implications of such understandings of behavior can have tremendous and far-ranging effects on how we ask questions about all kinds of behavior.

Watching an animal such as Stripey for a long period of time in

Old squirrel nest at Unruh farm.

natural conditions raises many questions that theories help to explain. It is important to realize, however, that we as humans view ourselves and animals "through a glass darkly," and many of our explanations will be wrong or will change drastically as we learn more. I felt this gap in my knowledge no more keenly than in the area of courtship, mating, and rearing of the young. I needed to find his nest and observe him and his mate (if he indeed had one) more intensely if I was to find the final answer to the question of his behavioral development and maturity.

With this in mind, my students and I began an intense observational program whose sole aim was to discover if Stripey and his mate had a nest with young. It was early March, 1991 and if Stripey had reproduced, he and his mate should be busy feeding an owlet or two. One of my students noticed on his all-night vigil that Stripey was now ranging wider in his nightly hunts. Was he expanding his range to secure more food? We also noted that Stripey's activity focused around a huge squirrel nest about two-thirds of the way down the hedge at Unruh's farm. Was this his nest?

While Stripey was away, we climbed up the tree to look inside the nest. There were no signs of any young, but bits of feathers and other material adorned its sides—a sure sign that owls were using it. Evidently owls do some home improvement to nests they commandeer.

We continued to watch throughout March but found no evidence that Stripey and his mate had any young.

There was strong site fidelity around the nest by both owls, but not a hint of any reproductive behavior in a week of continuous observation. Would Stripey pass this last test of his independence? Even wild owls have trouble achieving success in the mating game. Was I expecting too much of Stripey? Was he really a second-class owl on a second-class territory? Would he flinch and fly away at the first hint of trouble from another owl who wanted the territory and access to his mate?

My students and I began seeing other unidentified owls sitting on telephone poles on the edge of Stripey's territory. These were probably owls occupying neighboring territories, perhaps testing the borders of Stripey's territory due to the increased food requirements of raising their young. What kind of owl now occupied the Unruh farm? Was this a real owl or some strange combination of owl genes and human experiences?

This last question was still difficult to answer because Stripey showed signs that he recognized me but yet was a wild owl on his own territory. This situation is best illustrated by an experience with him the following spring. On April 11, 1991, I located Stripey sitting with his mate in the hedge at his usual place on the Unruh farm. The female quickly took flight, but Stripey remained on his perch as I approached, my receiver pulsating with the beeps of the signal from his transmitter. When I was about fifty feet from him, he hooted twice, and then as if to recognize to whom he was speaking, he began to cheep the begging call that so characterized his relationships with me. What a split personality! Are all owls able to be like this, or are owls, like people, individuals each having different abilities and personalities?

I was soon to have an opportunity to explore this question with another subject.

HOOTER—ANOTHER OWL, ANOTHER STORY

DUST IN THE AIR SUSPENDED

MARKS THE PLACE WHERE A STORY ENDED.

—*Thomas Stearns Eliot, poet*

◈ ◈ ◈ In my work with Stripey I had reached a kind of plateau. I had reared, trained, and released and followed him for over three years now. He had truly amazed me with his survival skills and behavioral development. Was he a special case? Would another owl develop in the same way, given the same environment? A call from a farmer north of Hillsboro would open up another trail in my journey to understand the psyches of owls.

Stuart Penner, a Mennonite farmer with a Mennonite name, called me one afternoon and said that he had discovered an owl chick in his barn while doing some electrical work. With the activity in the barn, it was highly unlikely that this owlet could survive there. This was my chance to raise another owl . The possibilities seemed endless for any behavioral comparisons with Stripey.

When I arrived at the Penner farm, it was cloudy. The rain that Kansas farmers so desperately depend upon to get the wheat started was beginning to fall. The barn was a tall storage shed not far from the house. I needed a rather long ladder to climb up to a rafter about twenty feet above the entrance to the barn. According to Stuart, a large female owl frequented the barn and he had earlier noted a nest containing three eggs. Only one hatched, which seemed to be odd. Perhaps a busy farm building is not the best place to incubate eggs. If the female is frequently scared off the nest, maybe only the toughest egg will hatch. Selection, it seems, begins at the egg stage, or even earlier.

But did just one egg hatch? If all three did, what happened to the other owlets? In birds of prey, siblicide and eating one's sibling are not uncommon. Gruesome? Yes, but such is the state of affairs in nature. The fortunate, most willfull, and best equipped prevail over the hapless and weak. However, the female owl had managed to incubate and rear at least one young owlet to the age of four weeks right in the midst of a busy farm operation. Such an astute female owl surely would endow her young with a good genetic foundation for a behavioral study. I carefully picked up the young owl, which was about the same age as Stripey when I found him.

It surprised me to see how nonaggressive this individual was—it gave no resistance to my gloved hand as I slid it under the chick's plump, downy body. Placing it in a cardboard box, I headed back for TESA—in the hope of beginning work on subject number two in my study of the effects of hand-rearing on great horned owl development.

From early on, Hooter (the name chosen by my daughters) was amicable and easy to handle. He readily ate mice but rejected scraps of meat. In this way, Hooter was different from Stripey, who readily accepted all forms of meat right from the start. With Hooter, it was mice or nothing, and this made it more difficult to raise him. I had to set and check all of my rodent traps and it became a full-time job to feed Hooter. I was again reminded of the commitment it took to raise Stripey, and it seemed that Hooter would be even more of a challenge.

Why was one owl different from the other? I can explain this only by saying that they were different individuals with different parents and different genetic histories. Increasingly, ecologists and animal behaviorists are recognizing this rather simple fact. While it is possible to talk about species-specific behavior in broad terms, you need to examine individuals to really understand behavior. Furthermore, I suspect that the really important aspects of population growth and social behavior happen at the individual level. With our emphases on statistics and experimental manipulations, ecologists have tended to miss these simple individual attributes. Perhaps we should step back from time to time and extensively watch an individual before generating our scientific hypotheses.

The differences between Hooter and Stripey were striking. There were differences in diet, aggressiveness, and killing behavior. Hooter ate only mice (no meat scraps), responded more to contact, was less aggressive. He (if indeed he was a he) did not hiss or clack his beak nearly as much as Stripey had done. He also did not kill mice at the same age as Stripey.

As spring turned into summer, Stripey became less and less approachable at the Unruh farm. He occasionally still gave the cheep sound as he flew away from me, but it was obvious that he wanted

Hooter.

little interference in his daily sleep or nightly hunts. Hooter, on the other hand, was slowly developing his hunting skills. Like Stripey, I kept him in the old owl cage in the barn and periodically let him kill mice and sparrows in a confined wooden box.

By late spring 1991 Hooter was beginning to fly short distances, and this aspect of his development was very similar to Stripey's. It became obvious to me that the big things—age of first flight, timing of feather development and molts, weight gains and spurts—were very similar between individuals of the species *Bubo virginianus*, while behaviors such as aggressiveness and exploratory behavior were very different. The physical components of development are rightly called "species-typical characteristics" while behavior, predictable within certain broad categories, varies notably among different individuals. This makes sense, since species are adapted for general roles in their environments while individuals must cope with a multitude of variables that change rapidly over space and time. Behavior provides the subtle adjustments that allow some to succeed and others to fail. Isn't that after all the way it is with us? We all come equipped similarly into the world but it's the way we respond to different opportunities that establishes who we are as individuals. Our genetics deals the cards but it is up to us how we play the hand.

It is now June, and the hot Kansas sun is turning a new wheat crop golden. Farmers in this area are readying for the biggest agricultural event of the year—the harvest. A new turn of events is also occurring in Stripey's life—John Unruh has decided to tear down the old barn. He and his wife are planning on building a house sometime in the future, on the land where the barn now stands. As I see the pile of old boards on the ground, I wonder if Stripey and his mate (who is still on the area occasionally) will shift their center of activity to the north, closer to the creek and lowland wooded area. This, of course, is a behavioral adjustment not preprogrammed into their brains.

Hooter, meanwhile, is rapidly developing the species appearance of a great horned owl. He still does not have the horns yet, but the downy feathers of his younger days are gone and he is beginning to show many adult behaviors. Like Stripey, he caches food in the corners of his cage when he's had his fill of mice and road-killed rabbits.

A peculiar sort of relationship is developing between Hooter and our dog Abby, an Australian shepherd we acquired after Buffy's death. Hooter readily approaches Abby, and the two will actually play together and Hooter occasionally grooms the fur on Abby's back. This, again, is completely different from Stripey, who had wanted nothing to do with Buffy; in fact, there had been direct antagonism between the two. As far as Stripey was concerned, Buffy and the cats did not exist for anything more than mock attacks during his training sessions. Hooter approaches Abby at every opportunity and the attraction seems to be mutual—Abby looks forward to the times when Hooter is out of his cage. Our Siamese cat, recalling the rough treatment he received from Stripey, wants nothing to do with Hooter and, strangely enough, Hooter does not approach the cat, either.

Hooter seems to be a lot less aggressive than Stripey, and slower in the development of his hunting skills. By midsummer Stripey was readily killing rodents and birds placed in his cage while Hooter is loathe to attack, doing so only when very hungry. What can account for this difference? Was it perhaps just a slight difference in the amount of time that they were exposed to their mothers? Stripey was found by me in late March and Hooter in early April. Stripey, however, might have been with his mother a few days longer than

Hooter and Abby.

Hooter, as he was slightly larger when I found him. In some birds, especially waterfowl, there is a critical period of just a few hours after hatching during which behavioral imprinting on the parent bird occurs. Did Stripey have this imprinting time while Hooter did not? Is Hooter a female and Stripey a male? Frustrating. Nevertheless, these are certainly two different owls, and I wonder about Hooter's ability to make it on his own.

Stripey, on the other hand, offered me no such worry. Late one warm June evening, Jan and I stopped by the Unruh farm to check on Stripey and he was sitting on the silo. Recognizing me, he began to cheep and stayed in the area rather than fly away as he usually did. Would I be able to lure him down with a mouse? I took Jan home and brought back a dead cotton rat. Stripey was not the least interested and I left with him sitting on the silo like a king surveying his kingdom.

If Stripey had a kingdom, Hooter had an opportunity. It was late June and time to release Hooter. I fitted him with a transmitter and elastic harness and placed him in the same tree near the pond where I released Stripey. He sat on the branch and began to play with nearby leaves in the same way as Stripey had done. Play and exploration, I believe, are standard equipment in all owls. To see the similarities here was very interesting, and one could not have told the difference between the two owls in this regard. Later that evening, I found Hooter on the ground in an exposed area near the barn. I decided to place him back in the cage with a road-killed rabbit, with the door open so he could leave when he finished eating.

The next morning Hooter was still in the cage, content to be in the area he knew as home and kitchen. Leaving the door ajar, I left to go check on Stripey, wondering if Hooter would venture out and become a "brancher," hiding out in the grass, weeds, and thick trees as Stripey did at that age.

Arriving at the Unruh farm, I was disappointed to learn that Stripey's transmitter had gone dead. I located him visually and he cheeped, but no signal registered on the receiver. How could I catch him? Returning to TESA, I brought back to the Unruh farm the large raccoon trap that served as Stripey's feeding station on the barn. Perhaps he would enter it again and I could trap him. I baited it with dead mice and set the trap at the base of the tree where he perched, and I left for TESA.

Later in the evening I found Hooter sitting on the barn. This was a prime opportunity to train him to come there to be fed. I threw a dead cotton rat on the metal roof, which responded with a clang. Hooter immediately flew to a nearby apple tree—the noise had apparently scared him. I left him cheeping in the tree hoping he would fly back to retrieve the cotton rat.

The next morning I went to see if Stripey entered the trap. No such luck. I set the trap every day for the next week. Stripey avoided it no matter where I put it. He evidently was wise to my methods. My grand plan of conditioning him to the trap so I could use it later to catch him was not working out. Stripey was no dummy and, although I felt frustrated, he impressed me with his slyness.

Hooter was developing some good skills of his own. He was now exhibiting the typical branching (hiding) behavior of his species that seemed to be part of his genetic makeup—a survival kit that is apparently issued to every great horned owl. This is logical since juvenile owls must hide yet be found by their parents for feeding. As for me, I used his signal to find and feed him just as I had done with Stripey. He also began to frequent the feeding stations on the barn and in front of the house on the swing set. By the end of June he was beginning to roam wider on TESA, but to the east hedge and beyond. He returned to the barn area often and occasionally sat inside on the cage where he was first kept.

On July 2, 1991, I found Hooter in the barn near his cage. He was very hungry, so I put him in the cage with some meat scraps to see if he would eat them. As I left, he began to feel the pieces with his beak but did not swallow anything. Yet by evening, he had eaten most of the meat and was contentedly sitting in his cage, evidently preferring its security, for now, to the unknown world outside.

That evening I went to Unruh's farm to see if I could find Stripey. John had mowed and hayed the pasture, and what had been a pasture with grass up to my waist now looked like a manicured golf course. As I walked by the dry pond I heard a familiar "cheep" coming from a spreading oak with its branches fanning out low to the ground. There, on one of the lowest branches, was Stripey, moving from side to side like a metronome, obviously very hungry. Had the mowing destroyed his supply of mice? While I began talking to him, he suddenly dived at me and just missed landing on my shoulder. He was obviously desperate for something to eat, so here was my chance to catch him and refit him with a transmitter. While he cheeped in a nearby tree, I quickly ran back to my van and drove to TESA to get some meat, a pair of leather gloves, and the trap.

When I got back to Stripey, the sun was setting and it was becoming dark, and he was in a tree near the dry pond. When he saw the meat scraps I was carrying he began to move his head in circles to allow his eyes to focus on the morsels. I held out a piece, and he immediately flew to the ground, walked up to me, and reached for the meat I held in my hand. Hunger had dulled all the wariness he had shown earlier. When he was next to me, I took my other hand and began to reach for his legs. Knowing this old technique of mine, he immediately jumped backwards, and I felt my chances of grabbing him dwindling. This was not going to be easy. To deaden my hopes further, Stripey flew back up to the tree and continued to watch me, especially my hands, which held the meat.

It was now getting fairly dark as the sun sank beneath the horizon and the orange glow so characteristic of Kansas sunsets began to turn dark in the western sky. Then I got an idea. I returned to the van and located a halogen flashlight under the seat. If I could get Stripey to land on the ground again, perhaps I could shine the light in his eyes, blind him momentarily, and grab him more easily. It was worth a try.

Again, I lured Stripey down to the ground by throwing a small piece of meat on the stubble of the cut hayfield. He literally inhaled the meat in a single gulp. Now his appetite was whetted. He came right up to me as I tantalized him with a bigger piece of raw beef in my hand. As he grabbed onto the meat with his beak, I shined the flashlight into his eyes. Releasing the meat, I quickly made a lunge for his legs. Eureka! A perfect grab, and I had a screaming great horned owl flapping like a Thanksgiving turkey being hauled to the chopping block. I quickly used my other hand to quiet the squawking owl, folding in his wings and bringing him to my chest. His talons were safely beneath the leather of my gloved hands and I quietly said a prayer of thanks that my lunge had hit the mark and not an inch lower.

Reaching the van, I put a cloth over Stripey's head and put him into the trap. He immediately shook himself, went to the back of the large trap, and gave me a hiss accompanied by a sequence of bill clacks so loud that the sound hurt my ears. So much for old times. He was mad.

Back at the garage, Jan was less than enthusiastic about trying to put a new transmitter on the hissing, clacking tinshemeth that sat in the trap on the workbench. I pulled out transmitter 151.347 that had just arrived from Dan Stoneburner's telemetry shop in Georgia, and prepared an elastic harness. This transmitter had a battery designed to last eight months. Giving the transmitter to Jan, I opened the door to the trap and confronted the angry individual within. I pulled my finger out of one glove finger and presented the empty leather to Stripey. He immediately seized it with his talons and rammed them completely through the place where my finger had been. With the other hand, I grabbed him above the legs and pulled him out of the cage. Like an old rattlesnake handler, I had become fearless in handling Stripey. I guess experience can dull our fears, but I suspect the importance of my task was the more effective sedative.

Most literature dealing with the handling of great horneds says that the owls do not use the beak in a defensive mode. Stripey had not been informed of this. He elicited many "Ouch!"es from me as he pinched my gloved fingers while I frantically tried to position him so Jan could slip on the harness and transmitter. In thirty seconds, my experienced transmitter-fitting spouse had deftly done her work, and Stripey was ready to be released. I put him back in the trap to let him cool down and perhaps eat his fill of the meat for which he had temporarily given up his freedom. He hissed, clacked his beak, and puffed up as viciously as I had ever seen him. He did not even look at the meat, so consuming was his anger. When our dog Abby walked

Wild Stripey in coon trap.

into the barn, Stripey went almost berserk and literally filled up the trap with his puffed-up body, hissing like a volcano. Abby, used to the amorous advances of Hooter, was completely bewildered and slinked off to assess the situation.

Hooter was still in the barn sitting in his cage. Before releasing Stripey, who now appeared to be as dangerous to another owl as Jack the Ripper, I closed the cage door to keep Hooter out of danger. After a check on the transmitter signal, I released Stripey into the familiar environs of TESA. Would he stay around or immediately return to the Unruh farm or go somewhere else? The answer to this question from a scientific point of view was important enough to overcome my reluctance about releasing Stripey far from his home.

It was dark when Stripey flew out of the garage at TESA. He landed in the top of a tall cedar near the driveway, where he immediately began to look around and take in the surroundings as if to reset his computer and establish his bearings. He then flew to the pond area, paused a while, then was off to the northern boundary of TESA, where he spent the night in the hedge.

The next morning Stripey was still in the north TESA hedge, sitting in a tall osage orange tree. Knowing that he was hungry last night and had not eaten, I offered a dead cotton rat by throwing it in the air. No deal—he sat there as if in a sleepy daze and looked off to the north toward Unruh's farm. Why was he not responding to the food that had led him into my clutches the night before? Had he caught something himself and satisfied his hunger? Was he so mixed up that he had forgotten his hunger? He then flew off to the east and spent the rest of the day in the East Hedge.

Hooter was still in his cage in the barn. I played with the idea of releasing Hooter and monitoring both of my owls, but I feared for Hooter's life. Even though the behavioral observations would have been interesting, my concern for the safety of both owls prevented me from doing this particular experiment. Sometimes human kindness wins out even in the cold mind of a scientist.

Stripey was still in the east hedge of TESA at 7 P.M. that evening. I decided to watch him for an extended period, since he was again near the South Woods and the resident TESA owls, who now had *two* strange owls in their territory. After about ten minutes, Stripey flew to the South Woods border. Immediately, I heard one of the resident owls hoot seven times in succession. Stripey then flew to the south border of TESA and remained there until about two in the morning, when he flew north away from TESA to the Bartel farm.

The next day, July 4, I found Stripey back on the Unruh farm. He had declared his own independence of TESA and reestablished his home country, traveling over two miles during the night to do so, and thus demonstrating a homing ability. While this was not as awesome as the feats of migrating birds (owls do not migrate in our region), it nevertheless impressed me. I again received his strong signal on my receiver.

Homing is a phenomenon found in animals in whom you least expect it. Once I spied a short-tailed shrew scurrying across my living-room carpet. After I captured it, I discovered the small hole that it used to enter the house next to my Trombe wall, a concrete solar collector on the front of our earth-sheltered house. I gave the animal a haircut to mark it and released it about five hundred yards from the house. The next night it was back crawling across the carpet. I performed this procedure four times before it finally did not come back. The last release point was half a mile from the house! Amazing for a creature less than two inches long.

When I returned to TESA, I opened the door to Hooter's cage. He immediately leaped up on the door and flew to the lagoon area, where he landed in an osage orange tree. Obviously, his fixation on the cage was waning. He too, like a growing teenager, was exploring and beginning to stretch the boundaries.

The rest of July was rather uneventful. Stripey stayed at Unruh's farm and Hooter explored TESA. Hooter was still very dependent on the feeding stations, as Stripey had been, and kept me busy catching mice and laying out meat scraps that he still ate only reluctantly. However, he was beginning to show signs of killing behavior as he readily plunged down on the live mice I presented to him. He was also able to kill house sparrows that I caught for him in a bird trap—if I first handed them to him. His search image for prey was becoming readily established. He and Abby kept up their occasional friendship but the meetings were not nearly as amicable as in the beginning. Hooter occasionally hissed and puffed himself up—his computer programs were shifting more to the default mode and early exploration or play drives succumbed to survival "software." No doubt the occasional hooting of the resident TESA owls had a part in this maturation process as well. As in Stripey's case, Hooter now confined much of his activity to the northern boundaries of TESA. If anything, the resident owls were more intense about Hooter, having been primed by the presence of Stripey.

Richard Wall and I began to build a room addition to our house, and we often saw Hooter fly around the barn and house as we finished a day's work. Since my schedule was now filled with carpentry and construction duties, I kept a less close watch on Stripey, whose signal continued to come predictably from the hedge area at Unruh's farm.

Upon completing the room addition to our home, my family and I decided to go to Ohio and Michigan for a visit. Although I had asked a friend to stop by and put some meat out for Hooter, he was on his own for about two weeks—his first test of independence. No doubt 'real' owls face such weaning times. I'm not sure if anyone knows for sure, though. If Stripey was any example of how difficult it is for a young owl to become independent, I strongly suspect that the process is a long and gradual one.

When I returned from our trip in mid-August, I hurried to hook up the receiver and locate Hooter. I had more concerns about this tamer owl than I did about Stripey. I need not have worried. He was on the ground near the north TESA hedge. Abby and he must still be interacting, because Hooter came right up to the dog as we approached. He had eaten all the meat at the feeding stations but was hungry, and quickly gobbled up the meat scraps I gave him. Evidently some of his pickiness disappeared with his experiences in the real world.

But where in the world was Stripey? I could not pick up his signal at the Unruh farm. Had he moved again? Given his attachment to the place, this seemed very unlikely. Had the transmitter died? It was a new one, and that seemed only a remote possibility. I started to become worried when I had not found Stripey by the time school started in early September. I decided to do an intense search of the Unruh farm. Late on a Thursday evening I flushed up an owl in the hedge north of the dry pond. I could not tell for sure, but it acted like Stripey, flying to the same perches that he used. If it was Stripey, the transmitter had somehow malfunctioned—not a rarity in the annals of wildlife research. Anything mechanical can and will go wrong. I left the Unruh farm questioning how I would ever catch Stripey again given the traumatic time I experienced just weeks ago.

I still had another owl back on TESA who was raising questions of his own. Surprisingly, I located Hooter in the South Woods right under the beaks of the TESA owls. He had been keeping to the northern boundary of TESA, something I had not expected. Was he losing some of that timidity? I also noted that Hooter was developing more aggressive play behaviors. I rolled hedge apples along the ground and he attacked them, piercing them with his talons and getting the sticky juice all over his feet. Stripey, to my recollection, never attacked rolling hedge apples. He practiced on the dog and cats—who were perfectly safe with Hooter. Individual differences!

At Tabor, this was the year that I got to teach my favorite course, Animal Behavior, and my students made good use of Hooter and the turkeys that I had reared from eggs. It was time to release the turkeys, who had been going through some interesting developments of their own. The hens were suddenly laying eggs and the male was getting a red "beard" and gobbling. For an animal behavior lab, I decided to put a transmitter on one of the hens and release her and her companions. The transmitter I put on her back was one equipped with solar cells. Turkeys are more likely than owls to get out into sun, so this technology fits their lifestyle better. Also, the bigger back of the turkey allowed me to mount the transmitter on a piece of white foam that kept the unit above the feathers. We were able to follow the turkey for two weeks, after which we never found her again. Turkeys range widely within an area and keep to the ground. Owls, because of their site fidelity and aerial roosting, make much better animals for study by telemetry.

Wild turkeys raised from eggs found on TESA.

The last week in September brought an unexpected and sad end to my study of Hooter. On September 25, I presented him with three live mice. He swooped down off the barn and killed and ate all three. It pleased me to see him come along so well since I had had early doubts. I left him sitting on the barn, and even he looked proud of his accomplishment. He had a good start on a pair of horns and he was filling out to look like a first-class owl. I looked ahead to my interactions with him since he provided an ideal replication of my observations on Stripey.

The next morning I picked up Hooter's signal from an unanticipated direction. Instead of being near the barn or in the east TESA hedge, his signal came from north of the house near a telephone pole. I went out there and saw something lying at the base of the pole. It was Hooter, dead and stiff. He had apparently flown up to the electrical transformer that fed electricity into our house and was electrocuted. It was the same transformer that had shocked Stripey in January 1989.

All the feathers around his beak were scorched, indicating that he must have probed around the transformer with it. His own curiosity, so adaptive in the world of nature, had killed him in the highly powered technological world of man. Stripey had barely touched the two terminals with his wing tips and just got a jolt. Hooter took a full charge to the head. One owl was taught a lesson and another one was killed. There is a randomness to this world which is as difficult to explain as to accept. Machiavelli gives a fitting epitaph for Hooter:

> . . . a wild beast, . . . which, naturally fierce and accustomed to live in the woods, has been brought up, as it were, in a prison and in servitude, and having by accident got its liberty . . .

APTURE

TIGER, TIGER, BURNING BRIGHT

IN THE FORESTS OF THE NIGHT,

WHAT IMMORTAL HAND OR EYE

COULD FRAME THY FEARFUL SYMMETRY?

IN WHAT DISTANT DEEPS OR SKIES

BURNT THE FIRE OF THINE EYES?

ON WHAT WINGS DARE HE ASPIRE?

WHAT THE HAND DARE SEIZE THE FIRE?

—*William Blake, writer*

❖ ❖ ❖ I took Hooter's body to my lab at the college and wrapped it in plastic and put it into the freezer. As I lowered the lid, my enthusiasm for more research was about as cold as Hooter's stiff body. It would have been intriguing to further compare Hooter with Stripey. Also, what would have happened if Hooter had wandered into Stripey's territory at the Unruh farm? I potentially could have had two hand-reared owls interacting, each with a transmitter. Perhaps they would even have mated. The potential for more information was exciting, but now all I had was one dead owl and another with a dead transmitter.

Could I ever catch Stripey again? I wouldn't blame him if he flew away at the sight of my van entering the drive at Unruh's farm. When I went there the next evening, I did notice an owl fly out of a tree near the dry pond. Was it Stripey? I tried to follow the dark apparition as it glided over the hedge row and down toward the creek. As I threaded myself through the brush and to the waterway that ran along the hedge, I suddenly recognized the familiar "cheep." There he was, sitting in the top of one of the hedge trees looking at me and cheeping.

This was highly unusual—he usually did not want anything to do with me when his mate was around. As I got closer, I could see the antenna of the transmitter extending out above his tail feathers. It obviously had quit before its time. Dan Stoneburner, whose advice and technical skill are as good as anybody's in the business, was very gracious and had sent me two transmitters to replace this one that failed. If only I could get him again and replace it.

Stripey stayed in the tree and I decided to return home, get some meat, and try to lure him down again. Could I do it? The odds were extremely slim but I decided to try. So far so good. When I returned, Stripey was still in the tree where I left him. I decided to entice him before I lured him to the ground. I took small pieces of hot dog and threw them in the air. Just like old times, Stripey flew out and grabbed them in his talons like an outfielder catching a baseball. The small pieces of hot dog enhanced his hunger and he began to cheep. I threw a larger piece out into the plowed wheat field next to the hedge. He flew out and rapidly gulped that piece down too. Then I threw a piece closer to me. Automatically he flew to it and likewise ate it. Next, I decided to go for it. I threw my entire supply of two hot dogs at my feet, and Stripey flew immediately to the bonanza. Just as he was about to fly off with his larder, I grabbed the antenna that protruded quite handily from his tail feathers. The transmitter made a good handle if not a perfect signal generator. Immediately I felt two talons go through the leather of my gloved hand holding the transmitter. Luckily they missed my fingers and I quickly grabbed both of his legs with my other hand. I had him again at last.

He flapped once or twice and immediately settled down as I began to walk with him to the van, which was about a quarter mile away, up through the hayed pasture. Once I arrived at the vehicle, I held on to the owl with one hand and drove with the other. Wondrously calm, Stripey caused me little trouble during the trip back to TESA. At the house, I got out of the van carrying my little captive. Kerry spotted me first and ran to get Jan, who, knowing what to do in these situations, opened the garage door. I walked in. Jan closed the door behind us and quickly readied a harness for the transmitter that had been on Hooter. At first, I wanted her to use one of the new transmitters but on second thought decided to let her continue. It was fitting that Hooter have something in common with Stripey.

Hooter's transmitter was a light replaceable battery type and we merely put in a new hearing aid battery. When we checked for a signal, however, there was none. Did the electrical charge that killed Hooter burn out the circuitry of the transmitter? On double-checking the situation, I discovered that we had merely put in the battery upside down. It worked fine, and now Stripey carried a transmitter that I could change in the field without having to bring him back to TESA. I had done this with Hooter. Again, it seemed appropriate that Hooter contributed to Stripey's future welfare.

Before releasing Stripey, I tried to feed him the hot dogs that he so dearly wanted. But now he wanted nothing to do with them. His only interest was in escaping from what he must perceive as a bizarre chamber in which he is manipulated and outfitted with a small box on his back.

Given his propensity for being recaptured and refitted (this was the twelfth time), one might wander about his long-term memory and possibly his intelligence. I have a hunch that owls only remember those things that are significant, such as prey and where one's enemies are. Perhaps I am successful with him only because I am insignificant to him. I do not fit into those memory banks that only have slots labeled food, shelter, and mates. Maybe this is not so bad.

Upon being released, Stripey flew to the same tall cedar as he had done a few weeks earlier, got his bearings, and this time he flew straight for the South Woods. Had he forgotten about the resident owls? He stayed there for about an hour and then flew from TESA back to the Unruh farm. Talk about learning significant things. How to get home is one of them.

This turn of events was a goldmine for discussion by my animal behavior class. When we went out to find Stripey three days later, there he was, in the same area at the Unruhs', on the same perch,

Replaceable battery transmitter.

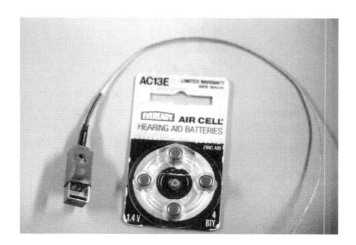

doing almost all the same things that members of his kind have been doing for millions of years.

It was now mid-October and the leaves in the trees at the Unruh farm were a mixture of oranges, reds, disappearing greens, and yellows. Some of the trees were already quite bare, and Stripey was not able to hide so well from me as I approached, my receiver pulsing with every signal that came from the transmitter on his back. In these situations, Stripey showed his bag of tricks in a most interesting fashion. This time, he flew to the very edge of his territory on the fringe of a wheat field. When I followed him, he swooped low into the ridged, low waterway designed to carry runoff water from the fields to the creek. Like a bomber trying to avoid detection by radar, he flew off to a clump of grass, landed, and crawled into it. There he waited for me to leave. With my antenna pointed right at him, I knew where he was and could have walked after him. Alas, after such clever maneuvering, it did not seem fair to follow him any further, so I let him hide while he was still confident in his cryptic skills.

A couple of nights later, I saw another owl with Stripey—presumably his mate. She was in the hedgerow near the old squirrel nest and Stripey was about twenty yards away. As she flew to the north, Stripey departed toward the east in the direction of the Dalke farm. Evidently my owl had a territory that was attractive to this female— a big selling point for a potential mate. Female owls fly around from territory to territory listening to the hooting. If they do not hear a pair dueting, they know that a male is alone and his calls advertise his whereabouts. She then supposedly stops by for a look-see and he begins to court her by performing a sort of dance and presenting her with food items, which probably serve to exhibit his abilities as a hunter. This is important because if they raise a brood he is the one responsible for feeding her while she sits on the eggs—and then the young after they hatch. Mate selection by a female is thus critical to her reproductive fitness. In this case I hoped that her judgment was good.

For some reason, fall was the season when crows liked to mob Stripey. Every time he flew from my advances, there were "instant crows" all around him—cawing and swooping at him, relentlessly trailing him wherever he went like a tail on a kite. Stripey must have disliked leaving his hiding places, acquired under cover of night, and open himself up to this kind of pestering and humiliation. If I did not know where Stripey was, I often could look for a group of mobbing crows or jays, and there he was. Great horned owls place a high priority on mob avoidance. Concealment may be equal to predator skills as a selection force producing the amazing hide-and-seek abilities of these animals.

The end of October 1991 produced a cold front that came marching down from the Canadian north. The springs and falls in Kansas are among the most comfortable you can find, but these periods of tranquillity can turn unexpectedly nasty. Tornado-spawning storms can erupt at any time in the spring, and Alberta clippers, such as the one now passing through, can make life in the fall miserable for owls and people alike. This particular front resulted in record cold temperatures and a coating of ice on the landscape. How was Stripey coping?

I worried that a record temperature drop like this might just catch him and his thermoregulatory adaptations by surprise. I need not have worried. After the storm passed, I found him in his favorite winter microclimate—a tree in a dip behind the dam of the dry pond, out of the wind and exposed to the warming rays of the sun. When I sat down here, I could actually remove my hat and coat and still feel warm; but walking just a few feet up the slope, my ears nearly froze. Stripey was no dummy and I admired his choice of perches. Above all, however, I admired him.

$\mathscr{O}$F OWLS AND SCIENCE

THE TRUTH IS, THE SCIENCE OF NATURE HAS BEEN ALREADY
TOO LONG MADE ONLY A WORK OF THE BRAIN AND THE
FANCY: IT IS NOW HIGH TIME THAT IT SHOULD RETURN TO
THE PLAINNESS AND SOUNDNESS OF OBSERVATIONS ON MA-
TERIAL AND OBVIOUS THINGS.

—*Robert Hooke, scientist*

❖ ❖ ❖ Discovering things like Stripey's thermo-
regulating behavior convinced me all the more that Stripey was indeed a competent owl and was not all that hampered by being hand
reared. Why then are there so many horror stories about imprinted
owls? A usual story goes like this: An owlet is discovered in early
April on the ground by a human and is taken (illegally by the way)
home. There it is reared to the juvenile stage (usually on a near-star-
vation diet of hot dogs and other human food) by its well-meaning
but underequipped and sometimes undercommitted surrogate parent. The screeching young owl drives the family crazy by the end of
May or June and is put into a cardboard box, taken to a distant
wooded area, and released.

There the young owl flies away from the cardboard box amid the
good-byes of Mom, Dad, and the kids, who are proud of their decision to let the owl go but don't have a clue of the hell their former pet
will face. The young owl does not stand a chance. It does not have a
search image for prey items, and it has little or no experience in killing its prey—something it needs before it has any chance of survival.
Some may say that nature equips her children to survive through
genetic preprogramming. Above the level of insects and other invertebrates, this does not hold true. Learning plays a vital role in giving
expression to genetic tendencies, particularly birds of prey and other
predators who have complex feeding behaviors.

Very soon our hypothetical young owl encounters the resident
owls who unmercifully attack and chase it, probably into an adja-

cent area owned by another set of owls. Not having the social aware-ness needed to avoid these angry conspecifics, it gets bounced from place to place and suffers the terrible psychological stress that comes from the complete rejection by others of your own kind. Animals live in a social environment that is every bit as harsh as the physical and climatic surroundings. An individual lacking the savvy to recog-nize and deal adaptively with others of its species is as much at risk as one who becomes naked in a snowstorm.

Totally famished and completely drained of any confidence, the owl resorts to begging from humans, who think it is "tame." Need-less to say, most humans are not well informed about the natural history of great horned owls. For most of our history, most of us humans have viewed owls as omens of death—dark creatures of the night who, being pets of the devil, are insidious vermin worthy of our fear and hatred. In recent times, owls have lost most of their "wickedness" but are still considered chicken hawks who deserve nothing but a bullet between the eyes. It is still uncommon to find an individual who values a bird of prey for its vital role in the web of life.

Starved into a crazed cheeping, our sorry young owl will come to a house with the night light on and the human family sitting around the table eating supper. It lands on the porch railing and begins to cheep and screech the calls it instinctively elicits to get food from its parents. Terrorized, the man of the house or an older brother will grab a shotgun and shoot the "crazy, probably rabid thing". So ends the gruesome tale. Lesson: do not pick up and raise young owls un-less you are a scientist trying to answer questions that will help all owls by helping us to better understand their behavior.

I have many questions. Is the high death toll of hand-reared owlets really due to imprinting on humans? Does exposure to humans throw some sort of mental switch that, once it clicks, produces irreversible damage? Are young owls (and other wild animals for that matter) really doomed because of an untimely exposure to humans? The no-tion almost seems magical or mythical, yet it is the conventional belief among scientists and others studying raptor biology and care.

In 1899, Congressman Willard D. Vandiver addressed his col-leagues and friends with the now well-known phrase, "Frothy elo-quence neither convinces nor satisfies me. I am from Missouri. You have got to show me." Well, I am not from Missouri but my Kansas owl beseeches me to follow the Missourian's suit. My experiences with Stripey have raised my doubts about the conventional wisdom of the proponents of imprinting.

I suspect that many so-called imprints are not animals switched into believing they are humans as they are creatures with behavioral deficits, who, given the chance, could develop normally. In my view they should be called "deficit birds." They are human-oriented and dependent because they are denied experiences that would allow their genotypes to develop in natural ways. With the aid of radiotelemetry and feeding stations, I suspect that many "imprints" could finally make it on their own as much as "normal" wild birds—and even mate and reproduce. There are many birds so old and long dependent on human care that we suspect that their spirit is long dead—extinguished by the smothering hand of man. Who knows: given a radio transmitter and a constant supply of mice on a feeding station in an area free of competitors, they may become phoenixes, rising from the ashes to dispel long-held and untested beliefs about their chances in life.

How could we begin to find an answer? Surely there have been many young great horned owls who, like mine and Bernd Heinrich's, though reared by humans, have become competent "real owls" because they were given freedom and the right experiences. The records of these animals could be scientifically examined and the timing of the various exposures to humans compared to see if there are similarities or differences. Also, those individuals and rehabilitation centers that have imprints could radio-tag these animals and monitor their fates in situations with readily accessible food at feeding stations. The risk of losing an animal is there, but my hunch is that a vote of those at risk would be affirmative.

In the world of science, if you want to see what others think of your ideas, you either publish a paper or you go to a meeting of those who do research or work in your area of interest. Scientists, like owls, generally have histories of experiences that shape their interests and lead them into careers. Some scientists merely follow the careers of their parents, being, as it were, genetically adapted and environmentally enriched. Others have lived close to the heartbeat of nature by having wild animals for neighbors. Still others, in their formal education, come across individuals and experiences that excite their interests and lead them into a life of animal watching. I have yet to meet a scientist who went into the field to become rich. Those individuals who pursue science from a materialistic base are akin to the ill-begotten owl just described. They stand little chance of surviving because they lack the basic survival skills needed to succeed in science—a driving curiosity and a love of nature.

From my youth, I was preadapted to become a biologist. I grew up on an Ohio farm and had goats, horses, groundhogs, dogs, cats, and many other animals as companions and pets. My search image for the prey of my academic interests had been given plenty of exposure to nature. I also had some good role models. My brothers Don and Ken and cousin Dick, who were nine to fifteen years older, were science majors in college and involved in teaching. Don was my high school biology teacher and Dick was a professor of animal behavior at the College of William and Mary. I majored in biology at Spring Arbor College in Michigan and went on to Michigan State University to specialize in the study of animal behavior. There I studied rodent behavior with two leading animal behaviorists, Rollin Baker and Jack King. Later, in my doctoral program I went to Kansas to study prairie rodents and to teach at Tabor College. Here is where I connected with Stripey who expanded my interests to owls. Now, in order to further understand him, I needed to make some contacts in the area of raptor behavior.

Earlier in the year, I had received a brochure from the Raptor Research Foundation near Tulsa, Oklahoma, announcing a national meeting in Tulsa of scientists and rehabilitation professionals who study and work with birds of prey. Tulsa is about a five-hour drive from Hillsboro. I decided to go and see if I could learn anything about owls and imprinting. The meeting announcement listed many well-known researchers, and I was excited as I departed for Tulsa on a Wednesday afternoon in November.

Humans today have much larger home ranges than those of our ancestors. Except for periodic emigration, our species has probably never wandered more than fifty to one hundred miles from home until modern times, and the world used to be a much smaller place. Our behavioral adaptations most certainly developed within the context of a much smaller area and social environment. Maybe this is the reason that we feel a bit of uneasiness when we have to leave our home territory. As with Stripey having to leave TESA, we all need our "resident owls" to chase us into new frontiers if we are to properly mature. In this case, a question about imprinting and owls led me to the south to the land of sooners and land rushes. It all seemed appropriate.

When I arrived in Tulsa after going through what seemed to be endless toll booths, it was dark and I needed to find a motel. As Stripey must have done, I began to look for signs of a habitable place for the night. For him, it might have been a concealed perch in a cedar or a hollow cavity in a snag. For me, it was a sign along an exit that said "Motel—Reasonable Rates." After traveling what I sensed to be too far, I gambled and took an exit that did not have any signs but looked like it should have motels. I immediately found myself in an older run-down area of town near some railroad crossings. It did not seem to be a suitable habitat for me and I continued on with a close eye on my fuel gauge—it read almost empty.

As Stripey moved through unknown territory he must have felt some of the same anxieties that I felt driving through the outskirts of Tulsa. Where should I stop? How much fuel do I have? What kinds of dangers lurk in the shadows? Seeing a bright sign up ahead in a well-lit area, I decided to stop at a motel that appeared to be clean, not too fancy, and which cost twenty dollars per person per night. These clues hit all the right buttons for me, as would "high," "concealed," and "out of the wind" for Stripey.

I spent a somewhat restless first night. It was bitterly cold for Oklahoma and I had neither enough heat nor blankets. A cold draft blew through the cracks around the door and I had to sacrifice a pillow to block the breeze. While placing the pillow by the door, I noticed a cockroach scurry across the floor. I stepped on it but the tough little cousin of the grasshopper did not miss a beat. Amazing. I should be so tough—and maybe I would have to be, before this trip was over. I was getting what I paid for. This was okay for one night, but I would not want to live here. And so it must be with the various owls. Some territories have plentiful prey, high perches, many nests, and access to water. Others have lesser amounts of these owl amenities. If an owl has the resources and ability to pay the price, he can secure the high-priced area; if not, he settles for less and waits for a better tomorrow.

As I peered out the frosted window of the motel, I could detect the faint yellow beams of the sun breaking through a hazy but clearing Oklahoma sky. The cars and trucks that fueled the economy of Tulsa were busily moving on the freeway next to the motel. I called the fancy downtown hotel where the meeting took place and asked about room rates and parking. In short, the territory was well stocked and the price high. Glancing hard at my credit card, I made a reservation. There was no way to meet and talk to people without staying in the hotel. At a scientific meeting, the formal paper presentations are the main attraction, but the real science occurs around the coffee tables and lounges.

It usually works like this. You sit down by a person you know is studying the animal or group of animals you are interested in. You introduce yourself: "Hi, I'm Max Terman and I work with great horneds." Next comes the expected, "What are you studying?" After you give a short description of your own subject, the expert you want to quiz will either talk in detail about his or her work or will tell you about Bill or Alice such-and-such who is working on the same thing. Then you start the process all over with Bill or Alice. Most textbooks and even published articles are months or even years behind what is really going on at the frontiers of science. Attending meetings is a way to explore the real frontiers. This does take time, however, and the expense is daunting unless you have a grant or a position at a research university with deep pockets. I had neither, but I did want to learn more about owls.

Coming from a small college, I often invite puzzled looks from scientists working at larger, research-oriented institutions. Colleges, especially small ones, are noted for teaching, not research, and why am I here if I don't have to be? Below the surface of this question is the reality of life at a big-time university these days—get a grant and publish or perish. At small colleges, you teach or perish. Both situations are tough, but the pressure is definitely more intense at the research universities. Many a young assistant professor blesses the day he or she gets tenure because it is then that the motivation switches from external to more internal. At any rate, our hats should be collectively tipped to all those at both small and large institutions who study owls, or whatever other organism, because they are usually more interested in how it survives than in how they themselves can survive the trials of academia.

As I went to paper sessions and talked to others, it became apparent that there were people of both stripes at this meeting. Some were there to play the games of academia while others were truly interested in the mysteries of nature. One of the latter was Frances Hammerstrom, a noted natural history author and lover of nature. I had the pleasure of her undivided attention for about thirty minutes outside a room where paper after paper dealt with either the bald eagle or peregrine falcon. When I told her about Stripey, she immediately told me of the many great horneds she had reared that "had made it just fine" in the fields around her old farmhouse in Wisconsin. The only one that she recalled did not make it was struck by lightning as it sat on a post—hardly a fate that could be blamed on his upbringing. I got the feeling that this woman and I agreed that the owls we had raised were neither harmed nor doomed by their interactions with us. She, like Bernd Heinrich and I, had given the owls their freedom and had kept them fed until they left on their own accord. Our conversation concluded as a young admirer handed her a copy of one of her books and asked for an autograph. It was a fitting closing to a memorable conversation.

Later I met Carl Marti, a well-known scientist who had published widely on a number of different owl species. He told me about an owl in Iowa that had been hand reared and kept at a rehabilitation center for injured raptors. It escaped and had secured a mate before it was recaptured while trying to beg food. I wondered what would have happened to that owl if it had been given prey items at a feeding station while it honed its hunting and mating skills. Such adventuresome projects are difficult to carry out in towns or cities, but even there it would be interesting to see the results.

During the five-day meeting I met many special people, both scientists and others involved in bird rehabilitation. While rehabilitation work is not conservation (in the words of Bernd Heinrich, "conservation deals with 'statistical owls')", "rehabers," as they are commonly called, perform a necessary service and have helped thousands of injured raptors and other animals get back into the wild. They have also heightened public awareness of wildlife issues by working at facilities such as the Raptor Research Center at the University of Minnesota, and the facility I was to visit on my way home, the Sutton Avian Research Center near Bartlesville, Oklahoma. Others from the meeting were invited to visit too.

As I packed my bags and prepared to leave the hotel, I looked out the window to see a parking garage with a flat roof covered with trees and shrubs and even a patch of tall grass. The architects and engineers had planned the facility in such a way that even in the concrete jungle, a bit of greenery could flourish. It gave me a little hope that perhaps in the future the concrete and steel energy sieves, which witness to our lack of foresight, will be replaced by a new generation of buildings. Green castles graced with singing birds that fly in from well-planned greenbelts and natural corridors that let nature extend her tree-lined fingers even into the hearts of our biggest cities. Impossible, you say—what bird would want to live on a high rise? Peregrine falcons have taken up residence in metropolises such as Minneapolis, Salt Lake City, and Denver and, according to papers given at the meeting, they are thriving. Anything is possible and nature is far more accommodating than we think.

Soon I was leaving the interstates of Tulsa and making my way down the gravel-covered side roads that lead to the Sutton Avian Research Center. I was in yet another world of rocky outcrops, rolling hills, precipitous bluffs, tree-lined creeks, and patches of farmland. The modern headquarters building of the center was at the end of a long, winding drive that ended on a hill overlooking a wide expanse of the rugged countryside. Ideal for a raptor center!

I was one of the first of those attending the meeting in Tulsa to arrive. As I waited in a large room lined with books on wildlife, I struck up a conversation with a young woman who was a graduate student at a large eastern university. She was at the meeting to get some ideas for a research project on raptors. Although her interest in science was high, it soon became evident to me that her hopes for using her degree were low. "Jobs in wildlife are scarce as hen's teeth," she lamented, "and when one comes open, hundreds apply." How could she ever support herself in the field she loved? Knowing that she was right prevented me from giving her a perfunctory reply. However, I do see on the horizon a time when people with skills in stewardship of the environment will be as highly regarded as those now in medicine or entertainment. When clean air, water, soil, and wildlife become scarce, we will have no alternative but to place a high priority on them. If we as a society can't recognize this simple fact, we will deserve the desolation that will surely come and even already threatens.

After the others arrived, the director of the center led us on a tour of the impressive facilities. There were labs for veterinarians to perform operations, and research labs and a library. There was a huge barnlike building with rows of spacious rooms that had exterior walls of screen that provided the avian occupants with a view to the outside. Birds of many species were housed in these facilities. As I walked the hall and peered into the viewing ports, it was interesting to see the unique behaviors of the occupants. In one room housing some vultures, we had to be careful when we entered because the birds tried to defecate on us from their high perches. This "aim-pooping" as our guide called it, was a characteristic behavior of this species, no doubt useful in warding off both predators and nosy scientists.

Another room housed an "imprinted" Jerkin (a gyrfalcon from Manitoba, Canada) that was kept with humans for over seventeen years. Raptors have surprising life spans in captivity—an eagle owl in Europe is reported to be over sixty years old. Evidently this Jerkin had adapted well to captivity as it was in excellent condition. It responded amicably to its owner, the director of the center, with cheeps and bows—"misdirected sexual behavior," said one bespectacled woman decked out in official-looking tan clothes. Again, I felt like I was from Missouri, but this was not the time nor place to raise my questions about the truth of broad generalizations.

In an adjacent building, what seemed like millions of Japanese quail of all ages lived for no higher purpose than to be food for raptors being housed at the center. Thoroughly mesmerized, I viewed the platforms, rotating feeders, and complex temperature-control equipment that led one of these quail from egg to the gullet of an eagle. Down the hall were a series of port holes leading to a room that allowed young birds to eat without ever seeing their human caretakers. This was supposed to prevent them from being imprinted on the human form. In some cases, puppets resembling the chicks' mothers fed them through these port holes.

Seeing the extremes to which these scientists and professionals went to avoid the imprinting "curse" caused me to wonder how my owl ever made it. Of course the people who run these centers have a lot more experience with raptors than I do, and it would be presumptuous for me to say that their efforts are extravagant. I do, however, take the privilege of a scientist (and a Missourian) and ask for evidence.

Still, the people I met at the center were gracious hosts and have my full support in the work that they are doing. One could do worse with one's money than to donate it to the worthy cause of rehabilitation. Equally worthwhile, however, is to route one's coins to organizations such as the Nature Conservancy, which care for whole populations or the many "statistical" raptors by buying land and conserving habitat. Both types of organizations are needed.

Pulling out of the center onto the winding country road, I temporarily became disoriented and drove five miles in the wrong direction. A quick glance at the sun's position gave me the proper direction and I was soon heading north, leaving the multicolored Ozark-like beauty of the Bartlesville area for the waving sea of grass that is Kansas. I arrived late at night. It was good to get back home and I, like Stripey, enjoyed the security of being among familiar surroundings and with my kin. Like the Unruh farm and its hedges were to Stripey, TESA and my secure house were to me—comforts that soothed both body and mind.

I felt good about my excursion into the professional world of raptors. The meeting was different from others I had attended in my specialties of mammalogy, behavior, and ecology. Raptor meetings are a unique blend of the theoretical and the practical, the scientific and the anecdotal, professors and community people. I had learned much, and Stripey and his world held a new fascination.

$\mathcal{S}$CREECHY AND THE KING OF THE SILO

SAVE THAT FROM YONDER IVY-MANTLED TOW'R

THE MOPING OWL DOES TO THE MOON COMPLAIN.

—*Thomas Gray, poet*

❖ ❖ ❖ When I arose the next morning, I immediately went to check Stripey at the Unruh farm. Attending a meeting and hearing research reports does something to get you motivated. Your scientific batteries recharge and the details of field work take on new importance. "No man is an island"—an oft-turned phrase that denotes a basic fact about our species. We need community to thrive. The thoughts and ideas of other people feed our souls, and we starve without them. Even owls require companionship from time to time.

November is a month punctuated by cold hints of winter winds and the hoots of great horneds. Stripey was again in the business of courting a mate, and she was with him as I approached on this cold, clear morning. Both were sitting near the old squirrel nest and evidently hated to move, as they sat tight until I was almost upon them. The female flew first, and then Stripey, reluctantly it seemed, followed. They flew to the lowland area and disappeared from view, only to come swooping up together in a distant tree by the waterway. As I watched them through my binoculars, the contrast with the caged birds at the raptor center leaped suddenly into my consciousness. Although Stripey would not be fed quail and would have to put up with the cold winds and periodic food shortages, I doubt that he would change homes.

TESA is not only my home but it is a wildlife study area. Through its grassy slopes and along hedge rows run trails lined with nest boxes. One of these nest boxes is on a tall metal tower that formerly held a wind pump. Still feeling my renewed scientific fervor, in late November I began to look inside these boxes and record the occupants or signs of animals using these boxes.

TESA nest box.

Sign on TESA's border.

One cold but sunny Saturday morning, I climbed the rather rick-ety steps leading to the large wood duck nest box at the tower's apex approximately twenty-five feet up, opened the door, and looked in. There, sitting on a mat of leaves, was a screech owl. It was in a state of torpor and beside it lay a half-eaten house sparrow. With my gloved hand I reached in and picked up the little owl who offered no resistance. Carefully cradling the little bundle in my hand, I de-scended to the ground and carried the owl to the house to show Jan and the girls.

Screech owls look for all the world like miniature versions of great horned owls. They have feathered horns and yellow eyes but lack the fierce and aggressive temperament. After my nerve-shaking bouts with Stripey, it was a real pleasure to handle this little creature, who merely remained silent and placid as the girls stroked its soft feath-ers. By this time, he (or she) was coming out of the stiff and slow movements of its torpor. I never suspected that owls might do this—go into torpor, a state of slowed metabolism and inactivity—but it makes perfect sense for a food-limited predator to shut down its en-ergy demands in winter. Hole nesters, like the screech owls, can af-ford to do this more than great horneds who must sit on more ex-posed nests and perches. I suspect even great horneds shut down somewhat.

Screechy in
nest box.

Well, here was a perfect opportunity to look in on the life of another species of owl. I decided to fit Screechy, a name the girls gave him, with a small radio transmitter. Since I had none on hand, I took Screechy to the college and fed him live mice and sparrows while I waited for a small transmitter that I ordered from Dan Stoneburner in Georgia. Screechy took readily to captivity and lived in a cardboard box in a large cage. He came out at night and killed his prey, which was always gone when I checked on him in the morning. My students kept records on the amount of food he ate, and they monitored his weight gain. Although he ate like a trooper (seven sparrows, three mice in five days), he hardly gained an ounce. His metabolic rate must be in perfect balance with his appetite. I wish I were so lucky!

Stripey, meanwhile, was still at his nest at the Unruh farm. There was, however, one difference in his behavior. He began hooting at me as I walked up to him. Was he warning me to stay away? The signals were mixed as he initially hooted, then cheeped as he flew off. I did not see any signs of his mate until mid-December. Then, surprisingly, I saw him with two other owls! All three were sitting in the hedge near the nest. Upon my approach, they flew to the lowland area, but then Stripey reversed his path and flew to near the dry pond where I had parked the van. He turned and focused on me, and for a long time we just looked at each other. I did not try to get any closer—I felt thankful to be this close given that this owl was almost four years old. Finally, he gave me a long cheep and flew off. I did not know it at the time, but this was the last sound that he would direct at me for a long time.

What was going on? Owls are solitary, only tolerating another owl to mate with—what was he doing with two companions? I have no explanation for this event. Perhaps this was just a visit by a stranger, but why did Stripey tolerate it? Was he able to attract two females? Questions, questions!

In two weeks, the transmitter arrived for Screechy. It was a small black box with a thin antenna that barely weighed six grams. I took the transmitter and Screechy back to TESA. What a difference compared to Stripey. No biting, screeching, and only a few bill clacks that were barely audible. He seemed relaxed with the elastic harness, a smaller version of the one on Stripey. It would be fascinating to work with a screech owl, and I looked forward to following him on his nightly rounds. To compare his life-style with Stripey's would be very interesting.

I put Screechy back into the tower nest box. He stayed there all day and came out at 8:00 P.M. at dusk to sit on a nearby tree. He stayed in that area all night—moving barely fifty yards from the nest box. He would invariably spend the day in the nest box for the first week of my observations.

Unlike Stripey, it was possible to get close to Screechy at night. When I shone a flashlight on him, his whitish gray feathers reflected the beams, and it was very easy to locate him in the dark background of the hedge trees. This seemed somewhat ironic because screech owls are better than great horned owls at blending into their surroundings. During the day, it was almost impossible to see Screechy sitting in a tree—so nearly did his profile match the tree bark against which he hid himself. Seeming thoroughly shocked that I was able to locate him, he often would not move until I almost touched him.

Screechy readily ate sparrows that I placed in his nest box, a place that, I would learn later, was vital to his survival. I wondered if he would reduce his home range in response to the supplemental food. I began my experiment by giving him one sparrow every day and then monitoring his movements. I did this for two weeks. Then I stopped feeding him and monitored his movements for two weeks. During the two weeks I fed him, he stayed within one hundred yards of the nest box. Two days after I stopped, he was in a new area in the South Woods. Food availability evidently has some effect on the range of his movements, and my "quick and dirty" project showed promise for this nest-box, telemetry, and supplemental-food approach to studying foraging behavior in screech owls.

Screechy's new nest was in a small hole about fifteen feet up a rotting ash tree in the South Woods. Later I found him in a rotten log leaning against a tree directly south of TESA, and still later in a stump of a tree about one-quarter mile south of TESA across a wheat field. From here he returned to the nest box. His home range was thus defined. The nest box was his main home, with the tree holes being second homes, used when needed. This arrangement persisted until mid-January, when a fox squirrel commandeered the nest box. Screechy still remained in the area but did not use his former nest; instead, I found him sitting outside during the day, on posts or huddled up against tree trunks. I suspect that this is unusual for screech owls, especially if they like to shut their engines down during the day.

Screech owl camouflage.

This lack of access to his nest box, I am sorry to say, probably led to his death. In late February, I found Screechy lying dead on the ground, thin and gaunt—his death no doubt hastened by his inability to store food and conserve energy in his squirrel-occupied nest box. Competition for food, for nest boxes, for the requisites of life. Some die, some live—this is the nature of nature.

That evening, Gary Myers, a close college friend and now a colleague at Tabor, called and said that the red version of the screech owl (screech owls, like many other species, often exhibit morphological differences across their geographic range) was inside in a birdhouse at their house in town. The death of my screech owl and the uncommon sight of a red screech owl on the same day—the coincidences in nature amaze me.

No such fate befell Stripey. He gave every evidence of being in control of his fate on the Unruh farm. On New Year's day around dusk, Jan, the girls, and I drove by the Unruh farm on our way to a friend's house for a visit. There, on a telephone pole by the road, sat Stripey, hooting for all he was worth. I could see the white tips of the harness on his transmitter as he craned forward, shoved his tail in the air, and pushed out his throat patch to give every hoot its full expression. I slowed down, and he flew from the telephone pole to the old silo, where he continued his hooting as if he were in a calling contest. Meanwhile, another owl flew from a nearby tree to near the dry pond—probably his mate. What was all the commotion about?

Further down the road, we discovered the reason—another great horned owl was sitting on the telephone pole on Stripey's territory and hooting at him. We were in the midst of a border dispute and I can only imagine the contents of the exchanges. E. O. Wilson, a Harvard biologist famous for his theories in sociobiology, estimates that animal species on the average have about forty displays by which to communicate with one another. It is thought that the sender of the messages tries to manipulate the receiver into acting in a way beneficial to the fitness of the sender. If this was the case, Stripey was in the midst of trying to get his neighbor to stay off his property and away from his mate—and he seemed to be doing it quite well. Kerry remarked that Stripey seemed to be "king of the silo." This was obvious to both her and the other owl, which flew off to the south away from King Stripey.

Silo at Unruh
farm, where
Stripey
hooted at an
owl intruder.

One week later, I got another surprise at the Unruh farm—two owls were again sitting with Stripey. They flew together to the Dalke farmstead and sat on three big round bales of hay in the farmyard. Who was this other owl? My best guess is that it was another female. Female owls, like those of many other bird species, fly around to select the best male they can find for mating. The reasoning goes like this: females produce and incubate the eggs, and invest a great deal of energy in rearing the young. They, therefore, have more to lose with bad mate selection than the male, who essentially risks only his sperm, which is produced in great quantities and is comparatively cheap in energetic terms. The females that choose good mates (good genetics and hunting skills) will be more successful in rearing offspring than those who do not. Males, conversely, try to mate with as many females as possible, constrained only by the demands, in most species, of helping to rear the young. Sociobiologists believe this is the main reason why owls are monogamous: the male is limited to one mate because he has to help raise the young.

Were these females evaluating Stripey? Did he have a good enough territory? Was his hunting prowess so impressive that not one but two females courted him? I could not know, but it was fun to speculate (which is sometimes all we as scientists are able to do on this matter of mate selection).

The end of January 1992 was highlighted by an extraordinary warm spell that brought in one of the warmest Kansas winters on record. The transmitter on Stripey's back was also setting a record—it must be a good battery since it was lasting much longer than expected. I knew that I would have to refit Stripey soon, but how could I catch him again?

He had to be getting wise to my lure-down-and-grab method. In the last months, he had been as unapproachable as I had ever seen him. His flight distance (the distance from me to him when he took off) was at least one hundred yards—farther then it had ever been. If I was ever to get him again, I would have to trap him.

This was not going to be easy. Stripey was close to four years old now—a wild owl, a natural predator, an owner of a territory, a potential mate, and an important link in the web of life.

PART OF THE WEB

WHAT HE TRUSTS IN IS FRAGILE; WHAT HE RELIES ON IS A
SPIDER'S WEB.

—Job 8:14

❖ ❖ ❖ William Least Heat-Moon, who writes elo-
quently of the Kansas Flint Hills in his book *PrairyErth*, quotes Philadelphia journalist Jay E. House: "So far as we know, no modern poet
has written of the Flint Hills, which is surprising since they are perfectly attuned to his lyre. In their physical characteristics they reflect want and despair. A line of low-flung hills stretching from the
Osage Nation on the south to the Kaw River on the north, they present a pinched and frowning face to those who gaze on them. Their
verbiage is scant. Jagged rocks rise everywhere to their surface. The
Flint Hills never laugh. In the early spring when the sparse grass first
turns to green upon them, they smile saltily and sardonically. But, as
spring turns to summer, they grow sullen again and hopeless. Death
is no stranger to them. For there nature struggles always to survive."
Such was the area where Stripey had his territory.

Stripey's territory consisted of a mosaic of brome grass pasture,
wheat fields, hedge rows, and Cottonwood River tributary bottom-
lands. It once was an untorn ripple in the vast fabric of rolling prairies that was the back and spine of the North American continent.

Today only the Flint Hills immediately to the east of Hillsboro
and its harboring county of Marion (named in honor of the American
Revolutionary war hero Francis Marion of South Carolina, the renowned "Swamp Fox"), survive to retain the identity of the Sea of
Grass, the Great American Desert that greeted the eyes of Coronado.
The immensity of it widened the pupils and stirred the hearts of
early American explorers such as Lewis and Clark, and of Zebulon
Pike. Pike, who with his soldiers entered these central plains of Kansas in 1806, was the first person to map and record observations
about what he saw. He wrote: "Passed very ruff flint hills. My feet
blistered and very sore. I stood on a hill, and in one view below me

saw buffalo, elk, deer, cabrie [antelope], and panthers." The millions
of bison fed the stomachs of the plains Indians, who for thousands of
years lived off its bounty without compromising its character.

So featureless was this treeless stretch that the early Mennonite
settlers (whose descendants now make up most of Marion County
and the city of Hillsboro) plowed furrows between farms so they
would not get lost. Sondra Van Meter, in her book *Marion County,
Kansas: Past and Present*, tells of a furrow which stretched twenty-
eight miles between Marion County and McPherson, the nearest
county to the west. How things have changed! The prairie is now
almost all gone except for the Flint Hills.

The Flint Hills today are like a triangular strip of unbroken velvet
twenty to eighty miles wide that crosses a vast patchwork of settle-
ments and farmland from Nebraska to Oklahoma. It is six million
acres of grass that was once so tall in places that men on horseback
disappeared below the waving seed heads. It is one of the few
remnants of the original true prairie ecosystem inhabited by such
creatures as the plains grizzly, cougar, bison, elk, prairie dog, and
black-footed ferret. Today, the richness bequeathed to the Flint Hills
by the creatures of the past feeds 120,000 cattle that produce twenty-
two millions pounds of beef annually.

The plains of central Kansas are like a blanket of seaborn sediments, covering a sleeping mountainous giant—the Nemaha
Ridge—who boiled and heaved up from the depths at the time of the
continent's birth. The ridges and buttes we see now are eroded lime-
stones and shales left behind by the ancient Permian seas that came
and retreated over the giant's tortuous and heaving body for millions
of years. The sediments of these seas and outwashes are now thousands of feet thick, burying the shoulders of the giant who still occasionally tosses in his sleep, creating tremors to remind us that he is
only sleeping. Perhaps in the future, this giant will push his jagged
head through the blanket to protest what we have done to the fabric
that was once so wonderfully whole.

A wooded branch of the Cottonwood River forms the northern
boundary of Stripey's home range. It is where I first observed his
hooting and where he serendipitously led me back to the high
ground. William Allen White, a Kansan and one of the nation's most
beloved journalists, wrote in his newspaper *The Emporia Gazette* in
1925: "In all the world there is no more peaceful, prosperous scene

than in the 'bottom lands' of the thousands and thousands of Kansas creeks. Here are the still waters, here are the green pastures. Here, the fairest of the world's habitations."

Stripey would agree, for he was now part of those ancient and still operating processes that produce the web of life—the ecosystem with its food webs and transfers of energy and nutrients. Like the big animals in the prairies of old, great horned owls are major predators. When viewed over an owl's life span, the number of prey it consumes appears to be mind-boggling. In one year, one owl could eat about fifty to sixty squirrels or an equivalent number of rabbits, mice, shrews, bats, rats, muskrats, gophers, weasels, mink, skunks, woodchucks, opossums, or porcupines. It could also harvest from the system birds such as blue jays, woodpeckers, crows, starlings, blackbirds, sparrows, and even ducks, geese, grouse, hawks, and other owls. The potential impact on these animal populations is significant in itself. But consider that each of them has its own impact. A crow eats many songbird eggs, for example. The reverberations of a night's hunting by Stripey go far beyond only him.

By enabling this owl to inhabit the hedge trees of the Unruh farm, I indeed had an ecological impact as well. Ecological systems are like this—the actions of one affect the lives of many. This is the heartbeat of nature. There is no set end or beginning, only the flow of energy and materials from plant to animal to soil to plant. Beautiful, dynamic, and unpredictable, yet patterned, ordered, and exquisitely practical.

On my way home on a Friday evening in late January 1992, I spied a bundle of gray feathers lying along the road just north of the Cottonwood River running along Stripey's territory. I stopped and saw that it was a barred owl, a competitor of great horned owls where the two species overlap. In Kansas, barred owls, however, are specialized to hunt the forested lands while great horneds are generalists, preferring field borders and more open habitat. This barred owl must have been hunting the deeper gallery woodlands that lined the Cottonwood and collided with a car when it swooped down to cross the road. The U-shaped flight pattern of owls so well adapted for hunting is tragic along a roadway. His body, however, would not go to waste. I would use it to bait a field feeding station for Stripey.

I was glad that Stripey's home range did not include any significant stretches of busy roads. His main roosts were in the silo on the Unruh farmstead, the hedge trees near the dry pond, the hedgerow near the nest, the lowlands created by overflows from the Cotton-wood River, and the isolated trees that fringed the borders between pasture, wheat field, and waterway. It was at one of these perches in the hedge row that I placed the huge raccoon trap that had been Stripey's feeding station on the barn at TESA. Would he still enter it in the field?

I wanted to see if Stripey would use this trap as a feeding station in the same way he had been trained to use it on TESA. This would be a much easier way to catch him in the future to change the battery in his transmitter. I even devised a wire hook by which I could pull the transmitter from his back and stretch it through the holes in the trap to replace the battery. This would reduce the chance of injury to both owl and scientist, and I theoretically could follow him as long as he lived on the area.

A long-term study of a free-ranging owl had much potential, so I strategized as I placed the carcass of the barred owl in the trap the next morning. Stripey had been roosting by the dry pond and flew away as I drove my van all the way down the pasture to the hedge-row. I did not do this very often since I did not want to make tracks in John Unruh's hay field. Amazingly, the transmitter was still working, but I knew it would not be long before it quit. My link with Stripey would be broken unless he started to use the feeding station.

For four days, the barred owl carcass remained undisturbed even though Stripey was in the hedge about seventy-five yards from the trap. Had he learned to avoid strange things like this new "wire box"? Apparently not, because the next day I found the remains of the barred owl on the ground just below the trap. It had the distinc-tive marks of a great horned owl kill—feathers plucked and body and flesh gone. This was good news—perhaps I would be able to catch him again when his signal went dead. My baits of sparrows and mice were sometimes left and sometimes taken. However, I still had my doubts about whether I could catch him again. I envied those days on TESA when I could catch him just by calling his name.

Occasionally I would sight a great horned on TESA and my heart would jump at the thought that it was Stripey. A quick check with the receiver or a look for the transmitter harness tags on its back revealed it to be either a TESA owl or a transient looking for an empty territory. I wondered how often the TESA area changed own-ership. Probably not very often, but it was hard to know. Great horned owls were often killed on the busy road near TESA. These dead owls were apparently not the TESA owls who chased Stripey away. I doubted if Stripey would return to TESA even if he could, given the high quality of the territory he now possessed.

Home is good, but it's not necessarily the best place for both owls and humans. In my own pilgrimage, I often wondered how I got to Kansas from the wooded forests of Ohio. Life is dynamic, always changing, and the offspring of both owls and humans must respond to its opportunities and challenges. Stripey had been chased from TESA by resident owls, I from Ohio by job offers and career choices. These are the differences between men and owls.

The warm winter of 1992 in Kansas resulted in an early February return of bluebirds to TESA. We've had bluebirds on TESA since I put up the nest boxes two years ago. It was always a joy to see these beautiful birds flashing their radiant blue backs to us as they flitted against the sun, coming right up to the house in their nest-gathering activities. Their gentle, friendly manner was a direct contrast to the elusive Stripey, who remained frustratingly unapproachable at the Unruh farm.

It was now late in the mating season, and by now Stripey should have had a nest with young if he reproduced. Although I saw his mate in the hedge near the big nest, there was no sign of the young owls that I so much wanted to see. His range seemed to be shifting to the buildings and old hay bales of the Dalke farm. I checked with Dan Dalke again to see if he had seen any sign of a nest. He had not, although he sure had heard enough of their "confounded hooting" the months before. It was not out of the question that Stripey had young, but I saw none of the signs. He would be making many feeding flights to the nest, and with my transmitter locations being taken every day, I would have surely seen them. Owls, however, are masters at disguising their actions and I could not absolutely rule out that he was successfully evading me.

The end of February also marked the last gasp of the electrical current in the extraordinary battery that powered Stripey's transmitter. I cannot give a free commercial at this point for batteries, since I have forgotten the brand name. Maybe batteries, like owls, have some that live long and others that die off short. I dare say, however, that the variability in biological organisms exceeds that in batteries. Variation is the stuff of evolution, and it appeared I had a winner with the owl on Unruh's farm. Whether he was a winner in the true test of evolution—reproduction—was still in doubt. Without a transmitter to follow him, it was even more doubtful that I could answer this question. Time to set the trap.

On a Monday morning in early March, I set the trap with a real prize, a road-killed raccoon. A signal-less Stripey and his mate flew from the nest area to the lowland. He had learned to eat large animals placed on the barn feeding station at TESA, and I hoped this bait would be irresistible to him. It was not. The trap remained untouched for more than a week. I removed the now reeking carcass and buried it nearby. Fickle animals, these owls—I wonder if they knew what I was about? They almost snickered as they flew from their perches in the hedgerow. I was grateful, however, that Stripey and his mate stayed close together—I saw both of them almost every time I checked the trap.

Stripey's mate, like almost all female birds of prey, appeared larger than her mate. Female great horned owls can be up to a third bigger. She often flew down to a cottonwood tree in the lowland and watched me as I followed Stripey. He occasionally would join her and seemed smaller in comparison. Why is this size difference found in these birds of prey?

Great horned owls have what is known as "reversed" sexual dimorphism (size difference by sex). In most animals with a size difference, the male is bigger. It is he who must fight other males to mate with the rather choosy females. Females are usually smaller, being well adapted for camouflage and care for the young. There are a number of scientific explanations. Perhaps the larger size of the female owl is an advantage in the protection of the nest and eggs on which she sits for long periods of time while the male feeds her and the young. Possibly the male is smaller to allow him to be more agile in pursuing smaller prey needed to feed the young. Later, the female could specialize on larger prey and they could thus exploit the niche more fully and not compete with each other. Whatever the reason, I was glad for the difference because it made it easier to distinguish him from her—especially now that his transmitter no longer worked.

I faithfully set and checked the trap every week for the rest of March and into May, but with no luck. The cotton rats, sparrows, and other road-killed animals were left untouched. If I was to catch him, it would have to be by other means. I removed the trap and concentrated on finding him and his mate by foot searches of their favorite perches.

How I missed that radio signal! Without it Stripey had the advantage—no contest. Many times I spent hours looking for him fruitlessly, all the time realizing that he was no doubt sitting close by watching me through his still, yellow eyes. On occasion, however, I would stumble on him and his mate by surprise, and they would usually fly to the lowland, then sit and watch me. I tried to photograph them several times, but they hardly showed in my photographs since they were more than three hundred yards away and I had no telephoto lens.

Classes at the college were drawing to a close, and the summer was fast approaching. I was scheduled to go again to AuSable Institute in the North Woods of Michigan to teach the animal ecology course. Although I would not be able to study Stripey for three months, I would be able to write the final chapters to this book since I would have plenty of time between class meetings and would be able to be alone in a cabin by Big Twin Lake.

On June 8, 1992, Katy and I drove to the Unruh farm for a last look at Stripey. I had not been able to catch sight of him for the previous three weeks and the chances of seeing him now were slim. But Katy and I were used to taking chances together. Her seizures appeared suddenly when she contracted viral encephalitis when she was two years old after a trip to the Rocky Mountains. Perhaps it was a tick bite—we don't know—the mystery of it perplexes our family most every day. Any family that has a chronically ill child with a disease of unknown origin knows the meaning of patience, persistence, and miracles.

We almost lost Katy in that Wichita hospital in 1982. A year earlier her identical twin Kerry came close to death from a bacterial infection in her eye. Life is so fragile for both people and owls. Every day that we live is a special gift—perhaps biologists are more in touch with this reality since forces we study determine life and death every day.

I held Katy's hand firmly as I looked out over the fields for a sign of the owl I had so long studied. Stripey had provided a diversion from the tension-filled days of hospital visits, EEGs, drug tests, CAT-scans, and fears of possible brain surgery. I half hoped that he would cheep and fly over Katy and me, giving us a last good-bye before I headed off for Michigan. We walked down the hedge by the large nest—nothing but blue jays and Harris sparrows flitting among the branches. On to the bank that overlooked the lowland area with its large cottonwood snags—no sign of Stripey. No miracle today. I drew Katy closer to me and looked into those eyes which have had so much apprehension for the future. "Sorry, honey, but it looks like he's gone." I could see the disappointment well up in her. She has had so many tough battles that I really would have liked her to win this one.

Katy's seizures are for the most part controlled with medication, but she still struggles with the occasional welling up of strange feelings and emotions brought on by some unknown turmoil within her. Like Stripey, she probably feels a contradiction in her life, one that we pray may someday be answered. But also like Stripey, it is possible to persevere and overcome our handicaps and claim the joys of life in spite of our circumstances.

As we were about to leave, Katy grabbed my arm and said, "Dad, why don't you hoot and see if he hears you—maybe he's just sleeping." Well, why not—I had become quite a good hooter (and cheeper) over the years. I cupped my hands, drew a deep breath and boomed over the Kansas landscape—"hoo-hoo-whoo-hoo, whoooo-whooo." I waited and scanned the trees with my binoculars. The trees were fully leafed out and it was impossible to see an owl unless he wanted to be seen. Katy's hand jumped within mine. "Dad—there he is—look over by the tall snag!" As I looked toward the west, a familiar form spread its four-foot wings out wide and flew in a big swooping arc out over the wheat field and to a distant tree. There it landed and shook itself in the way only owls can do—from the bottom up, from the tip of its tail to the top of its horned feathers. Miracles, both small and large, do happen.

It is somewhat perplexing to know where to draw things to a close. Stripey continues to perform his role as top predator on the Unruh farm, and I may yet be able to capture him and follow his movements. I think I will try, but perhaps my chances are not too good. He is sly and deserving of his freedom. Stripey has elevated my appreciation of owls and their behavior. We as scientists have considered them to be less than they are. Far from being stimulus-bound automatons, they are well-adapted creatures, each an individual, molded by what I believe is that unseen Hand which cradles us all. Shalom.

$\mathscr{C}$OMPARISONS AND CONNECTIONS

THE FIRST TWO WEEKS IN THE YOUNG HORNED OWL'S LIFE
HAVE A SINGULARLY PROFOUND EFFECT UPON ITS FUTURE
DISPOSITION. RECENTLY HATCHED OWLETS ACCUSTOMED
TO NO SOURCE OF FOOD OTHER THAN THEIR HUMAN ATTEN-
DANTS CAME TO RECOGNIZE THEM SOMEWHAT AS THEY
WOULD THEIR OWN PARENTS, EVEN DISPLAYING WHAT AP-
PEARED A GREAT DEAL LIKE TRUE AFFECTION. ON THE OTHER
HAND, AN OWLET REARED BY ITS PARENTS THROUGH APPROX-
IMATELY ONE-FOURTH OF ITS GROWTH NEVER DID REALLY
TAME, THOUGH IT TOLERATED DISCREET HANDLING.

—*Paul Errington, wildlife ecologist*

◈ ◈ ◈ The following week I left Jan and the girls
for AuSable Institute and the North Woods of Michigan where I
would be able to teach and write in a world of bogs, marshes, forests,
water, and sand. Given a cabin on the shores of Big Twin Lake, I was
kept company by eagles, loons, mallards, and an assortment of professors and students. A perfect place to draw things together.

A natural question to be asked is how does Stripey compare in his
behavior and development with what we know about wild owls and
other hand-reared great horned owls? Before answering, let me give
a short recounting of my conversations with people and my interactions with the literature on great horned owls. This provides a peek
at the nature of the scientific enterprise as it is practiced by both
professional scientists and interested laymen alike.

A misconception about research in ecology is that it must be practiced by people with Ph.D.'s who work at colleges and universities.
No doubt the bulk of published research comes from these individuals, but significant work is done by interested amateurs, especially
people who enjoy bird-watching. Adrian Forsyth, in an article in the

Orion Nature Quarterly, describes a notable example of someone outside traditional science who contributed significantly to the field of behavioral ecology—Margaret Nice, a mother of five children and avid bird-watcher who lived in Columbus, Ohio in the 1930s.

When the Nices moved to Columbus, Margaret was reborn as a naturalist. Her resolve took a form that most people must have considered eccentric. She devoted eight years of her life to a study of the song sparrows nesting in the tangled fields and brush around her house.

Working a few hours every day, she banded the sparrows and laboriously mapped their territories. She noted when they returned, when they sang, how females chose territories, which males won fights, who mated with whom, how many offspring they fledged, where the banded young dispersed, the effect of cowbird brood parasitism, and how weather affected these events. She continued on, year after year, building up a lifetime profile of individuals and a population. Nice eventually banded and followed the fortunes of 136 individuals, learning to recognize many by the distinctive elements of their songs.

Her study was published by the Linnaean Society in New York under the title *Studies in the Life History of the Song Sparrow.* Ornithologists proclaimed it to be the best study combining field work and scholarship of that time.

Fieldwork and scholarship are the two legs upon which our understanding of nature moves from vague descriptions and anecdotal accounts to real knowledge. Scholarship must occur within a community of learners, and no one person can possibly ask all the questions or pose the many hypotheses that could account for even one of the behaviors that I had observed in Stripey. I had many conversations with other people who worked in animal behavior such as Maury Wiegel, Craig Weatherby, Pat Redig, Frances Hammerstrom, Bernd Heinrich, Dan Stoneburner, Dick Terman, Richard Wall, Virleen Bailey, Mitchell Bird, John Zimmerman, Don Kaufman, Chris Smith, Jim Reichman, and many other scientists, rehabilitation professionals, and interested persons who had raised owls. Their comments often led me on a journey to new books and articles and different ways of thinking.

The first stop along the trail to scientific understanding begins in the library. I spent many hours in the libraries at Tabor College, Kansas State University, and other universities looking up material in the popular and scientific literature. I consulted recent textbooks, scientific articles, and conducted computer searches. I found the literature on great horned owls to be massive, but surprisingly little was available on the specifics of behavioral development in hand-reared or tame owls. Only the popular literature contained accounts in any detail.

Bernd Heinrich's account of his experiences with Bubo in *One Man's Owl* was perhaps the most useful for my purposes; I've referred to his records of Bubo many times in the effort to understand my own owl.

Another good source of information on captive-reared horned owls is Ronald Austing and John Holt Jr.'s informative book, *The World of the Great Horned Owl* (1966). The authors provide interesting accounts of the many great horned owls they've raised and released, for example:

> Of all the horned owls we have raised, Old Hoot has been the most interesting and the most sociable; he was the only one that failed to revert to the wild state after becoming a self-sufficient hunter. Old Hoot is still with Ron, although he is kept in a roomy cage for his protection. In the spring of 1964 he was ten years old.

Like Stripey, all of Austing and Holt's captive-reared owls used a feeding station to supplement their hunting. Unlike the other owls who generally left by October, Hoot kept coming back long into the following spring. He seemed to enjoy human company. When he finally did leave for a few days in the spring, Holt and Austing thought he had finally reverted to the wild. Not true—he had flown three miles away and had frightened a local family to death by peering into their home on a dark night, alarming a man, who, fearing for his wife and children, had taken after Old Hoot with a bat. What follows is an amazing tribute to the toughness of this individual bird:

> We drove to the man's house to claim what remained of Old Hoot. When the lid of the can in which he had been thrown was removed, we were astonished to find that Old Hoot was still alive! He was dazed from the blow, however, and it was three days before he regained his equilibrium and was able to stand erect. For his own protection we decided we had better confine Old Hoot, who had lost all fear of man. We built him a roomy cage and decided to keep him indefinitely.

Two years later, the authors moved to a distant part of the county and kept Old Hoot in a cage where he hooted back and forth with the resident owls. Since he seemed to be getting more wild, they decided to release him again:

> We considered the fact that the resident owls, in defense of their territories, would probably drive Hoot away the moment he left our yard. Perhaps this would give him the sort of urging he needed to make him become a wild owl. When we released him, he circled the house twice and came back to perch in the old walnut tree. There he sat for about five minutes as if to get his bearings. Then he flew away across a field and disappeared in a woodland not far away.

One month later Hoot showed up at a house in a small town three miles away. This time he was lucky—the people were friendly and did not beat him, and instead they called the authors who came and recaptured him. He was returned to his cage only to escape again one year later. This time he was gone five weeks. Austing and Holt's hopes were raised again, but alas, he returned to the same house in the same town! Recaptured, he was returned for a second and last time.

The authors' accounts of the development of the many young great horned owls raised by them parallels quite closely my itemization of the events of Stripey's life. Austing and Holt mention perching, play and flight development, defensive behavior, bill clacking, hunting and killing behavior, activity cycles, thermoregulatory behavior—even the fact that owls vary in their behavioral development: "Young owls obtained when they are more than four weeks old do, as a rule, tend to be less tractable, and when captured after six weeks of age they are savage and unresponsive and usually remain that way. Nearly all our young horned owls came to us before they were a month old, when they were much easier to work with." Perhaps this is an important point to remember with Stripey—timing of exposure to humans is critical.

I found only one other book that discussed hand-reared horned owls—Farley Mowat's *Owls in the Family* (1985). This is a delightful book more oriented toward children but it still gives much useful information on the behavior of his two pet great horned owls, Wol and Weeps. And in the professional literature, I found only one paper that dealt with tame owls—a short article by Kimmel and Zwank entitled "Post-release survivorship, dispersal, and food habits of captive reared Great Horned Owls" (in *Proceedings of the National Wildlife Rehabilitation Symposium* vol. 2 [1983]: 104–108). After waiting nearly three months to get it through the interlibrary loan, I found that the information was good but the study lasted only five months and was of limited value in my quest to understand Stripey. Another paper, Scott and Carpenter's "Release of captive-reared or translocated endangered birds: What do we need to know?" (published in the more easily available journal, *Auk*, vol. 104 [1986]: 544–545) provided a good review of the questions surrounding the captive rearing of birds. However, nowhere in my search of the scientific literature did I find a long-term study using telemetry that followed one or more individuals for an extended period of time. As far as I knew, my observations on Stripey were unique.

I will briefly recount what is known about wild owls and their natural history in order to launch my comparison of Stripey with other owls. There are many books from which one can get this information. In the most recent, *North American Owls* (1988), noted ornithologist Paul Johnsgaard gives a good account of the major events in the life history of great horned owls. Twelve subspecies of the species *Bubo virginianus* range from western and central Alaska, central Yukon, northwestern and southern Mackenzie, southern Keewatin, northern Manitoba, northern Ontario, northern Quebec, Labrador, and Newfoundland south throughout the Americas to Tierra del Fuego. A truly widespread species! The particular subspecies that occur in Kansas are *Bubo virginianus virginianus* (eastern Kansas), *B. v. occidentalis* (northwestern Kansas), and a mixture of the two intergrading through the rest of the state. The diversity of subspecies reflects the variety of habitats in Kansas, and I suspect that Stripey's gene pool was as rich as his vocabulary.

The vocalizations of great horned owls are extraordinarily diverse and difficult to characterize due to individual variation in the number of syllables and the lack of strong accenting that is typical of other owls (such as the barred owl). Therefore it's not surprising that Stripey had his own individual vocabulary and timing of vocal development. His sonograms revealed an elaborate sequence of tonal hoots, and his many moods were accompanied by short barks, chuckles, growls, laughs, whistles, screeches, and screams. Like Bernd Heinrich's Bubo, Stripey was a good vocal representative of his race.

Hooting typically occurs from the time of the harvest moons of autumn through early spring, when females and males engage in singing duets. Male calls are more prolonged and elaborate than female calls, and they are lower pitched, deeper, richer, and more mellow. The female initiates the duet with a three-second call of about six notes given at intervals of about fifteen to fifty seconds. An answering male returns a call of about five notes, lasting about three seconds and often superimposed on the female's (thus a duet). Such dueting probably cements a pair bond and warns off intruders. Rehabilitators report that injured adult owls will often not mate with other captive owls because of previous commitments to another owl—so strong is the relationship.

Stripey certainly hooted after he established his territory on the Unruh farm. Bubo, while not seen with a mate, was apparently much more vocal than Stripey and, after two years of age, virtually filled Heinrich's cabin with incessant hooting. Perhaps great horned owls that live in forests such as those around Heinrich's cabin in Maine are more vocal than Kansas owls. This would be a good subject for study, since vocalizations are subject to a variety of selective factors in the environment.

One cannot help but wonder if the openness of the prairie affects the development of a species. According to Henry Fairfield Osborne, a scientist and writer quoted by Least Heat-Moon in *PrairyErth* (1991): "It is on the plateau and relatively level uplands that life is most exciting and response to stimulus most beneficial." Harvard biologist E. O. Wilson suggests in his book, *Biophilia* (1990), that humans have a decided preference for open, grassy environments with water and scattered trees. Asked to rate the attractiveness of landscape photographs, the experimental subjects of University of Washington zoologist Gordon Orians and psychologist Judith Heerwagen consistently chose those with low-branching trees that are broader than they are tall—a shape that is characteristic of the savannah and prairie. I'm not sure about us humans, but horned owls do reflect regional differences in their choice of habitat.

In all areas of their range, great horned owls are extremely varied in the type of habitats they select. At minimum, they need a roosting site, a nesting site, and a hunting area. Roosting sites are generally conifers because they provide maximum concealment. Nesting sites, while variable, are usually the old stick nests of other birds or squirrels. Hunting areas are typically open, with scattered trees for perching. Stripey, from TESA to Hiebert's Pasture to the Unruh farm, selected open areas with concealed perches. These types of sites are plentiful in the Kansas countryside. Stripey was also found on occasion in dense woods such as the South Woods near TESA and the Franzen creek area. Information on Bubo's selection of habitats was not available since he was not followed outside of the author's cabin area.

Some ecologists believe that great horned owls select timbered areas for breeding habitats. A short-term University of Minnesota study using telemetry (see Johnsgaard 1988) observed that owls used fields and forest edges for hunting and used forests for all other activities. Stripey, once he settled at the Unruh farm, did not use the wooded creek area extensively. Perhaps his mate tended a nest there, but that was unlikely, since Stripey would have been delivering food constantly and I would have picked up these excursions in my night radio locations in February and March.

Home-range sizes of great horned owls are also variable and depend on local environmental factors. Another telemetry study of wild owls in Wisconsin (Johnsgaard 1988) estimated a home-range size of about eight hundred to nine hundred acres for adults and sixty to eighty acres for fledglings. Other studies indicate that defended territories (different from home ranges) average about one hundred and fifty acres. Kansas has a higher density of great horned owls than most states—averaging a pair per square mile, compared to a pair per five to ten square miles in other states. These figures compare favorably with my observations on Stripey. He roamed over an area of about two square miles in his initial comings and goings from TESA. When he finally secured a territory (the Unruh farm), its size was about one hundred acres.

I wonder if the concepts of home range, territory, and optimal foraging need to be redefined depending on whether the animal in question has settled or not. Once Stripey secured the Unruh farm, he did not range beyond its borders (except for the times I forcibly removed him to TESA, after which he homed back to the Unruh farm). Many animals take time out from their usual patch to sample the prey abundance in other patches. According to ecologist Richard Brewer, grassland birds do this more than birds of most habitats. They keep tabs on other habitats in the vicinity by "flying off their territories and looking things over, and they may shift to a new site even within a breeding season." Stripey certainly did this in his first two years, flying from TESA to the other parts of his range. Once he settled on the Unruh farm, this sampling of habitats probably ceased. Habitat sampling may characterize young owls searching for a territory, but I doubt if it occurs much in older, established owls.

Great horned owls in the northern parts of their range are known to move significant distances. Some older Canadian owls move south as far as Iowa and Nebraska in times of food shortage. Those in southern regions are mostly sedentary, not moving more than ten miles or so from where they were born; these are usually young owls dispersing from the territories of their parents. Stripey moved about two miles to the north of TESA to find his territory. Whether he will move again, say in a time of severe food shortage, is unknown, and it's one of the major reasons why I would like to catch him again and refit his transmitter.

Studies of banded wild owls, show that 50 to 80 percent or more of the young die in their first year. Most are shot by humans; others are killed on the highways by cars, some are trapped, and some are electrocuted by power lines. Rarely does an owl seem to die of natural causes. Katherine McKeever, in her book *Care and Rehabilitation of Injured Owls*, recalls that "in more than twenty-two years and the admission of well over three thousand raptors, only two individuals (other than nestlings) were received following 'natural mishaps.' All the rest were the victims of human civilization and its tools, guns, cars, traps, high wires, towers, windows and poisons. Some were the victims of direct human interference at the nest."

Of the few owls that survive the first year, 28 to 32 percent die by the end of the second year with the same mortality rate in following years. In other words, of one hundred young owls dispersing from home, only about fourteen to thirty-five are alive at the end of two years, ten to twenty-five after three years, and only about one after ten years. If these estimates are true, Stripey is indeed one of a select few. Hooter's death by electrocution as well as the owls I've found along the highways underscores the truth of these estimates. I hope Stripey can continue to live on for many more years. In captivity, great horneds have lived for about thirty years. In the wild, an owl probably can't expect to live more than fourteen years.

As already mentioned, the diet of the great horned owl shows that it is an opportunist and has generalist tendencies. It eats animals of all kinds, with rodents and birds being tops on the menu. Records show that owls take house cats, geese, herons, and pheasants. The great horned owl's ferocity in killing prey is vividly reflected in A. C. Bent's account of observations by a naturalist in Washington in the early 1900s: "The largest bird that I have known the Horned Owls to kill is the Hutchins Goose, which came from the game farm of Dr. Shaver. The killing must have taken place in the water, as the body of the goose was in the lake with the head and neck on a floating log. The method of killing so large a bird was by ripping up the neck, as the head and body were uninjured; the victim is several times as heavy as the murderer!" The average size of prey for a study of Colorado owls, however, was about five to six ounces—rat size.

The talons of great horneds have the strongest grip of any owls (even the larger snowy owl) and require a force of 13,000 grams (about 30 pounds) to open the self-locking grip. Bent's account of a great horned owl that was shot out of a tree in June 1927 shows its survival tenacity. Though it was unable to fly, it still eluded the hunters—they found only a few secondary feathers. Later in the year, the same hunters in the same area shot yet another owl:

> . . . the most superb owl we have seen in this land of owls, splendid not only in size and general condition, but covered with a blanket of pure white fat of a depth which would have been surprising on the fattest of waterfowl. By chance we skeletonized this specimen, and found that, at some earlier date, the ulna had been completely shattered for a length of about an inch and a half, and had knit, at a somewhat false angle, in a large, perforated bony mass. The principal metacarpal bone had also been smashed, and had knit in a similar way. The probability that this was the missing owner of the secondaries was very strong. Such a condition presupposes other 'ills we know not of' for the side and back must have been badly peppered. The owl had been able to maintain life without flight for a considerable length of time, in spite of the abundant coyotes, and either kill some prey under the same conditions or endure an amazing fast and still regain its superb condition within one short northern summer.

To develop into such a bird must require a measure of uncommon meanness. But Stripey never tried to harm me in his first two years; he was easy to handle and very gentle, even enjoying my company. He especially relished being pecked on the bill and having his head scratched. As he got older and more free and independent, this behavior changed until he was, for all practical purposes, wild toward the end of his third year. Bubo, likewise, was tame and friendly to Heinrich but became more independent during the last summer of their three-year relationship.

Bubo, however, was more aggressive than Stripey. He attacked other people—something that Stripey never did, even on his territory. Individuals vary in aggressive behavior. There are stories of great horned owls attacking people, particularly joggers who enter their hunting areas. Whether this is generalized aggression or just misplaced hunting behavior is debatable. There seems little doubt, however, that some individuals are more prone to initiate attack than others, just as in our own species. Great horned owls are dangerous birds, and one is well advised to give them a healthy dose of respect, especially to females with young.

Fortunately, Stripey was never able to sink his talons into me when I recaptured him. No doubt he could have injured me if he had been able to secure a hold. Whether he would have—this I don't know for sure. Even for an owl it must be difficult to launch a mortal blow to a friend. When he did grab my glove on occasion, he meant business, and the only way to extricate him was to drop him. Maybe this information will come in handy for some future owl handler who has the misfortune of having an owl locked onto his hand or arm!

Great horned owls are apparently the least successful of their kind in catching prey by hearing alone. Vision seems to be important, and successful hunting requires some light. The highest hunting success occurs on moonlit nights and during the dawn and dusk hours. Some ecologists believe great horned owls are descended from diurnal hunters and have accentuated the vision-oriented strategies of their ancestors. The size of their eyes in comparison to the body would seem to confirm this speculation. Their eyes are about as large as ours yet their total body weight is only about three to four pounds! Because humans are diurnal creatures, few (save for us owl watchers) are aware of what ecologist Richard Brewer calls the "day-night pattern of ecosystem organization."

The details of courtship behavior in great horned owls is sketchy at best since only a few anecdotal accounts exist. Both sexes supposedly hoot and bow while drooping their wings, cocking their tails, and rubbing their beaks. Copulation is most likely brief and follows a solicitation call of the puffed-up male who then treads on the back of the female. Stripey displayed actions that suggested sexual behavior several times. He landed on my feet on a number of occasions and emitted twittering calls, often exhibiting parental-care-like behaviors around the artificial nest at TESA, at a nest at Hiebert's Pasture, and in the barns at TESA and the Unruh farm. He also showed incubating behavior after one of his recaptures. All of these behaviors occurred in both the breeding and nonbreeding seasons (March, April, May, October, February). The elements of courtship behavior were certainly in his repertoire, but it is doubtful that these came together when he needed them most. Whether they will happen in the future I do not know. Heinrich reports that Bubo exhibited amicable behavior but he was not aware of any sexually oriented activities. Some "imprinted" owls are said to attempt to "mate" with human forearms, heads, and so forth, but the details of these behaviors are sketchy or incomplete.

Great horned owls are territorial for much of the year and paired birds will patrol an area. Their nests are spaced according to the presence of other owls and, perhaps, of red-tailed hawks. Adult owls probably lead a solitary existence from early July until early November. Males begin to hoot vigorously in early winter to disperse rivals and attract females. Breeding starts with egg laying in January or February. Adults care for the young through August (sometimes later), after which pair bonds break up.

My observations leave little doubt that great horned owls are territorial. The resident owls on TESA tolerated Stripey's presence only from May to about October. Their hooting occurred almost any month but intensified from November through February during the mating season. After he established his territory, Stripey rarely went beyond its borders, and during the mating season his defense escalated. During the nonmating season, he was quiet and did not hoot and may have allowed other owls to trespass. Stripey was seen with a mate from September through May, indicating that this mate-attraction business may start quite early.

Stripey remained dependent on me well through the first year and into the second—much longer than an owl's dependency under natural conditions. In this regard he had a special advantage over most owls, which die during the first year. There probably is tremendous selection pressure on juvenile owls during that year, and only the best make it through to see another.

Owl nests are usually far from human disturbance, although some nest in barns, silos, or even grain elevators. There is great variability among owls from different regions—some will even nest on the ground or on rocky ledges. Stripey invariably settled in areas that had large abandoned nests, usually of hawks or squirrels. He preferred stick nests about twenty or more feet high in inaccessible places, including my artificial nest at TESA and nests at Hiebert's Pasture, Peter's Hedge, and finally, the Unruh farm. He perched near barns at TESA, the Bartel farm, the Unruh farm, and at the Dalke farm. Perhaps because he was reared in a barn his search image was affected in this regard.

Since Stripey has not reproduced I cannot comment on clutch size (number of eggs in a nest) or any aspects of incubation or parental care of the young. Perhaps he is yet to become a parent. Possibly some great horned owls do not reproduce until well after their third year, so maybe there is still hope for Stripey.

Developmentally, Stripey's growth appears to have been right on target with the published data. At five to six weeks he had well-feathered wings, and soon after he began to move around his cage. He started to fly in June of the first year (at about ten weeks of age) and exhibited all the behaviors of young owls who hide in the brush waiting for their parents to feed them. This tendency is surely genetically programmed, as is the behavior of food caching, which he first displayed in his seventh month. Heinrich's Bubo was also a food hider from early on, storing excess food in June of his first year of life. Food caching in great horned owls is rarely documented, and Bubo and Stripey might be the first to confirm this behavior. I would like to study this habit in more detail with another owl. My next trip to AuSable provided another subject. But its message wasn't about food caching.

It is now July. The Michigan countryside around the AuSable Institute is lush and wet. Life of all kinds thrives in the bogs, marshes, lakes, and forests. What a contrast to Kansas and its hot summer winds and grassy prairies. Even here, you can find great horned owls. A small pond is near the institute. A clearing, created by the lumbering activities of beavers, surrounds the brown, acid water. A student working on a botany project told me that she saw a large owl who quietly watched her from a distance of about ten yards—it did not fly and stayed put all day. I could not pass up a chance to go and see one of Stripey's kin who inhabited the North Woods.

Joe Sheldon, an ecologist at AuSable, went with me to search for the owl. We found it sitting quietly and motionless beside a log on the edge of the pond. It was obviously sick or injured since it did not move when I touched it on the back. Then I saw that its left eye was infected and filled with pus. Its lack of muscle mass on either side of the protruding keel indicated that it was starving. The owl, no doubt, was unable to hunt with its injured eye. We brought it back to the lab and tried to feed it, clean its eye, and warm it up. I could not revive it, and it died about an hour later, its right eye not even closing as its body slowly wilted in death.

I examined the owl's body closely, noting the huge yellow eye that was still admitting light into the lifeless body. I parted the feathers on its facial disk and noted the large ear slits—designed to detect the faintest movements of a deer mouse on a dark autumn night. The feathers on the wings were fringed for silent flight. The razor-sharp talons at the end of heavily musculatured legs were magnificently engineered to pierce and lock in on the body of a prey. What a piece of work!

Yet this bird, with all of its imposing gear was dying alone. There was no hope of help from any of its own kind. Compassion, concern, empathy, kindness, mercy, pity—none of the emotions associated with humanity were part of its world. This owl, like Stripey, was part of an existence that feels neither obligation nor responsibility, only self-preservation. We, on the other hand, must do better. In the words of ecologist Richard Brewer, "We have the responsibility for protecting the earth [not] because every species is kin but [because] we are the only one that knows it."

Perhaps this is the ultimate message of Stripey's kind to me: "We both are made of stardust, you and I, and we feel the same whisperings deep within. You have been given the gifts of virtue and grace. I act out of need alone and selfishness drives my fate. Esteem me highly, marvel at my skills, but also behold yourself. Your kind has the world in its grips! Control your selfish bent—we are interdependent! Be a steward—for you alone may image the Divine!"

REVELATION

THE WAY TO TRUTH IS SIMPLE AND EASY TO EXPRESS,

TO ERR AND ERR AND ERR AGAIN,

BUT LESS AND LESS AND LESS.

—*Anonymous*

❖ ❖ ❖ It is difficult to end a book of this nature. Its main character continues to defy normal literary conventions by introducing new acts into the play that impede closure. I have not been able to catch Stripey and have stopped my regular visits to the Unruh farm to study him. I continue, however, occasionally to walk around the farm from time to time in hopes of seeing him. The old barn has been torn down and John Unruh has built a new house in its place, but Stripey is still there. John and his wife proudly report that he has hooted and called his mate almost every night since the pair moved in near the end of October, 1992. If by chance I happen on him, he rapidly flies off without even a word. I often spy another owl with him and assume it is his mate, although I still have no evidence of reproduction. He is carrying on his own life now, and I, happily, am not needed anymore.

On one occasion, however, our interaction was rekindled. It was mid-October and the day was warm—a south breeze passing through the Kansas prairie, making for an almost perfect autumn day. I drove up the now graveled driveway of the Unruh farm that led to John's new home. He and his wife knew why I was there and immediately informed me that Stripey had been hooting in the nearest hedgerow last night. As I walked the hayfield that led to the owl's favorite spot, I peered into the trees scattered around the pond hoping to catch a glimpse of him. Not a sign. As I picked my way through the thorny branches of the osage orange trees and entered the grassed waterway bordering the hedgerow, an owl suddenly bolted from one of the hedge trees and flew rapidly off into the distance. "Well, there he goes—just as usual." I proceeded to walk on in the hope of seeing his silhouette in a far distant tree.

Stripey at the Unruh farm hedge.

Suddenly another owl jumped up from the grass and alighted on the very top of a tree about fifty feet away. Quickly I lifted my binoculars, hoping to see the tell-tale signs of the transmitter harness that would tag this animal as Stripey. I could not see his back, as this owl was looking straight at me. My doubts vanished as it began to emit some short hoots that quickly changed into long cheeps. It *was* Stripey! Afraid to go much closer, I sat down in the grass, relishing the moment of contact I had been seeking. Here was positive proof that he still recognized me!

Would he fly if I tried to come closer? Never was I able to get closer than about fifty yards in my previous sightings this fall—and he had never shown any desire to interact with me. Cautiously I rose from the grass and walked up to him. He did not fly off but continued to cheep at me and scan my hands and body with his telescopic eyes. I talked to him for about twenty minutes before he looked off in the direction of his mate and flew away.

Since this last meeting, I've had high hopes of seeing Stripey every time I visit the Unruh farm. Only rarely do I catch a glimpse of him, with his old gnarled transmitter antenna sticking up from his back. Many questions remain unanswered. I knew Stripey was surviving, but did he *really* have a mate? Would he reproduce this spring of 1993, his fifth year? Since I could not catch him to replace the transmitter battery, it seemed that these questions could never be answered.

What a shame! Over five years of following a hand-reared owl, and I could not answer the most important question—could he mate and reproduce? Without this information, I could not establish that an imprinted owl could overcome his unusual upbringing and rejoin the world of wild nature. This is often the case with ecological research—many studies of the animal world begin, then end with interesting but frustratingly incomplete answers. Nature yields her secrets grudgingly, and we ecologists must often settle for what little she provides. I reluctantly decided that this was the case with Stripey. I typed up the final pages of the manuscript about this owl and me and began the search for a publisher.

I decided to focus my research skills on other topics. Since I love to play golf, I became involved in the ecological study of golf courses. Golf courses take up a lot of land—could they harbor wildlife as well as golfers? Do we humans have to exclude all forms of life but our own from the areas we occupy? With some creative habitat manipulation, couldn't we maintain "links" with the rest of nature? I

Prairie Dunes Country Club, Hutchinson, Kansas.

searched for a naturalistic golf course in the area to study. In Hutchinson, Kansas, about an hour's drive away, I found a country club called Prairie Dunes that was a virtual wildlife sanctuary, where dickcissels coexisted with golf balls. My students and I began our work there, and I placed Stripey on the back burner.

One Sunday morning in March 1993, however, owls took center stage once again. Dan Dalke, a farmer living next to the Unruh farm, called to say that a great horned owl was nesting in his barn—he had discovered it while removing hay bales to feed his cattle. The owl did not move and just "looked at him." Since Dan was familiar with my owl research, he thought it might be "my" owl. After church, I drove over there.

As I entered the small barn, I looked around at the scattered bales of hay pushed against the walls. I had difficulty seeing in the dim light—the sun barely shone through the cracks between the weathered boards. Where was the owl? Right by the door, a stack of hay bales extended close to the roof, and on the top bale, I discerned two feathered "horns" and two huge yellow eyes dimly profiled against the wall. Dan had organized some of the bales to form steps up to the owl sitting in a shallow depression on the top. The moment of truth had arrived. If this was Stripey, would he recognize me? Was I risking losing an eye—or worse—from an attacking wild owl? From below I talked to the owl in low tones, calling out "Stripey" and making the cheeping sound I had trained him to recognize. No reaction. I began to climb the bales, warily guarding my face with a gloved hand. The owl rose up and started to hiss while erecting its feathers in a threat display.

As the the bird turned, I noticed something that gave me more courage. Below the erect feathers there was a white piece of elastic. This *was* Stripey! I cheeped with more feeling and even threw in some hoots. The feathers relaxed and the hissing ceased. I gradually extended my gloved hand to Stripey, and he gently began to caress it with his beak. Just like old times. My owl had returned and was nesting in a very convenient place. Nesting? Stripey?

With my gloved finger, I slowly probed under Stripey's breast feathers. To my astonishment, there were two round, white, golf-ball-sized eggs! This was too much. Dumbfounded, I descended the

Stripey on hay bales at the Dalke farm.

hay bale staircase down to the floor and sat on a bale, watching my newly found owl. Did male owls incubate eggs? That great horned owls are monogamous and both sexes feed the young is well known, but does a male also sit on the eggs? Utterly confused, I decided to go back to TESA to find some meat for Stripey in an attempt to strengthen the old bond between us.

When things are destined to happen, it is strange how everything just falls into place. When I got out of the van at TESA, one of our cats came running across the drive with a small cotton rat in its mouth. I immediately commandeered the rodent from the surprised feline and drove back to the Dalke farm, leaving a bewildered cat in my wake.

Stripey was still on the nest—seemingly glued to the eggs. As I climbed up to him, he again hissed in typical owl fashion. As I revealed the cotton rat, his demeanor immediately changed. Stretching forth his beak, he snapped at the creature. I quickly moved it to the far end of the hay bale. Stripey then rose off the nest moved toward the rodent. The two round white eggs were totally revealed to me.

Sitting on the eggs.

As Stripey secured the rat in his beak, he began to emit choking sounds. They were very similiar to those he had given earlier when I was still observing him on TESA and at the old barn at the Unruh farm. These sounds were somewhere between a hoot and a chuckle, and their meaning was clear. They were signs of contentment, perhaps even an acknowledgment of an act of kindness. I spent almost two hours on top of the hay bales caressing and "beak-pecking" this unusual owl.

But what was this owl—male or female? I had been so sure that Stripey was a male. I based this on his behavior (such as the territorial hooting and attacks on the stuffed models) and the sonogram I took of him on Craig Weatherby's sonograph. But here "he" was sitting on eggs, and male owls, according to the available literature on the nesting behavior of great horned owls, do not incubate the eggs. The female sits on the eggs and the male delivers food to her.

During the next three weeks, I visited Stripey almost every day either before classes or on my way home. On each visit, I brought meat or rodents from the lab. He began to anticipate my arrival and

"The meeting of two personalities is like the contact of two chemical substances: if there is any reaction, both are transformed"—C. G. Jung.

cheeped as I walked into the barn. I began to become more and more convinced that Stripey was a female. Only rarely did I observe him (her?) to be absent from the nest and off the eggs. I also noticed that rodents that I did not deliver were at the nest. A deer mouse, prairie vole, cotton rat, and even a rabbit adorned the nest. Evidently, Stripey had a male owl helping *her* during the incubation, and this pretty well settled my doubts. Stripey is, and was all the time, a she.

I must admit that it is pretty hard for a biologist to eat crow on this sex identification thing with Stripey. Perhaps I can be forgiven in some measure, however. Short of a laproscopic examination of the reproductive organs, it is extremely difficult to sex a great horned owl. There are differences in size, but unless you have two owls of known sexes to compare side by side, it's difficult to know for sure.

Observing behavior is the only alternative. So apparently female owls attack and are attacked by other owls, look for unoccupied habitats, and defend territories and vocalize just like males. The only other explanation is that Stripey is a male now acting like a female, and I find this hard to accept.

Where is the other owl? If only I could see them up close together—then I could compare sizes. But no such luck. He is around—the presence of the eggs is proof enough. I was so sure that Stripey was smaller than his (I mean *her*) mate. So much for observing at a distance: we see what we want to see. The only cure for this mental myopia is hard physical evidence. It is difficult to admit a mistake but persistence pays off. English poet Robert Herrick put it well: "Attempt the end, and never stand to doubt / nothing's so hard but search will find it out." Science is supposed to be hypothetical and self-correcting, but does it have to be so humbling?

Stripey incubated her eggs for about three weeks from the time I discovered her in the barn. I was amazed at how approachable she was. She displayed none of the aggression that one would expect from a winged tiger sitting on her eggs. When I arrived at the barn, she greeted me with a cheep, accepted the food I carried, emitted her choking sounds, ate the meal, and settled on the eggs. I could stroke her and was even able to examine the transmitter with its now dead hearing-aid battery.

The last transmitter I had put on Stripey was the kind that had a replaceable battery. All you had to do was slide the old one out and shove in a new one. Since Stripey was so easy to handle while she sat on the eggs, I decided to take the opprotunity to put her back on the air waves.

With a new zinc-air hearing-aid battery in hand, I went to the barn and climbed up to Stripey, who, as always, was sitting dutifully on the nest. I gave her a mouse, and while she was occupied with it I quickly slipped the old battery out of its slot. When I tried to put the new one in, however, it slipped right through the slot and fell out. By this time, Stripey had finished her meal and quickly gave a sharp peck on my ungloved hand. Ouch! I knew these batteries were of the right size—the slot must have widened and would not hold the battery.

What could I do? Although Stripey was approachable and could be petted, she did not like having the transmitter on her back manipulated. She pecked hard at me, and it was going to be tough to try to adjust the slot size on the transmitter while it was still fastened to her. I could remove the harness and replace the whole transmitter, but this was really risky. There was no way that she would stand for the replacing of an entire harness—I'd have to grab and confine her, and this would put too much stress on her. After much thought, I discovered that I could squeeze the battery into a vise, increasing its diameter to fit the slot in the transmitter. There was no sweeter sound than the return of the beep of the transmitter in my receiver. However, the fingers that manipulated the controls on the receiver were now black and blue from Stripey's powerful beak pecks.

During Stripey's incubation time, I was able to observe, photograph, and videotape her. I even brought my classes from the college out to observe "the owl." On each visit, Stripey cooperated fully. While she was on the nest, I was able to climb up to her and point out such things as the eye membranes, facial disk, ear openings, fringed feathers, and other aspects of owl morphology. Oddly enough, however, she did not produce an abundance of pellets at the nest site. I only found a few, indicating that she flew outside to void these bits of undigestible bone and hair.

The blessed event occurred on March 23, 1993. Stripey's reproductive fitness was confirmed by a slight break in the egg shell. A little owlet conceived by a hand-reared imprinted female and a wild male breached the egg case and entered the world of great horned owls.

As I watched the little raptor struggle to get out, I was tempted to remove bits of the shell to help it along. But I resisted: struggle is the theme of its existence and it needed all the practice it could get. Eventually the last remnant of shell was flipped aside, and a wet, rather ugly-looking owlet numbered itself among the living. A day later it was joined by its sibling from the other egg. Two for two! Both eggs were fertile! Amazingly this imprinted owl of mine was able to accept a mate, breed, conceive, lay, and incubate eggs to hatching. But this was the easy part—could she possibly meet the demands of feeding two bottomless pits to maturity? I only knew too well what it took to raise just one great horned owl. But she had a helper, and she would need him!

I have been a biologist for over thirty years and I have never been witness to anything like this. The growth rate of great horned owl chicks averages almost 25 grams per day. That means an owl chick weighing 100 grams on Monday will weigh 125 or more grams on Tuesday. I began to doubt the accuracy of my scales in the face of such numbers. This rapid growth rate is reflected in the data in the table, collected over six weeks while the owlets were in the nest.

Owl chick on scale.

A prodigious amount of food is required to support this kind of growth. Not only did Stripey have to feed her chicks, but she had to meet the rather large demands of her own metabolism. I decided to supplement her food supply any way I could, by bringing in meat scraps, mice, and other animals. Stripey gladly accepted dead house sparrows, starlings, snakes, and road kills. Her mate, whom I never saw at the nest, must have wondered where this windfall was coming from.

One of the most poignant things for me was to observe the gentle way in which Stripey fed her young. She tore off small bits of meat from a prey item and gently nudged it in front of the beak of the chick. Sometimes she would have to persist in her efforts, adding choking sounds to the slight nudges. So here we see the proper context for these sounds of contentment—they are urgings of a mother to her young. Why did they also occur in the other contexts of my

Weight Gain of Owl Chicks (in Grams)	Date	Owl Chick 1	Owl Chick 2
	3/26/93	83	53
	3/29/93	123	83
	3/30/93	152	105
	3/31/93	185	130
	4/1/93	230	165
	4/2/93	273	175
	4/3/93	289	205
	4/6/93	415	215
	4/8/93	545	395
	4/12/93	560	420
	4/13/93	570	410
	4/14/93	610	520
	4/15/93	710	635
	4/16/93	800	645
	4/19/93	820	650
	4/20/93	850	670
	4/21/93	900	690
	4/22/93	910	700
	4/24/93	920	725
	4/25/93	940	740
	4/26/93	990	840
	5/1/93	1025	925
	5/4/93	1100	1000

observations of Stripey? Who knows—perhaps all sorts of adult behaviors first get practiced by youngsters producing them out of context. Isn't this what juvenile behavior means?

That Stripey was a good parent was very satisfying to me. I did not
want to throw a monkey wrench into the process of her motherly
development. Her brain must hold entire genetic programs that are
devoted to this behavior. Where else would it come from? I did not
show her how to prod a young chick to eat, or how to nestle it beneath her when a chilly wind blows. Wouldn't it be nice if humans
were wired like this? Or would it? There is something special in
being responsible for our behavior that would be lost in the mechan-
ics of genetic determination. This may be the essential difference
between humans and owls and other forms of life.

Stripey's chick in aggressive "fan" display.

I knew it would not be long before the young would be out of the nest and on their own. Putting transmitters on them after they had left the nest would be difficult if not impossible. Young owls are very adept at hiding, and if I was to keep track of them I had better put the transmitters on them now while they were still in the nest. Both owlets were rapidly losing the downy cream-colored feathers of their first growth stages and were acquiring the brown feathers of the adult. They were also becoming more aggressive and hissed and clacked at me as I measured and weighed them. After six weeks, the business of putting them in a cup and placing them on the scales became too much to handle, and this aspect of the project came to an end.

With both hands, I picked up the larger of the two chicks and climbed down the ladder I had placed beside the nest. All the way down the young owl was clacking and trying to snare me with its talons. These owls were much more difficult to handle than Stripey. Being with one's real parents (even though one was Stripey) certainly had an effect on behavior. Either the "tameness" of a human-reared owl was turned off, or the wildness of a natural owl was turned on in these chicks. To be sure, I would not be relating to these owls as I had done with their mother. There was no identification with me even though I had fed and handled them extensively.

I placed the hissing and threatening little owl on a hay bale and gently looped the harness over its head and up and around its wings and tied a knot to secure the transmitter in place. What a difference experience makes! Two minutes and the transmitter was snugly in place and functioning. I then did the same with the other owlet. The whole business was done in five minutes. As I looked at the two little raptors sitting quietly in the nest, I remembered the trial and error ordeals I had had with their mother's equipment. The elastic harness—this simple technique took me months to acquire, but what a difference in the results! I did not have to worry about lost transmitters or injuries due to a faulty attachment. Stripey paved the way for her young even in this most unusual circumstance—just one of the many sweet ironies that gave me pleasure in this owl project of mine.

Once owls reach a certain size, they do not remain in the nest, but hide under grass, brush, and the cover of other nearby places,

Author with
young owl.

Stripey and chicks on grain elevator.

depending on the parents to find and feed them. Since I had transmitters on the owl chicks, it was a simple matter to find them and check
on their progress.

Both owlets looked good. Stripey and her mate were evidently
doing a good job of parenting, and my additional inputs were just
gravy. Even so, I felt that I was making a contribution to the huge
investment that I had in Stripey by insuring the survival of her offspring.

Stripey, however, grew more aggressive. She attacked me once
with her talons as I approached her to give her a mouse. She was
evidently feeling the stress associated with the increased demands of
fledging her young. I decided to back off my intimate involvement

with them and was content to just track them with telemetry. It was a real joy to be able to go out to the Dalke farm, turn on the receiver, get a fix on the signals, and locate the owl family. Most of the time I'd locate them behind the barn on an old grain elevator. I had to keep my distance, however, since Stripy was very protective of her hand-some offspring. (It is interesting that Stripey aggressively defended the owlets now but not when they were eggs and hatchlings. Perhaps the investment in the chicks was now so high that aggressive de-fense was warranted—an observation that conforms to sociobiologi-cal theory.)

It wasn't long before I lost the signal to Stripey and one of the young. Evidently the batteries had lost their power or the transmit-ters malfunctioned. I was able to track only the young owl with transmitter 151.083. The owl family now moved away from the barn area to an old brush pile, where I was able to follow them because of the strong signal. Usually when I located the chick's position, the other owls were not far away.

The principal of the local junior high school lives on a farm nearby, and one day he brought over a great horned owl that was in a stupor, found in a cattle feeding trough. I was able to feed the owl once in a while, but it refused to move. Evidently something was wrong with its nervous system—maybe pesticide poisoning. I decided to release the owl near Stripey and the young in the hope that Stripey's presence would prompt it to fly and maybe return to its own territory.

I placed the new owl on a fence post where it sat dutifully—not moving, just looking from side to side. Stripey reacted to the station-ary owl immediately. She flew to within one hundred yards of the dazed intruder and began to hoot. The startled owl jumped down from the post and scooted into some tall grass. This reminded me of Stripey's reactions to the TESA owls years earlier. Now Stripey was the resident, and acted accordingly. But once the dazed owl disap-peared from sight, Stripey flew off—a far cry from the relentless pursuit of intruders by the TESA owls. Maybe Stripey was less ag-gressive than they because of her human-influenced upbringing. Regardless of the cause, the rather mild interaction was interesting to me. I removed the dazed owl from the premises and returned it to TESA to its holding cage. It died two nights later from unknown causes. Pesticide poisoning often has effects like this.

        Toward the last week of June I discovered .083 in a hedge on the Hamm farm. It must have been trying its wings and went exploring just as Stripey had done at the same age. Stripey kept returning to the home site. Evidently this leave-and-return pattern is characteristic of the dispersal behavior of young owls.

We left on vacation in July for Michigan and Ohio. During our absence from Kansas, the Midwest received the brunt of the torrential rains that flooded out the central part of the country, particularly Iowa and Missouri. On our return route later that month, we stopped in Booneville, Missouri, and were shocked at the high water and devastation. Kansas was not spared this onslaught, either, and five to ten inch rains and the flooding of lakes and rivers became commonplace.

Back home, I began to hunt for .083. I found it still on the Unruh farm, but near the west border. It was sitting in a small tree often chosen by Stripey. I wonder if the roosting sites are passed on to the young by the parents. The young owl, now fully grown, swooped out of the tree and flew about five hundred yards north to the island of trees on the northern border of the Unruh farm. Though there was no sign of Stripey, Dan Dalke reported that the owl family was still intact, and that the young owls were still begging food off the adults. In October, he noted all four owls on the barn roof, with the young owls screeching for food. These young owls were staying around longer than most of the accounts in the literature indicated; usually they are dispersed from the parents around the end of summer.

Soon after this, I lost the signal to .083 and was never able to locate it again—a common outcome when tracking a wild owl. I did not look for Stripey again until December 1993, when I found her and her mate (no antenna on its back) in a tree near the pond on the Unruh farm. The mate immediately flew off when I got to within one hundred yards, but Stripey, her antenna wire still clearly visible, stayed and began to cheep at me. Later, this cheeping turned to hooting. She stayed near me for about an hour before she flew off to the north, to the area where her mate had flown.

After a long hiatus in my owl watching, I again located Stripey in March and once more in December 1994. For the purposes of this book, this December meeting was my last contact. Both Stripey and her mate were in the hedgerow near the pond. On my approach her mate immediately flew off, but she was very approachable, obviously recognizing me. After securing an "emergency" hot dog from John Unruh, I again attempted a midair feeding. Would she remember how to do it? No problem. Stripey and I executed the ol' toss-and-grab play flawlessly, like two old athletes practicing a favorite pass at a class reunion. After catching the hot dog, Stripey landed on a branch and began to eat the strange but vaguely familiar morsel. Where was her transmitter? I scanned her back with my binoculars. No sign of the gnarled wire or white elastic. The transmitter was there in March but by Christmas she had somehow shed it. Now she was truly unfettered both by the transmitter and her human upbringing. The cast-off transmitter signaled the official end of her connections with me and punctuated the reality of her wildness.

This bird was in great shape, showing the full stature of a dominant female owl with every exuberant shake of her richly colored feathers. Watching her, I was filled with the special feelings of a special relationship, and I felt proud and honored. Stripey had found her place in the world and had reproduced her own kind, the ultimate challenge of every living thing. I had gained a profound respect for the complexities of creation and a renewed appreciation for the uniqueness and responsibilities of humankind. And now I had also found a publisher—the same one that had made Bernd Heinrich's owl famous.

After seven years, this animal and I still have a relationship that is unprecedented in the annals of owl literature. I don't know how much longer I will be able to locate her and continue to renew our relationship. I plan to go out to the Unruh farm about every other month or so with a mouse or piece of meat. Will she stay around? I hope so. But if I do not find her again, this journey into the world of an owl is an experience I will never forget. Very few of us have the opportunity to get such a personal glimpse into the world of wild animals and contrast it with our own or that of other animals.

How do I paint the last strokes in this painting of an owl and a man? As I reflect on the image, several patterns appear on the canvas. Most striking is Stripey's amazing triumph over "human imprinting" marked by her successful reproduction. Next emerges her complete identification with her own species. But highlighting the whole portrait is her continued openness to me, an alien species who trapped, tagged, transported, and otherwise manipulated and helped shape her life.

The final messages from this owl? Lay hold of life, take heart and persevere! Do not become bitter over injuries and injustices. In times of trial, even an owl can draw on resources of considerable depth. Stripey's amazing journey over tough terrain is a clear indication that real significance comes not from seeking life's gentle slopes but from climbing its canyons.

"He was a bird of death. He has experienced the human world from an unlikely perspective. He and I share a viewpoint in common: our worlds have interpenetrated, and we both have faith in the miraculous"—Loren Eisely on his crow (*The Immense Journey*, 1957).

◈ ◈ ◈ POSTSCRIPT

I WAS ALWAYS, AS I STILL AM, TRYING TO FASHION A PIECE OF
LITERATURE OUT OF THE LIFE NEXT AT HAND.
—*William Dean Howells, author*

THIS STORY will not grant me an ending. On a Saturday night in early March 1995, Dan Dalke called to say that there were, again, owls in his barn. His son had chased some out while doing his evening chores. Old feelings of excitement leaped up within me as I again contemplated interacting with Stripey. Caution swept over these feelings, however, as I remembered just how dangerous great horned owls can be. Would Stripey remember me? Would she let me get as close as she did in 1993 and allow me to handle the chicks? Even though I had already sent off the "finished manuscript" to my publisher, a postscript would have to be written.

How am I going to go about this task? Stripey surely would be protective of this, her second genetic investment in her evolutionary fitness account. Maybe the more young you have, the more vicious you get. Visions of deep neck gashes and not so surgically removed eyes crept nightmarishly through my mind as I went to sleep and planned how I would again join my human world to that of owls.

On Monday morning, with a hot dog in my pocket and a flashlight and video camera slung from my shoulder, I again drove down the back driveway to Dan Dalke's barn. The Kansas winter was just barely hanging on, and a mist of nearly freezing rain greeted me as I opened the door of my Geo Prism (I had sold the van), grabbed my equipment, and tippy-toed through the mud to the barn.

Dan had put in more bales this year, and the stacks of hay filled more of the barn than before. The atmosphere of the barn, dark as always, enhanced the goosebumps now forming on my neck. Dan, an electrician, was not at home but had left a wooden ladder about ten feet from where Stripey was thought to be nesting. Grabbing the flashlight and climbing slowly up, I suddenly stopped and hunched my head. Hiss, hiss, and a flutter of wings came from below my feet!

What the heck? Three Muscovy ducks jumped out of the bales and flew to the ground and indignantly waddled out of the barn, shaking their tails behind them. Why would any duck in its right mind sleep in the same haystack with a pair of owls? Obviously any sense of survival had left these ducks with the wild heterogeneity of their gene pool.

Collecting my wits, I continued my trek up the ladder. This time a real hiss came from the darkness of the familiar corner, and, after I turned on my flashlight, the profile of a sitting owl came into view. She hissed but did not move. I began talking and cheeping in the old style. Immediately, the air went out of the hissing bulge of feathers. Stripey settled down and calmly looked at me. My pulse rate reacted in kind, and the two of us just stared at each other, relishing the moment of reunion.

Remembering that acts and deeds stand for more than good intentions in the world of owls, I shook myself from the trance and slowly pushed a hot dog over to Stripey. She raised up, exposing two white eggs, and pulled the hot dog close to her. She did not eat it but immediately began the clucking sound that I had noticed when she nested in 1993. I videotaped her sitting on the eggs, with the hot dog protruding from under her breast feathers.

Should I dare try to pet or finger-peck her bill as I had done in times past? It had been two years since she and I had had any physical contact. I moved the ladder so that I would be directly in front of her after I ascended the fifteen feet to the nest. I slowly began the climb, wary of four razor-sharp talons on two feet descending on me at any instant. Clack, clack, clack—the sharp, loud tapping of an angry owl came not from Stripey but from outside and behind me. There, sitting on a fence post in the nearby horse corral, was a pulsating and bouncing great horned owl. I immediately jumped from the ladder as the silent swish of air from its attack blew by my descending head. The newcomer owl landed on a beam and hooted at me three times, and it then focused his attention on Stripey. Finally he and I had met. This encounter, however, had all the kindness afforded an old boyfriend of a long since married sweetheart. If I could only get to my camera to record this momentous event. Too late— the owl flew over to Stripey and disappeared behind the bales of hay.

Finally collecting my courage and realizing the need to get the male on video, I slowly moved the ladder away from the nest back to its former position. With flashlight and camera in hand and my well-being at risk, I climbed the ladder and extended my neck to catch a glimpse of the pair I had so long tracked and viewed from afar. The tunnel of light from the flashlight fell only on Stripey, contentedly sitting on her eggs. The other owl was gone, apparently having exited through a crack in the boards on the other side of the nest. He was nowhere to be seen.

Was this Stripey's mate? Had he somehow communicated with Stripey, and had she quieted him so he could leave? Or was this bird one of the offspring from past years coming back to help its mother? Unlikely, as helpers at the nest occur in other birds but probably not in owls. There was no sign of any transmitter harness on this second bird. No, this must be Stripey's mate and the other progenitor of the two eggs under Stripey.

I wonder if he had any sense of his mate's unusual past. How will this remarkable adventure of ours end? Here I am again, in the position once more to receive messages from an amazing owl.

◈ ◈ ◈ EPILOGUE

IT'S OBVIOUS THAT HUMANS ARE UNLIKE ALL ANIMALS. IT'S
ALSO OBVIOUS THAT WE'RE A SPECIES OF BIG MAMMAL,
DOWN TO THE MINUTEST DETAILS OF OUR ANATOMY AND
OUR MOLECULES. THAT CONTRADICTION IS THE MOST FASCI-
NATING FEATURE OF THE HUMAN SPECIES.

—*Jared Diamond, evolutionary biologist*

STRIPEY'S TWO EGGS nestled warmly beneath her downy feathers as I climbed down the ladder at the Dalke farm and headed for my car. Leaving the driveway, I felt a wave of melancholy sweep over me as I reviewed the incredible adventure this owl and I had lived. Could it have been eight years since I had rescued the owl chick from a city park? The story had been recorded in a book, and even though all the characters in our play were still performing, it was time for me to move on. Many things beckoned for my attention. The science division at Tabor was planning a new science building. My ecological research at Prairie Dunes Country Club had spawned a contract to write another book, *The Ecology of Golf*, which meant applying for a sabbatical leave and helping to find a person to take over my responsibilities at the college. Already I was filling my office with books and journals on landscape ecology, conservation biology, and golf course architecture, to focus on habitats on golf courses instead of owls on eggs. The world of owls, however, was not to release me just yet.

March in Kansas often brings deluges of rain to the prairie. When this happens, I like to survey the effects on Marion Reservoir, a bulge in the Cotttonwood River created by a dam designed both to supply water to and prevent flooding of the surrounding towns. My family and I decided to go on a picnic and observe the runoff effects from Hillsboro Cove, a busy camping area on a broad peninsula of old farmland jutting out into the man-made lake. The water level in the reservoir was still high from the tremendous floods of 1993, and the torrent of prairie runoff from the recent rains was gushing over the dam and down the Cottonwood—a prairie river that was now an on-again, off-again spout for the reservoir's regulated releases. As I dozed on a picnic table thinking about how the presettlement river must have looked, I noticed a dark-winged apparition fly out of the forked base of a nearby cottonwood tree. It was a great horned owl. I slowly walked over to the tree and peered into the space created by three branches spreading out to form its base. There, on a mat of leaves, were two round eggs, unmistakably those of a great horned owl. They looked just like Stripey's back on the hay bales in the Dalke barn.

This was such an ill-chosen place to raise a brood—right in a busy camping area and only five feet off the ground, in plain view of humans, cats, raccoons, crows, and a multitude of other nest destroyers. Unlike Stripey, this female owl had been unwise in her nest site selection. When the campers arrived next week, this nest had no chance of survival. Torn between letting the inevitable happen and trying to rescue the young owls, I decided to leave one egg and take the other to Stripey, who might adopt it. Birds are notorious for rearing unrelated young. In nature, females occasionally lay their eggs in the nests of others of their own kind or even other species. Cowbirds and cuckoos are well-known examples of birds that have surrendered parenting entirely to other individuals who, for some reason, care for the foreign young, even at the expense of their own offspring. Taking one egg, I went back to our van, summoned my family, and left Hillsboro Cove for the Dalke farm. As I drove away from the camping ground, the quiet, dark shadow flew back to the cottonwood tree.

Stripey was very approachable and readily accepted the egg I slipped under her. The warmth of her incubation patch contrasted sharply with the damp openness of the tree in the camping area. After I removed my hand, Stripey took her beak and positioned the new egg beside the other two, nestled down with a twisting motion of her body, and unassumingly resumed the incubation process. Now all I could do was wait.

One week later, on my way home from Tabor, I stopped in at the Dalke farm and hurriedly climbed the ladder to see what was going on. Two white, downy chicks were under Stripey. The third egg had not yet hatched, but I could tell there was life in it by holding it up to the Kansas sun and viewing an embryo moving within. Immediately my thoughts went to the other egg at Hillsboro Cove—what had been its fate? I quickly drove the eleven miles to the reservoir and walked up to the tree where the owl had laid her eggs. Campers had been there, as the trash barrels were full of garbage. As I approached the tree, on the ground lay a broken eggshell and a dead, little owl embryo, its beak gaping from a desiccated body. Just as I had suspected, the nest had been too vulnerable, the egg had been discovered, and perhaps a questioning but insensitive mind had satisfied its curiosity by throwing the egg to the ground. In the world of nature as well as our own, very few choices exceed the importance of selecting the correct place to rear your young.

The next evening, March 28, 1995, I noticed that three owlets were now beneath my hen owl in the Dalke barn. Because it had narrowly avoided the fate of its sibling, I decided to call the smallest of these Lucky. Lucky was about two-thirds the size of his new nest mates. I gave Stripey a rat and watched as she skillfully severed pieces from it for the young owls. Stripey began by feeding her own chicks, whose gaping beaks reached hers first. After they were satiated, Stripey fed Lucky. As I watched this young owl gulp down the meat given it by an adopted mother, my thoughts went to my own daughters. Adoption is a wonderful thing—somewhere in our being, we humans possess the ability to love and care for others not related to us. How about owls—would they do the same?

As so often happens when we look for human attributes in animals, we are sorely disappointed. During the next two weeks, Lucky did not keep up with the growth of his adopted siblings. They commandeered almost all of the food that Stripey's mate delivered to the nest. Even though the Dalkes and I supplied rats and occasionally tried to feed him, Lucky was unable to compete with his more aggressive nest mates and died. Even his body was eventually eaten by Stripey and her chicks. What a cold but efficient thing is nature.

While her chicks were small, Stripey was very approachable and nonaggressive, just as she had been with her first clutch. As before, I could easily weigh the chicks and, again, their rate of weight gain was prodigious—each grew from one hundred grams on April 1 to nearly four hundred grams on April 11. They soon began to resemble great horned owls, their eyes now becoming the characteristic yellow. As spring progressed, the warm Kansas sun switched on the power of the prairie ecosystems—and Stripey's belligerence. She became very aggressive, suddenly lunging at me with her beak and talons; the growing investment in her rapidly developing owlets no doubt precipitated this behavior. In a matter of days, I went from being a friendly visitor to a wary interloper keen to read her subtle moods. One day I could finger-peck her beak; the next she would rush at me with open talons. The only hint of impending danger might be a slight tip of her feathered horns or a sharper twitter to her voice. This is the way it is being a friend of owls.

Darrel Dalke, Dan's oldest son, reported that Stripey's mate attacked him in the evening as he attempted to get bales of hay to feed the farm animals. The family dog is now restricted from the barn area, lest his back become a target for talons. This treatment Darrel and his family endure because of their interest in these owls. Stripey could not have chosen a better farm to call home. I was happy to give the Dalkes an autographed copy of the book, which I'm sure is a very realistic read for the whole family.

It would not be long before Stripey's chicks would leave the nest, and I wanted to put a new, improved year-long transmitter ordered from Dan Stoneburner on one of the chicks to track its movements. Just when do owl chicks leave their parents and where do they go? This question became part of a biology research project for Geoff Donaldson and John Babb, two of my biology majors at Tabor, who were going to observe Stripey and the radio-tagged chick over the next year. The short-lived transmitters I had put on Stripey's first offspring had not provided enough information. Perhaps this new transmitter would give better data. First, however, we had to put it on one of these well-guarded chicks. Stripey and her mate would never allow this in their presence—we had to do it when they were off the nest.

The chicks happened to be alone on the nest on the afternoon of May 4, when my wife, Jan, and I stopped by the barn. Warily I climbed the ladder—often looking back over my shoulder for any sign of Stripey or her mate. Reaching the nest, I quickly grabbed the legs of the nearest chick and rapidly descended with a hissing, flopping owlet acting like my parachute. As I scanned every porthole of the barn searching for an attacking owl, Jan weaved the elastic straps of the transmitter under the spread-eagled wings of the angry bird. In a minute, Jan attached the transmitter, and I scrambled back up the ladder, released the chick to its nest, and like a fireman flew back down. There was still no sign of Stripey. The beeping of the transmitter from the receiver matched the rapid beating of my heart and verified the success of our endeavor. A chick was tagged (we called it Lefty) that could be followed over the next year.

Geoff, John, and I really appreciated the transmitter on Lefty. The signal allowed us to easily find him, Stripey, and the other young owl who was invariably nearby. Even though Stripey was aggressive toward us, we still fed her with midair tosses of rodents and meat scraps. Tossed to Stripey from a safe distance, this supplemental menu no doubt helped meet the tremendous food demands of her offspring. During these food tosses, the offishness of her chicks made it difficult for Stripey to feed them. On one occasion, I tossed a mouse in the air, Stripey grabbed it and flew to Lefty who was nearby sitting on an old hay bale. Lefty was so busy hissing and threatening me that he would not take the food from Stripey, who persisted in pushing the food to Lefty's beak. Exasperated, the young owl flew to the top of a thin fence pole about fifty yards away. Stripey, driven by her instinct to feed her young, followed Lefty to the pole, landed on his back, and tried to feed the owlet while balancing on top of him— while Lefty continued to fan, hiss, and glare at me. This comic balancing act set up by familiarity and fear was almost too much for me. Chuckling and shaking my head, I sat on the ground watching this circus in the wild for about fifteen more seconds. As both owls flew off, I yearned for my camera. If I had carried it, one of the most extraordinary owl photos ever to grace an ornithological manuscript would have appeared in this book.

Stripey first moved her two young owls to the brush pile, then east about a quarter mile to Unruh's hedge, just as she did in 1993 with her first brood. Geoff and John tracked their movements until Tabor closed in the spring. As the hot days of the Kansas summer approached, I threw myself entirely into the task of learning more about landscape ecology and golf courses. After attending meetings in Wisconsin and Texas, I became totally engrossed in habitat connectivity, greenways, corridors, patches, and landscape matrices. Occasional book signings, speaking engagements, and the food-begging cries of young owls on TESA briefly brought Stripey to mind; but for the most part, she and I now had different lives.

Old acquaintances, however, have a way of reemerging. On the evening of July 21, Donna Dalke called and said that Stripey was in one of her chicken coops and would not come out. Could I come down and see what I could do? Dan and Donna met me at the driveway and we walked to a small shed housing about ten chickens. As

I looked into the darkness of the moonlit shed, all the chickens were hunkered down in their individual dens, each as motionless as a white-feathered rock. Stripey was sitting wide-eyed on the floor. "Stripey—what are you doing?" Hearing my voice, she let out a long "cheeep," flew right at me, veered to the right, flew out the door, and vanished into the darkness. Was Stripey using the Dalke chickens as a prey source? It was hard to say. Dan had noticed some beheaded chickens on the farm but never really saw owls doing the attacking. I felt badly about my owl (or owls) possibly killing chickens, but Dan and Donna assured me that having a famous owl around was worth the sacrifice. Such is the welcome this owl enjoys. Stripey does reciprocate, however. Since her arrival, Dan reports no problem with pack rats gnawing on wires on his tractors.

The summer passed and another school year began. Geoff and John immediately located Lefty's signal near the Unruh pond. In late October, they followed Lefty to a large wooded tract about two miles to the northeast. After this, they lost him. The transmitter had failed, or Lefty had moved out of range. I suspect that the latter is true, since the Stoneburner transmitter was not due to quit until the next spring. Geoff and John believe that the other chick left in the same direction but then headed more due east. Evidently, in Kansas, young owls, after some trial departures, disperse in mid to late autumn and continue moving until they find an unoccupied area. This agrees with my observations on Stripey and her first brood. However, I suspect that the dispersal times vary considerably with individual owls and ecological conditions.

Geoff Donaldson continued his interest in owls and kept visiting the Dalke and Unruh farms, occasionally getting a look at Stripey and her mate. One of the joys of being a professor is to see your students pursue one of your projects, and this one was indeed continuing. On February 26, 1996, Geoff reported to me that Stripey had again mated and was sitting on two eggs—and where else but in the Dalke barn, in the same place, on the same bales. The strong nest and home range attachment of an owl was one of the most fascinating observations in this study. The best was yet to come, however.

Stripey's fame was spreading in our community. When the first copies of this book came out in early spring, even the media became involved. Larry Hatteberg, a well-known and talented author and a reporter for KAKE-TV in Wichita (the same ABC affiliate that did the first TV story on Stripey back in 1988), called to see if he could do a

different kind of story on Stripey and me—one that was more philo-
sophical and of human interest—for his Hatteberg's People series.
This popular series, recorded in a book by Hatteberg, features unusual and interesting people in Kansas. My owl activities, not surprisingly, qualified me for this distinction. I was flattered, but would
Stripey cooperate? The filming date was set for April 16, one day
after my birthday and income tax day. Stripey's eggs had hatched on
April 1—would she still be in her approachable stage?

As has happened throughout this owl adventure of mine, things
went uncanningly well. Even with bright lights beaming down on
her and the chicks, Stripey cooperated fully. She stayed on the nest,
did not fly away, and was easy to handle. I was even able to get her
to perch on my arm in front of the camera as Larry interviewed me.
We were all, including myself, amazed at this wild owl. Stripey had
been on her own for over six years and here she was, sitting on my
arm in front of a TV camera. The very well done video is one of my
prize momentos. After the video aired, more than a few people came
to the Dalke farm to catch a glimpse of this now more famous owl.

For the continuation of this saga, I am indebted to Donna Dalke.
She took over for me as the human component of the story and began
to feed Stripey meat scraps and rodents using the midair catch
method. In fact, the entire Dalke family, especially their oldest son,
Darrel, began feeding Stripey. It certainly was the best of times for
my star owl. As it happened, she would need the extra resources.

Marvin Petersen, the local official for the Kansas Department of
Wildlife and Parks, walked up to my office with a wire cage on May
6, 1996. Inside the cage was a young juvenile great horned owl that
had walked into a clothing store in the nearby town of Marion. What
it was doing there is hard to say—probably in its dispersing activities
it had made a wrong turn into a world of suits and dresses instead of
hedge trees and grass.

Great horned owls have truly integrated with the human world.
They are one species that appears to be thriving on the increasingly
populated landscape of Kansas. At a book signing at the University of
Kansas, I was told of an owl that had raised its young on a flower
shelf on the second-floor balcony of a nursing home. The growing
owlets proved to be great entertainment for a watchful resident
named Mary, who shared the story with a friend who relayed the
story to me. I later met three Lawrence, Kansas high school students
who videotaped this owl and her chicks for a science project. A

reader in Oklahoma City, who happens to live next door to a golf course, sent me photos of a great horned owl family with four chicks, nesting in a basket on a backdoor ledge. These owls evidently had a first-rate environment for rearing a maximum number of offspring. I wish scarlet tanagers, prairie chickens, loggerhead shrikes, and a whole host of other threatened birds were this adaptable. Alas, they are not and depend on our common sense to save what natural habitats are left. I hope my initiative to include more wildlife habitats on golf courses will help in this struggle.

Nevertheless, this young owl in the clothing shop was out of fashion and was reported to the authorities. Officer Petersen, knowing of my work with Stripey, wondered if I could use this wayward bird in my project. I put down my book on golf course architecture, carefully maneuvered the owl into a large, white plastic bucket, and took it into my office. For ten minutes I sat staring at the young owl who glared back at me, its eyes level with the rim of the bucket. Although I did not know its gender, I decided to call the owl Calvin,

Family of owls from Oklahoma City. Courtesy of Teresa Andrus.

after the prominent maker of high-fashion jeans. But what would I do with Calvin?

Accepting an egg is one thing, but would Stripey adopt an owl chick of this size? The supply of food should not be a problem. It was worth a try. I put the lid back on Calvin's bucket, closed the computer file on my golf book outline, and took Calvin out to the Dalke barn. Stripey was gone. Her two chicks, although almost ready to disperse, were dutifully sitting on the nest. I gently dumped Calvin out on the barn floor. Immediately the talons thrust skyward and Calvin began hissing and threatening me. Mighty impressive for an owl found beneath a rack of dresses! I took off my ball hat and let him sink his talons into it—as many an owl had done before to this now air-conditioned headpiece. I then grabbed Calvin's legs and placed him in the nest with Stripey's chicks. They, being an especially gentile pair, merely moved to the side and accommodated the indignant interloper. These chicks were completely different in behavior from Stripey's last brood—another testament to individual differences, even between siblings.

After I climbed down the ladder, Calvin calmed down and sat quietly on the nest. Calvin was bigger than Stripey's chicks, a fact that became important later on. Before leaving the Dalke farm, I informed Donna of my latest adoption project. She smiled, said something about a new adventure, and began walking to the barn to get a look at Calvin. As I drove off, I wondered what Stripey would do to Calvin—accept him or eat him? I need not have worried.

The next day, Calvin sat contentedly between Stripey's chicks, unharmed and well fed. Calvin was apparently now part of the family. My sabbatical replacement, Dr. Ken Otter, a recent graduate of Queen's University in Canada, had arrived to look over the college and town. He was, as luck would have it, an expert in mating strategies in birds, specializing in black-capped chickadees. DNA fingerprinting studies seem to confirm that unwitting "adoption" takes place in the world of birds, although it does not appear to be a widespread phenomenon. However, in nature, most of this occurs through the exchange of eggs, not nestlings. Even still, many scientific experiments on parental investment use transferring of nestlings between nests, and these juveniles are commonly adopted by the host parents. Based on Ken's observations, there was a strong possibility that Stripey would add not two, but three new owls to the Kansas countryside.

Calvin with Stripey's chicks. (Calvin is on the left.)

As often happens in the world of science, slight differences in some factor bring about totally unexpected results. Calvin, being slightly larger, older, and more aggressive than Stripey's chicks, dispersed before they did. The next week I found Stripey and Calvin about five hundred yards away from the barn by the brush pile. Stripey's chicks were still in the barn and were starving—their begging calls completely ignored. For some reason, Stripey had gone off with Calvin and seemed to forget totally her own chicks! Evidently, Calvin's dispersal had switched Stripey's parental care program to the next level and her own chicks were excluded from the database. Could owl behavior really be this mechanical? How could Stripey desert her own offspring so glibly? Wonderfully complex in so much of her behavior, here she was simple, stimulus-bound, and disappointing. To say I was perplexed by this enigma understates my confusion.

I went home to get some food for the starving owls and met Katy standing by the front door. Upon learning what had happened, she insisted on coming with me back to the Dalke farm. Because they themselves are adopted, both Katy and Kerry were very interested in this new owl project. Both girls are now freshmen in high school. With the help of a new amino-acid-based neuroepileptic drug and the love of family, friends, and a supportive community, Katy continues to confront the considerable challenges that face teenagers today. Both she and Kerry have come a long way and we are very proud of them. When we arrived at the barn, Katy helped me meet the challenge of Stripey's orphaned chicks, who ate ravenously. Now what should we do?

"Dad, maybe Stripey needs to be reminded that she still has a family. Could we take one of the chicks out to her? Even owls forget sometimes." Good idea—I safely secured one of the owl chicks by its legs (I didn't have to use the old hat trick), hugged the rather complacent owlet to my chest, and we walked to the brush pile through an adjoining alfalfa field. Dickcissels, meadowlarks, and ladybird beetles were everywhere. For such a small area, the diversity of organisms on the Dalke farm is amazing. This display of life might be due to the farm's location on the landscape where a number of different habitat types come together. In the parlance of landscape ecology, maybe the Dalke farm is at a convergence point of intersecting landscape elements. Whatever the reason, this home site of Stripey's is a diversity "hot spot." These thoughts reminded me that I should be back in my office exploring how to facilitate these "hot spots" on golf courses. That would have to wait. My job now was to deliver an owl chick to its wandering mother.

I placed Stripey's chick on the old trailer bed near the brush pile. Stripey was nearby on the ground in the alfalfa field—no doubt feeding Calvin. Katy and I circled around behind Stripey and herded her to the trailer bed, where she landed beside her chick. Looking confused, Stripey nuzzled the chick with her beak, occasionally scanning the alfalfa field. Would this reunion jog her parental memory? Would she remember the chick still in the barn?

The next night I checked on the chick in the barn. It had not been fed. Stripey remained near the brush pile tending to Calvin and the chick we had brought to her. At least she was now feeding this chick! Should I take the other chick out to her? I decided to wait until the next night just to see if she would remember this genetic investment of hers still in the barn. It did not happen. Stripey did not even respond to the alarm calls given by the chick, who in its frenzy h~ ˙ wedged itself between the cab and bed of one of the farm ˊ Darrel Dalke rescued the chick upon hearing its cries.

I decided that Stripey really was stimulus-boun˸ˊ her parental behavior. Because of some ancie˸

in her kind by the realities of natural selection and population lim-
its, she responded only to the needs of the largest, strongest owl
chicks. The weaker ones were not a priority. In the ancestral history
of great horned owls, this strategy has worked for millennia.
Schemes that we might consider more fair, failed. In my humanness,
I expected something different—but should I? She was only following the dictates of what has shaped her kind over the ages. Kindness,
parental responsibility, a sense of fairness—do these really exist in
the world of an owl? I think not, and perhaps we are naive when we
place these human expectations on wild animals. Quite simply, the
worlds we live in are different. The motivations of an owl are not
those of a human.

I took the barn chick (whom I now reluctantly humanized with
the name Joe) out to the brush pile. Calvin and the other chick (let's
call it Hoot) were sitting on the nearby trailer. Calvin rapidly flew
away as I walked up with Joe. Hoot, not being as wild in disposition
as Calvin, flew to the ground and slowly slinked into the brush pile.
I put Joe on the trailer bed and fed him three mice. As I watched him
jump down and scurry under the brush pile next to Hoot, I wondered
what awaited Joe in the owl world.

Over the next three weeks, Donna or I invariably found Joe around
the brush pile or in the alfalfa field cheeping and very hungry. Evidently Stripey and her mate had all that they could handle with
Calvin and Hoot. There is a reason why great horned owls normally
lay only two eggs in the nest: this clutch size optimizes their survival. My attempts to stretch this number to three failed on two
occasions. As far as I could tell, Joe was on his own and completely
dependent on our handouts to keep him going. Fortunately for Joe,
Donna took on the job of feeding him (whom she called the Little
Guy) and kept him in fairly good health. Donna also began to feed
Stripey with midair catches. We never observed Stripey feeding
Joe, although this is a possibility since Joe hung around with the
other owls.

By midsummer, Donna was up to her neck in owls. Around dusk
all four of the owls frequently flew to the house to check on the
availability of food handouts. That must have been quite a sight!
After the grand arrival, Joe would usually come to Donna to take
food from her hand. Next, Stripey might beg for a midair toss. Sometimes the other owls would take Joe's food from him, revealing the
pecking order in the family. This company of owls would visit the

Donna Dalke feeds Stripey with a midair toss.

Dalke family not only during times of convenience; sometimes the group would convene in the evening, often very late. Dan has mentioned that his wife has jumped from her bed and turned into a "ghost in the night" to go out to feed the hungry visitors.

In late autumn, my curiosity about Stripey could not be satisfied by secondhand reports. I put away my landscape ecology research and Abby (my dog) and I went to the Unruh farm to search for Stripey. As I walked by a tree near the Unruh pond, an owl gave a familiar cheep and flew to the north. This was Stripey—each owl has a distinctive cheep that Donna and I soon learned to distinguish. Soon another owl rose from a nearby tree and followed Stripey in her flight to the north. Was this second owl Joe, or Stripey's mate? I could not get close enough to make a final determination. After all this time, though, that cheep was reassuring. Stripey was still alive and recognized me. My curiosity satisfied, I reached down and patted Abby on the head and left for the car parked on the road about a quarter mile away. Abby obediently followed right behind and, requiring no more than a mere nod from my head, jumped into the car Born of good stock (her grandfather was a grand champion Aust shepherd), Abby was so intelligent, calm, and easily con was a special dog, even to being an unlikely comp who met his sudden death on a utility pole. I in this epilogue that Abby also has died, hit by a truck on the thir-teen-mile road on November 2, 1996. I buried her beside Buffy, my first dog in this owl adventure, who also died on that same road. How Stripey has survived this highway is beyond me. Many an owl and other wild animal has met its death on this asphalt mortality strip. Roads, trucks, and automobiles—how we humans depend on them. But we also pay a price.

As I put the finishing touches on this epilogue, the lives of hu-mans and owls still incredibly intertwine on the Dalke and Unruh farms, the Kansas prairie, county of Marion. One of my most inter-esting discoveries was the permanence of Stripey's site fidelity. If she is at all representative of her species, once an owl moves into your life, you are indeed in for a long term relationship. Calvin and Hoot, as young owls must do, have left the area in search of their own territories and lives. I wish them well, and I hope Calvin stays away from towns. Apparently feeling the effects of his early aban-donment, Joe still hangs around with Stripey and her mate at the Unruh pond. John and Ilene Unruh have recently seen them both near their house. Stripey and her mate are engaging in hooting duets. Will Stripey rear another brood this year? Will Joe ever become inde-pendent and set out on his own? Like his mother, maybe his learning curve rises a little slower than his more normally treated comrades. Ironically, Stripey may now have to deal with her own "deficit bird"—mainly because of my intervention. But then, this story would not exist without my interventions. Perhaps this is the most human aspect of all.

It is now January 1997 and almost nine years have passed since our story began. I expect, God willing, that Stripey and I will have many more years of interacting in the future. I began this adventure seek-ing to understand the effects of human imprinting on an owl. De-spite being reared by humans, Stripey has still retained her true iden-tity, reproducing three times. Her behavior has been both complex and simple, wondrous and perplexing. In detailing her life, I also more completely defined my own. While I did not find the imprint of a man in an owl, I did discover something greater in me.

I began this epilogue with a quotation from Jared Diamond's fasci-nating book *The Third Chimpanzee*. It marks what is perhaps the most salient point of this story of a man and an owl. Why are we, in the words of Rene Dubos, "so human an animal"? Touched by the creative power of that eternal, invisible hand that stretches through the vast eons of time, the paths of humans and owls diverged and produced creatures with immensely different behaviors and proclivities. In my view, the essence of our humanity rings forth beautifully in the well-known verse in I Corinthians 13:13 NIV:

> And now these three remain: faith, hope, and love. But the greatest of these is love.

My experience convinces me that it is here that humans enjoy a gift that we have not found in other animals. Today, in the face of our social, economic, and environmental challenges, it is a poignant truth that both our fate and that of other creatures depend on how we humans exercise our gifts of wisdom and love. Will we flounder in our unreasoning selfishness and greed, or become responsible stewards of the wonders of creation? If this book about the remarkable world of one owl helps tip the balance in favor of stewardship, then I am most pleased and thankful. Shalom.

A thirty-minute videotape, produced by the author, chronicling the events in Stripey's life is available. Contact Max Terman, Department of Biology, Tabor College, Hillsboro, Kansas 67063 (by E-mail: maxt@tcnet.tabor.edu).

❖ ❖ ❖ APPENDIX: CHRONOLOGY

FOLLOWING are the significant dates and events relevant to this study. This material is provided for the benefit of those who might want to look for patterns in the events of Stripey's life. Refer to the map for a geographical perspective.

Date	Event	Location
3/20/88	Owl collected as a 3–4-week-old chick	Hillsboro City Park
3/21/88	Fed meat scraps, imprinted on humans	Tabor College
6/4/88	First trial flight to tree	TESA
6/18/88	Owl released with transmitter on leg	TESA
6/21/88	Mockingbird mobs severely	TESA
6/26/88	Leg transmitter removed	TESA
7/20/88	Ate insect, June bug	TESA
7/24/88	First dispersal to nearby woods	South Woods
8/12/88	2-day absence	South Woods
8/16/88	Fake attack on dog	TESA
8/19/88	Took and cached mouse; first signs of a hoot	TESA
8/21/88	First 3-day absence from rearing site (TESA)	South Woods
8/26/88	"Horns" more noticeable	South Woods
8/28/88	3-day absence	South Woods
9/1/88	Caching food	TESA
9/14/88	3-day absence	South Woods
9/20/88	Response to conspecific calls—intense stare	TESA
9/21/88	Next 3-day absence from rearing site	West Hedge
9/25/88	Aggressive attack on domestic dog	TESA
9/26/88	Resident owl vocalizing	TESA
9/27/88	4-day absence	West Hedge
10/1/88	Cached duck, perched on my foot	TESA
10/2/88	Flew at Kerry, very playful	TESA
10/3/88	Rich Wall groomed owl; owl roosts on shutter cover	TESA
10/8/88	Peered in window, chased dog	TESA
10/9/88	First chuckling vocalizations	TESA
10/11/88	Cached pheasant	TESA
10/13/88	First dispersal movement—10 days	Hiebert's Pasture
10/16/88	Dead owl found near Bartel farm	Hiebert's Pasture

Date	Event	Location
10/22/88	Stripey returns!!	TESA
10/23/88	KAKE-TV visits, Stripey released	TESA
10/24/88	Resident owl chases Stripey away at night	TESA
10/25/88	3-day absence	Hiebert's Pasture
10/28/88	Manipulative play, leg transmitter removed	TESA
10/29/88	5-day absence	Hiebert's Pasture
11/4/88	7-day absence	Hiebert's Pasture
11/14/88	3-day absence	Hiebert's Pasture
11/17/88	1-day absence	West Hedge
11/19/88	2-day absence, first snow	West Hedge
11/22/88	1-day absence	West Hedge
11/24/88	3-day absence	Hiebert's Pasture
12/1/88	First full hoot, roosts on shutter covers	TESA
12/4/88	7-day absence	Hiebert's Pasture
12/12/88	Mock attacks on domestic cats	TESA
12/14/88	2-day absence	Hiebert's Pasture
12/16/88	Less focus on house, at pond, buzzed me	TESA
12/20/88	Protected frozen possum, aggressive	TESA
12/21/88	Michigan visit; relied on feeding station	TESA
12/31/88	Fitted with Stoneburner transmitter 151.247	TESA
1/1/89	Elastic harness put on Stripey	TESA
1/3/89	Owl on ground, friendly	West Hedge
1/4/89	Roosting	Hiebert's Pasture
1/5/89	Owl in new location	Peter's Hedge
1/7/89	Antenna bitten off transmitter	TESA
1/8/89	Resident pair of owls hooting	South Woods
1/10/89	Owl not approachable	Hiebert's Pasture
1/12/89	Stripey almost electrocuted	TESA
1/13/89	Battery transmitter put on Stripey	TESA
1/15/890	Released, attacked, killed sparrows	TESA
1/16/89	Roosting near human habitation to north	Bartel farm
1/18/89	Hiding behavior in milo stubble	Hiebert's Pasture
1/20/89	Farthest dispersal movement	Franzen Creek
1/26/89	Seen with another owl in Peter's Hedge	Peter's Hedge
1/30/89	Flew away to Bartel farm	TESA
2/1/89	On TESA in barn, very cold	TESA

Date	Event	Location
2/2/89	Stayed 7 days, out of wind	South Woods
2/8/89	Other owls hooting in woods	Hiebert's Pasture
2/9/89	Students follow Stripey to TESA	Hiebert's Pasture
2/10/89	Second prolonged absence	Hiebert's Pasture
2/24/89	Stripey returns, tame; new transmitter 151.346	TESA
2/26/89	Stripey offish again, nonapproachable in South Woods	South Woods
3/23/89	Dispersal to new area	Nickel farm
4/2/89	Unusual clucking (barn)	TESA
4/9/89	Wild, fleeing behavior in creek area	Franzen Creek
4/11/89	Chased by resident owl from rearing area	TESA
5/13/89	Owl located in concrete rubble— roosting	East Hedge
5/14/89	Very amicable behavior to "human parent"	TESA
6/15/89	Very attracted to front area of house	TESA
6/19/89	Prolonged stay at TESA, 24 days	TESA
6/30/89	2d Michigan visit; relied on feeding station	TESA
7/25/89	Stripey molting; turkey eggs discovered	East Hedge
8/4/89	Obvious molting of feathers	South Woods
8/5/89	Returns to Hiebert's Pasture	Hiebert's Pasture
8/8/89	Returns to TESA	TESA
8/10/89	Resident owl hooting, excludes Stripey	Hiebert's Pasture
8/11/89	Stripey to Nickel farm	Nickel farm
8/15/89	Returns to TESA, hungry	TESA
8/17/89	Screech owls calling	TESA
8/21/89	Caught live deer mouse released in weeds	TESA
8/22/89	Stripey to Bartel farm	Bartel farm
8/23/89	Returns to Hiebert's Pasture	Hiebert's Pasture
8/26/89	Stripey back to TESA, artificial nest attracts	TESA
8/28/89	Leaves pellet in artificial nest	TESA, South Woods
8/30/89	Another owl hit on road, Stripey ignores	South Woods
9/2/89	Responds to recordings of resident owls	TESA, South Woods
9/3/89	Returns to Peter's Hedge	Peter's Hedge
9/5/89	Flies farthest west, to Craft farm	Craft Farm

Date	Event	Location
9/6/89	Returns to Peter's Hedge	Peter's Hedge
9/7/89	Stripey found near gopher burrow	Peter's Hedge
9/11/89	Transmitter failing	Peter's Hedge
9/12/89	I called Bernd Heinrich	Peter's Hedge
9/14/89	Returns to TESA, refitted with transmitter	TESA
9/15/89	Stripey often in front of house	TESA
9/16/89	At Peter's Hedge; monarchs migrating	Peter's Hedge
9/22/89	Stripey returns to TESA	TESA
10/1/89	Forced to Hiebert's Pasture; night visits to TESA	Hiebert's Pasture
10/2/89	Forced to north waterway by resident owl hooting	TESA
10/3/89	On Bartel farm	Bartel farm
10/4/89	Back to TESA, to South Woods	South Woods
10/5/89	Adept at catching cotton rat released in weeds	TESA
10/7/89	Manipulated material on artificial nest	TESA
10/8/89	Resident owls dueting; Stripey gone	Peter's Hedge
10/13/89	Stripey near barn at Hiebert's Pasture	Hiebert's Pasture
10/16/89	Allen Hiebert feeds Stripey	Hiebert's Pasture
10/18/89	Stripey in barn at TESA	TESA
10/20/89	Hooted when primed by my calls	TESA
10/22/89	Owl not approachable	Peter's Hedge
10/23/89	Stripey resident in Peter's Hedge for 14 days	Peter's Hedge
10/24/89	Trip to Williamsburg; relied on feeding station	Hiebert's Pasture
11/1/89	In Hiebert's Pasture	Hiebert's Pasture
11/9/89	Resident owls dueting	TESA
11/11/89	Stripey located in middle of plowed field	Peter's Hedge
11/13/89	Very tense, tranced, observant for resident owls	TESA
11/14/89	Back to Hiebert's Pasture	Hiebert's Pasture
11/15/89	Resident owl attacks Stripey in daytime	TESA
11/16/89	Stripey deep in South Woods	South Woods
11/17/89	Back to Hiebert's Pasture	Hiebert's Pasture
11/19/89	Night visits to TESA	Hiebert Pasture
11/26/89	Wild owl chased out of West Hedge	Hiebert's Pasture

Date	Event	Location
11/28/89	Stripey on shutters	TESA
11/29/89	Leaves for 11 days	Hiebert's Pasture
12/7/89	Stripey on Nickel farm far to west	Nickel farm
12/8/89	Stripey very offish	Hiebert's Pasture
12/10/89	Flies to neighbor's house for first time	TESA
12/11/89	Stripey sitting on frozen squirrel carcass; offish	TESA
12/12/89	Resident owls patrolling; Stripey endures	TESA
12/14/89	Stripey back to Hiebert's Pasture; record cold wave	Hiebert's Pasture
12/18/89	Buffy killed; Stripey in West Hedge	West Hedge
12/20/89	Michigan visit	TESA
1/1/90	Feeding-station meat eaten	South Woods, TESA
1/4/90	Stripey leaves TESA for 75 days	Hiebert's Pasture
1/7/90	Resident owls on TESA mating, wharrr call	Hiebert's Pasture
1/10/90	Stripey farthest away	Craft Farm
1/12/90	Crows mob in Peter's Hedge	Peter's Hedge
1/13/90	Stripey flies off with key case, avoids hunters	Peter's Hedge
1/15/90	Midair catches	Peter's Hedge
1/21/90	Stripey near in West Hedge, flew to H.P.	West Hedge
1/23/90	At Nickel farm; offish	Nickel's Hedge
1/27/90	Franzen Creek to Hiebert's Woods	Hiebert's Woods
1/30/90	Movement centered on creek in Hiebert's Woods	Hiebert's Woods
2/4/90	Transmitter dead, signal lost	?
2/27/90	Owl (Stripey?) by two huge nests in cedar trees	Hiebert's Woods
3/2/90	Two owls flew out of Hiebert's Woods to Peter's Hedge	?
3/16/90	New transmitter 151.345; odd behavior	TESA
3/17/90	Stripey now in South Woods	South Woods
3/19/90	To Hiebert's Pasture; night visit to TESA	Hiebert's Pasture
3/30/90	Back at TESA on barn with rabbit road kill	TESA
4/2/90	Back to Hiebert's Pasture for 7 days	Hiebert's Pasture
4/7/90	Stripey in West Hedge would not be approached	West Hedge

Date	Event	Location
4/15/90	Hiebert's Pasture and Nickel farm next 33 days	Hiebert's Pasture
5/24/90	At TESA, midair catches, attacked stuffed owl	TESA
5/26/90	Stripey deep in South Woods, hiding in rubble	South Woods
5/27/90	In barn; did courtship dance, flew to artificial nest	TESA
5/30/90	Back to Hiebert's Pasture	Hiebert's Pasture
6/2/90	At AuSable; Stripey on own, around TESA	TESA
6/15/90	Stripey sighted by Jan on TESA	TESA
7/25/90	Stripey in South Woods; attacked cat on barn roof	TESA
7/29/90	No response to stuffed owl near barn	TESA
7/30/90	Stripey ate fish—bullhead	TESA
8/2/90	Stripey alert to TESA owls' calls	TESA
8/6/90	Returns to Hiebert's Pasture	Hiebert's Pasture
8/13/90	At Bartel farm	Bartel farm
8/29/90	Signal lost	?
9/20/90	Dead owl found near Suderman's	?
10/8/90	Stripey returns; new transmitter 151.242	TESA
10/22/90	Easily handled, groomed	TESA
10/23/90	Disappears, cannot locate	?
10/26/90	New location	Suderman's Hedge
11/2/90	New location—north of Davis residence	Davis home
11/3/90	New location	Hamm farm
11/4/90	Returns to TESA	TESA
11/10/90	New location—woods north of Bartel farm	Bartel farm
11/12/90	Resident owl gave squawk call	TESA
11/17/90	New location—farm building area	Dalke farm
11/22/90	New location—hedge east of Hamm farm	Hamm farm
11/30/90	"Hit and run" visit to TESA	TESA
12/1/90	Very hungry, took hot dog	West Hedge
12/2/90	On patio cover at house	TESA
12/3/90	Mock attack of dog	TESA
12/4/90	Resident owl patrolling	TESA

Date	Event	Location
12/5/90	Cannibalism of owl carcass	TESA
12/10/90	On ground in front of house, very hungry	TESA
12/18/90	Cached possum under cedar on TESA	TESA
1/2/91	Near Hamm farm	Hamm farm
1/16/91	Resident owl patrolling TESA	TESA
1/23/91	New location	Unruh farm
2/6/91	Stripey at Unruh barn hooting	Unruh farm
2/9/91	Stripey puts mouse in nest near barn	Unruh farm
2/10/91	Another owl sighted with Stripey; behavior in barn	Unruh farm
2/15/91	Stripey hoots, "leads me back to barn"	Unruh farm
2/17/91	Strong site fidelity to U.F. hedge, woodlot area	Unruh farm
2/20/91	No signal from Unruh farm	?
2/27/91	With mate, flew off, perched together	Unruh farm
3/31/91	Another owl on telephone pole near 13-Mile Road	Unruh farm
4/13/91	Hooter aquired; Stripey at Unruh farm	Unruh farm
7/2/91	Stripey recaptured, new transmitter	TESA
7/4/91	Stripey homed to Unruh farm	Unruh farm
8/26/91	No signal from Stripey	?
9/13/91	Hooter in South Woods	South Woods
9/26/91	Hooter electrocuted	TESA
9/27/91	Stripey recaptured, fitted with transmitter	Unruh farm/TESA
9/28/91	Stripey homes back to Unruh farm	Unruh farm
11/19/91	Stripey and mate sighted	Unruh farm
11/23/91	Screechy found in nest box	Unruh farm
12/17/91	Stripey with two other owls	Unruh farm
1/24/92	Barred owl found on road	Unruh farm
1/31/92	Barred owl carcass eaten	Unruh farm
2/1/92	Screechy found dead	Unruh farm
2/10/92	Stripey and mate near Dalke barn	Unruh farm
2/18/92	Bluebirds at TESA	Unruh farm
2/21/92	Stripey south of Unruh farm near woods	Unruh farm
2/26/92	Transmitter signal lost	Unruh farm
3/23/92	Stripey and mate sighted	Unruh farm
3/31/92	Stripey and mate sighted	Unruh farm
4/21/92	Stripey; no mate sighted	Unruh farm
5/5/92	No sign of Stripey at Unruh farm	?

Date	Event	Location
8/1/92	Three owls with Stripey	Unruh farm
10/23/92	Stripey with mate, cheeped then hooted	Unruh farm
3/7/93	Stripey seen in Dalke barn on nest	Dalke barn
3/10/93	Battery replaced in transmitter	Dalke barn
3/23/93	Stripey's first egg hatches	Dalke barn
3/24/93	Stripey's second egg hatches	Dalke barn
4/19/93	Stripey off nest, chicks by themselves	Dalke barn
5/1/93	Transmitters put on chicks	Dalke barn
5/13/93	Chicks out of nest	Dalke barn
5/17/93	Stripey attacks me as I approach chick	Dalke barn
5/18/93	Stripey and chicks on elevator	Dalke barn
5/28/93	Stripey and chicks in brush pile	Dalke barn
6/2/93	Stripey and mate in hedge, chicks in brush pile	Unruh farm
6/21/93	Young of resident owls begging on TESA	TESA
6/22/93	Stripey's owlet dispersed to Hamm farm	Hamm farm
7/28/93	Stripey's owlet back to Unruh farm	Unruh farm
8/5/93	Stripey's owlets begging for food on Dalke barn	Dalke barn
8/11/93	.183 flushed from hedge	Unruh farm
12/29/93	Stripey with mate at Unruh farm	Unruh farm
3/12/94	Stripey alone on Unruh farm	Unruh farm
12/17/94	Stripey with mate; midair catch	Unruh farm
3/6/95	Stripey on nest, two eggs; mate attacked me	Dalke barn
3/7/95	Eggs of second brood hatch	Dalke barn
4/7/95	Lucky dies	Dalke barn
5/4/95	Transmitter placed on Lefty	Dalke barn
5/18/95	Owlets leave barn	Dalke barn
7/21/95	Stripey in chicken coop	Dalke barn
9/14/95	Lefty near Unruh pond	Unruh farm
10/20/95	Lefty leaves	Two miles north
2/26/96	Stripey on eggs	Dalke barn
4/1/96	Eggs of third brood hatch	Dalke barn
4/16/96	KAKE-TV filming	Dalke barn
5/6/96	Calvin placed in nest	Dalke barn
5/14/96	Calvin leaves barn	Dalke barn
8/7/96	Calvin leaves	?
9/14/96	Hoot leaves	?
12/11/96	Joe still around	Dalke farm

THE FOLLOWING books provide more information on owls, Kansas, the prairie, and what it means to be a scientist and naturalist.

Angell, Tony. 1974. *Owls*. Seattle: University of Washington Press.

Austing, G. Ronald, and John B. Holt Jr. 1966. *The World of the Great Horned Owl*. Philadelphia and New York: Lippincott.

Burton, John A. 1973. *Owls of the World: Their Evolution, Structure and Ecology*. New York: E. P. Dutton.

Craighead, John J., and Frank C. Craighead, Jr. 1969. *Hawks, Owls, and Wildlife*. New York: Dover.

Eisely, Loren. 1957. *The Immense Journey*. New York: Random House.

Everett, Michael. 1977. *A Natural History of Owls*. London: Hammlyn.

Heinrich, Bernd. 1987. *One Man's Owl*. Princeton: Princeton University Press.

Heinrich, Bernd. 1989. *Ravens in Winter: A Zoological Detective Story*. New York: Summit Books.

Heinrich, Bernd, and Alice Calaprice. 1990. *An Owl in the House* (young people's edition of *One Man's Owl*). Boston: Little, Brown.

Horn, Gabriel. 1985. *Memory, Imprinting, and the Brain: An Inquiry into Mechanisms*. New York: Oxford University Press.

Johnsgaard, Paul. 1988. *North American Owls*. Washington, D.C.: Smithsonian Institution Press.

Karalus, K. E., and Allan W. Eckert. 1974. *The Owls of North America*. Garden City, N.Y.: Doubleday.

Least Heat-Moon, William. 1991. *PrairyErth (a deep map)*. Boston: Houghton Mifflin.

Leopold, Aldo. 1949. *A Sand County Almanac*. New York: Oxford University Press.

Liers, Emil E. 1953. *An Otter's Story*. New York: Viking Press.

Maslow, Jonathan E. 1983. *The Owl Papers*. New York: Dutton.

McKeever, Katherine. 1987. *Care and Rehabilitation of Injured Owls*. Lincoln, Ontario: W. F. Rannie.

McKeever, Lawrence. 1986. *A Dowry of Owls*. Toronto: Lester and Orpen Dennys.

Mowat, Farley. 1961. *Owls in the Family*. Toronto: Little and Brown.

Reichman, O. J. 1987. *Konza Prairie: A Tallgrass Natural History*. Lawrence: University Press of Kansas.

Sparks, John, and Tony Soper. 1970. *Owls: Their Natural and Unnatural History*. New York: Taplinger.

Terman, Max R. 1985. *Earth Sheltered Housing: Principles in Practice.* New York: Chapman and Hall.

Tyler, Hamilton, and Don Phillips. 1978. *Owls by Day and Night*. Happy Camp, Calif.: Naturegraph.

Van Meter, Sondra. 1972. *Marion County, Kansas: Past and Present.* Hillsboro, Kansas: M. B. Publishing House.

Walker, L. W. 1974. *The Book of Owls*. New York: Alfred A. Knopf.

Wilson, E. O. 1994. *Naturalist*. Covelo, Calif.: Island Press.

Yolen, Jane. 1987. *Owl Moon* (children's book). New York: Philomel Books.

Zimmerman, John. 1993. *The Birds of Konza*. Lawrence: University Press of Kansas.

◈ ◈ ◈ *INDEX*